PROTESTS AND ONS

PROTESTS AND VISIONS

PEACE POLITICS IN TWENTIETH-CENTURY BRITAIN

James Hinton

HUTCHINSON RADIUS

Hutchinson Radius
An imprint of Century Hutchinson Ltd
62–65 Chandos Place, London WC2N 4NW

Century Hutchinson Australia Pty Ltd
89–91 Albion Street, Surry Hills,
New South Wales 2010, Australia

Century Hutchinson New Zealand Limited,
PO Box 40–086, Glenfield, Auckland 10,
New Zealand

Century Hutchinson South Africa (Pty) Ltd,
PO Box 337, Bergvlei, 2012 South Africa

First published by Hutchinson Radius 1989

© James Hinton 1989

Typeset by Deltatype Ltd, Ellesmere Port
Printed and bound in Great Britain by
MacKays of Chatham, Kent

British Library Cataloguing in Publication Data
Hinton, James
  Protests and visions: peace politics in 20th century Britain.
  1. Great Britain. Peace movements, 1895–1986
  I. Title
  327.1′72′0941

ISBN 0–09–173005–8

Contents

For Mark and Sasha

Preface

This book has arisen out of my own dual career during the 1980s as a peace activist and a professional historian. There is a remarkable absence of debate about peace movement history among peace campaigners – in sharp contrast to the often obsessive concern with origins characteristic of the labour movement. It is dangerous to neglect one's history, not because there are any simple lessons to be learned from it, but because its legacies are with us whether we recognize them or not. The history of the peace movement contains assumptions and traditions which are negative and disabling. By clearly confronting them, we will find them easier to deal with. But there are also positive elements to be found – strategies of protest and visions of alternatives, whose recovery can be empowering in the present, providing 'resources for a journey of hope'.[1] It is evidently a matter of opinion as to which are the positive traditions and which the negative. I have my own opinions, and make no secret of them. But there is, I hope, enough serious history presented in this book to enable others to construct their own distinct readings. Ongoing debates about the future of the peace movement could, I believe, be enriched by debates about the interpretation of its past. If this book does something to bring the past into the present in this way, it will have achieved its central purpose.

One reason why the peace movement lacks much sense of its history is that – unlike the labour movement – it has had little continuous institutional life, consisting, rather, of a series of shortlived outbursts – the *protests* of this book's title. Only in exceptional circumstances has public outrage broken through what a Whitehall official once smugly described as 'the normal apathy in the country in the matter of foreign affairs.'[2] Most of these outbursts improvised their own machinery of protest, specific to their immediate purposes.[3]

Nevertheless, there is a recognizable tradition of peace campaigning. While most peace movements have been explicitly non-partisan affairs, their campaigns have developed in conjunction with the Liberal and Labour Parties, as well as with the smaller parties of the left. Who was using whom – and for what – in these relationships, was a matter of constant concern both to peace activists and to politicians. More important, however, is the fact that, time and again, peace movements have provided a meeting place between the major currents of liberal and socialist thinking which go to make up British radicalism. Many of the leading figures of peace politics belonged to a tradition of liberal – and internationalist – socialism, which seems to me the most positive resource in Britain's political culture. Frequently, however, they found themselves embattled with a nationalist socialism – a socialism rooted in, and limited by, the power of the nation state – which has, since the First World War, done much to block the emergence of peace politics in the Labour Party.

Peace politics has dealt in *visions* as well as in *protests*. People were dismayed by the behaviour of governments because they had their own ideas about how Britain ought to act in the world. The history of these visions is, very largely, a history of attempts to articulate, sustain and renew a national identity perceived as antagonistic to that projected in official foreign policy. The 'alternative' identity was not always as removed from the assumptions of Britain's rulers as peace activists liked to think it was. One of my leading arguments is that, throughout the twentieth century, British peace movements made assumptions about the role of Britain in the world which owed more to the unconscious legacy of nineteenth-century imperialism, than they did to any realistic assessment of the basis on which a country which had lost the power to run the world could best contribute to building peace. As George Orwell remarked, in one of his masterly half-truths: 'Scratch the average pacifist and you find a jingo'.[4] I have scratched a good many pacifists in the course of researching this book and I have found, if not exactly jingoism, then certainly a remarkable faith in the power of the British state (and especially its Royal Navy) to set the world to rights. Peace activists have been as prone to delusions of imperial grandeur as have Britain's rulers. The Pax Britannica bequeathed a legacy of 'imperialist pacifism'.

But there was also an alternative tradition. Before 1914 both liberals and socialists shared a vision of a pacific, transnational European community. This was shattered by the First World War, which also marked the beginning of the end of Europe's global dominance. Losing faith in the ability of Europeans to create their own peace, many radicals turned to the emerging superpowers for help. It is, however, questionable how far a belief in American liberalism or Russian communism represented an advance over the older radical tendency to subscribe to the ideology of the Pax Britannica. In each case, wishful thinking tended to blind the radicals to the *raison d'État* behind the utopian rhetoric. From the Second World War, attempts were made to revive the concept of a democratic and pacific Europe as a focus of peace campaigning in Britain. There is an obvious continuity between 'Third Force' ideas of democratic socialism between the two superpowers in the 1940s, and the 'Beyond the Blocs' politics of European Nuclear Disarmament in the 1980s. Today, as the superpower grip on Europe begins to fade, new possibilities are opening up in Europe. In this situation, a major question confronting the British peace movement is whether it can overcome the traditions of nationalist socialism, 'imperialist pacifism', and what I will call – just this once – 'superpowerism'. Can the peace movement engage with a continental struggle to build peace, democracy and socialism in Europe and, by doing so, contribute to the transformation of what it means to be 'British'?

There is nothing innocent about the word *Britain* in my title. I have not attempted to deal with the history of peace politics in the smaller nations of the British mainland. I am concerned, rather, with the 'British' identity of the English. Within the political cultures of Scotland and Wales these issues pose themselves very differently. In small and historically oppressed nations, radicals find it possible to combine their nationalism with both socialism and internationalism in positive ways: ways that are simply not available to the English because the sources of English nationalism have been poisoned by the legacy of British imperialism. The most important task facing the peace movement is to play a part in enabling the English to discover themselves as members of a medium-sized European nation. It is not an easy thing to change a nation's identity. But peace politics has always been about the construction of national identity, and the history provides, not only obstacles, but also resources.

Why the term 'peace politics'? Partly, I use it to emphasize that peace movements involve not only protests and visions, but also *political* effort and intelligence in combining these and bringing them to bear on existing structures of power. Without visions of a world transformed, there can be no peace politics. But the issues of war and peace always present themselves as urgent, immediate and having to be dealt with in the here and now. Concern for mere survival governs the appetite for a new Jerusalem. Because peace is both a utopian dream and an urgent necessity, the constant goal of peace politics has been to build bridges between utopian thinking and effective action in the world as it is.

My other reason for using the term 'peace politics' is that I cannot, regrettably, say 'pacifist politics'. The word 'pacifist' did not acquire its modern, restricted meaning until the 1930s. Prior to that, since it was first coined at the turn of century, it had the more general meaning.[5] A pacifist was someone who rejected the doctrine that the best way to preserve peace was to prepare for war and who looked for the ultimate removal of force from international relations. Pacifists worked to build peace and to prevent war. But they did not necessarily reject the use of force in all circumstances, and most of them accepted that there would be occasions when war was justified. All those who opposed the First World War described themselves as 'pacifists', notwithstanding the fact that most of them were not opposed to the use of force in some circumstances. Those who were, used terms like 'non-resistance', 'absolute pacifism', 'extreme pacifism', or 'Christian pacifism'. The modern identification of 'pacifism' with what would earlier have been called 'absolute pacifism' was a product of the division of the peace movement in the 1930s over the appropriate response to fascist aggression. There was a struggle for the word, the absolute pacifists ran away with it, and they have kept it ever since.

I outline this etymological history because it has created a difficult problem for historians of peace movements. If 'pacifist' is used in its post-1930s meaning, we are left without any *single* word to describe the people or ideas under discussion. In this book I have frequently resorted to the term 'peace activist', but this is hardly satisfactory, not only because it leaves out the *inactive* (and non-absolute) pacifist, but also because the word 'activist' is itself a disputed one.[6] In 1956 A. J. P. Taylor, confronting the same problem, proposed a distinction between 'pacifists' (the absolute ones) and 'pacificists' (the rest).[7] As a stylist of distinction he had more sense than to clutter his own prose with this ugly tongue-twister, and buried it in a footnote. More recently 'pacificist' has been disinterred and put to extensive use by one of the most prolific and scholarly writers on the history of British peace movements – Martin Ceadel. I have chosen a more pragmatic solution. In discussing the period before the 1930s I have used 'pacifism' in its broader meaning, as it was used at the time, and without the inverted commas. In discussing the period since the 1930s I have generally avoided it by using the term 'peace activist', which, for all its drawbacks, I can at least pronounce. When I do use the word 'pacifist' without any qualification, I mean it in the more general sense.

This book represents an attempt to put two parts of my life together. I have many debts both inside the academy and outside. Without the generous sabbatical leave policy of the University of Warwick I could not have written the book. I have been greatly helped by the response of seminar audiences at a History Workshop Conference and at the Bradford School of Peace Studies. I have spent many happy hours refining the underlying arguments with fellow peace activists, sometimes on demonstrations, but mainly in pubs. I have had the services of an enthusiastic and understanding editor, Neil Belton. Logie Barrow, Meg Beresford, Julian Harber, Jill Liddington, Fred Reid, Martin Shaw, Kate Soper, and Ben Webb have read all or parts of the manuscript, and have saved me from worse errors of fact and judgement than those which remain. Finally I want to thank Yvette Rocheron, who not only gave me the courage to embark on the project in the first place, but also read and discussed each chapter with me as it came off the word processor.

1

Victorian Visions: Imperialist Pacifism

1914 was the turning point. It marked the end of the Hundred Years' Peace.[1] It opened the Era of World Wars which, for all we know, we still inhabit. What was absent between the end of the Napoleonic Wars in 1815 and the outbreak of the First World War was not, of course, war as such. Indeed war was endemic in a system of squabbling nation states and dramatic shifts in the European balance of power gave rise to many minor wars and some major ones. But none of these wars threatened to destroy civilization, to halt Europe's extra-ordinary economic growth, or to undermine the global expansion of its power. None of them was a 'Great War'.[2]

Before 1914 the popular agitations aroused in Britain by particular wars and threats of wars, were informed by an optimistic assumption that, whatever the folly of the moment, history was on the side of peace. War was an outrage, but it was also an anachronism. It did not call into question either the virtue or the viability of the international system itself. 1914 raised the stakes. What was now at issue was the survival of civilization. Agitations against particular wars continued, and occasionally – Spain in the 1930s, Vietnam in the 1960s – they diverted the peace movement's attention from the larger problem. But, in general, the wickedness of particular wars served merely to illustrate the wickedness of the system as a whole.

Nineteenth-century peace movements set out to improve the world: twentieth-century ones struggle to save it. Although much had changed, much also remained the same. It is impossible to understand twentieth-century peace movements without first examining the traditions on which they built. Nostalgia for the Hundred Years' Peace played a significant role in conditioning responses to the Era of World Wars – especially in Britain. British power had played a key role in sustaining the long years of peace. Small colonial wars, it is true, abounded. But these were widely seen as police actions undertaken in the name of civilization, not as wars. It was, to a significant degree, what proud Victorians said it was – a Pax Britannica. Where other nineteenth-century national-isms found their deepest meaning in war, the supreme power exercised in the world by the British enabled them to link their national identity above all to peace. It is hardly surprising that Britain's nineteenth-century role as policeman of the world continued to influence the twentieth-century mind. The legacy of this for the peace movement was a divided one: it resulted in a stronger peace movement than anywhere else in Europe, but one deeply scarred by often unrecognized im-perialist assumptions. This imperialist pacifism struck deep roots in the British political culture, and it haunts peace movements to this day.

When radical intellectuals tried to come to grips with the imperialist and militarist trends of the early twentieth century, no-one was more important to them than Richard Cobden. Cobden, a Manchester cotton merchant turned pamphleteer and politician, had articulated the key beliefs of nineteenth-century liberal political economy: *laisser-faire* and free trade. Together with John Bright, a cotton manufacturer from Rochdale, Cobden led the struggle for the abolition of the Corn Laws. From the outset he was concerned as much with the political as with the economic consequences of free trade, and he saw an integral connection between the Anti Corn Law League and what he called 'the Peace movement'.[3] The triumph of the League in 1846 marked, for Cobden, not simply a victory for the industrial bourgeoisie over the landed aristocracy, but a milestone in human progress. The repeal of the Corn Laws opened the way for the removal of all remaining protective tariffs. As other countries followed the British lead, universal free trade would inaugurate a 'world's revolution', breaking down the barriers between nations and laying the basis for a genuine world community:

> I see in the Free-trade principle that which shall act on the moral world as the principle of gravitation in the universe, – drawing men together, thrusting aside the antagonism of race, and creed and language, and uniting us in the bonds of eternal peace.[4]

Cobden rejected nationalist economics. It was an archaic delusion to believe that one country's gain was another country's loss. The free exchange of goods across national boundaries worked to the advantage of all involved. 'Commerce is the grand panacea which, like a beneficent medical discovery, will serve to innoculate with the healthy and saving taste for civilisation all the nations of the world.'[5] Through peaceful commercial intercourse the virtues of Victorian bourgeois culture would be diffused across the globe. Adam Smith's 'invisible hand' – 'that principle . . . set up in this wicked world as the silent arbiter of our fate'[6] – guaranteed that, in conditions of unrestricted competitive enterprise, each individual's pursuit of his own self-interest would serve the interests of humanity at large. The proper role of the state was to create and sustain the conditions of domestic and international law and order within which private economic activity could flourish. Government attempts – like those of the eighteenth-century mercantilists – to subordinate the activities of their traders to the 'national interest', only succeeded in impoverishing all concerned. Eventually, Cobden prophesied, as quiet penetration by the commercial spirit displaced dynastic and national rivalries:

> the desire and the motive for large and mighty empires; for gigantic armies and great navies . . . will die away; I believe that such things will cease to be necessary, or to be used, when man becomes one family, and freely exchanges the fruits of his labour with his brother man. I believe that, if we could be allowed to reappear on this sublunary scene, we should see, at a far distant period, the governing system of this world revert to something like the municipal system. . . .'[7]

There is no need to doubt Cobden's sincerity to recognize that his gospel of free trade coincided neatly with the needs of

British capitalism. Presiding over the world's first industrial economy, British businessmen had good reason to favour free trade. The fantastic productivity of their mills and factories enabled them to outsell all rivals, whether these were the developing manufactures of Western Europe and America, or the indigenous handicraft industries of the East. In the latter case, it is true, merely economic advantages were reinforced by the use of imperial power to undermine still further the capacity of local industry to resist invading Lancashire textiles. By and large, however, mid-Victorian prosperity rested on the unregulated activities of traders rather than the expansion of formal imperial controls. 'To trade with civilised men', Macaulay had remarked in 1833, 'is infinitely more profitable than to conquer savages.'[8] And, despite all the bluster of gunboat diplomacy for which he is remembered, the same perception informed much of Lord Palmerston's policy:

> We want to trade with Egypt and to travel through Egypt but we do not want the burthen of governing Egypt. . . . Let us try to improve all these countries by the general influence of our commerce but let us all abstain from a crusade of conquest which would call down upon us the condemnation of all the other civilized nations.[9]

Britain was at the peak of its power, a world-dominating state, and it was easy for the British to confuse the tenets of their nationalism with the universal interests of mankind. Nowhere was this more apparent than in attitudes to naval power. Following the defeat of its main rival in the French Wars, the Royal Navy patrolled the oceans of the world. Regimes in the Far and Near East were forced into commercial intercourse with Britain by the threat – or reality – of naval bombardment. Once these reluctant players had been forced into the game, however, it was reasonable to suppose that the Navy would no longer need to act as an international bully, but could confine itself to policing international waterways. In 1907 a Foreign Office mandarin penned a classic statement of the conventional wisdom. It was, argued Eyre Crowe, only because Britain was a free trading power, which used its navy to pursue a policy in harmony with 'the general desires and ideals common to all mankind', that the continental powers were prepared to tolerate her naval supremacy.[10] This belief that the Royal Navy served the interests of mankind, was not without influence among radical opponents of British foreign policy. Whereas a large standing army was generally seen as an instrument of tyranny, the projection of naval power overseas appeared to be compatible with the maintenance of civil liberties at home. 'Military dictatorships exist everywhere,' George Orwell later remarked, 'but there is no such thing as a naval dictatorship.'[11] Clifford Allen, leader of the conscientious objectors in the First World War, articulated a widely shared feeling while recuperating from a term in jail in January 1918:

> Long-sea walk. . . . All my boundless love for the sea came back to me when amongst the sea-weed-strewn rocks with sea gulls screaming as I used to hear them each Christmas. . . . I am glad – unashamedly glad that this virile sea-girt country is my native country. . . . I want my country to be great amongst the nations of the world – great by virtue of its loyalty to freedom and tolerance. . . . We C.O.s must somehow make it clear to our fellow countrymen that it was our very love of country that made us choose prison rather than see her sported [sic] and bound by conscription. No wonder there cannot be conscription for the Navy. A moment by the sea will show why. . . .[12]

Affection for the Navy was an important strand in British pacifism. It was, after all, naval predominance that enabled Britain to put down the Atlantic slave trade, an act of 'moral leadership' with which virtually every peace movement of the nineteenth and twentieth centuries has claimed an affinity.

Foreigners often found it difficult to appreciate that free trade served their needs. Freedom, it seemed, was the paradise of the strong. Friedrich List, whose *National System of Political Economy* (1841), laid the theoretical basis for German protectionism in the later nineteenth century, argued:

> . . . under the existing conditions of the world the result of general free trade would not be a universal republic but

> on the contrary a universal subjection of the less
> advanced nations to the supremacy of the predominant
> manufacturing, commercial and naval power.[13]

Denied tariff protection against cheap British goods, old handicraft industries collapsed, and indigenous modern industries found it difficult to get off the ground. The British, dominant in the world economy, could put nationalist economics behind them. Lesser mortals saw only self-serving cant in Cobdenite high principle, because only through the intervention of the state in regulating national economic life could they hope to compete on equal terms with the British.

Nevertheless there was some truth in Cobden's claims. In the long term, the creation of a world market was bound to stimulate worldwide industrial development. Moreover the continued growth and expansion of European capitalism depended on the maintenance of an effective world monetary system. Cobden's heroes were the traders, not the bankers who financed their operations. But the bankers of the City of London, exporting capital to every corner of the globe, came to play a central role in sustaining the conditions for economic growth. The export of capital enabled Britain to run a large trade deficit, providing markets for both primary products and, increasingly, manufactured goods. London's bankers used their enormous power behind the scenes to keep the world's major currencies in balance, masterminding what E. H. Carr was later to describe as 'a pseudo-international world economic order based on British supremacy.'[14] The fact that the long years of peace embodied only a 'pseudo-inter-nationalism' – an internationalism slanted in Britain's favour and squarely based on the power of the Royal Navy and the City of London – was not to prevent many people, radicals among them, from looking back nostalgically to the Pax Britannica after the world fell to bits in 1914.

Despite the triumph of free trade in 1846, Cobden had no reason to be complacent about the enlightenment of Britain's rulers. Political power remained firmly in the hands of the landed aristocracy. It was not until the end of the century that any significant numbers of politicians from non-landed backgrounds began to make their way into the political élite. This aristocratic domination was nowhere more apparent than in the conduct of foreign policy. When, in 1870, the institution of competitive examinations opened civil service careers to middle-class talent, the Foreign Office was exempted from reform. The diplomatic service remained, in Bright's contemptuous phrase: 'neither more nor less than a gigantic system of outdoor relief for the aristocracy of Great Britain.'[15] The emergence of a liberal world economy may have been the real basis of international stability: but this was hardly apparent to the men who ran British foreign policy. For these men what counted was the 'Great Game' of European diplomacy, the endless manœuvring on the international chess board – making and breaking deals, picking up rumours of secret clauses, playing off one rival against another. Britain's diplomats spent their lives with fellow aristocrats in the courts and chancelleries of the Great Powers – constructing, trimming and adjusting the secret machinery of peace: the Balance of Power.[16]

Nothing angered the Manchester School more than 'this system of foreign interference, protocolling, diplomatising, etc. . . '. In the name of the 'mischievous delusion' of the Balance of Power, thundered Bright, aristocratic governments had led Britain into 150 years of more or less continuous warfare, all of it pointless. 'We have been,' said Cobden, 'the most combative and aggressive community that has existed since the days of the Roman dominion. . .'.[17] Eventually free trade would create a pacific world community – but only when foolish aristocrats left off their meddling. Shortly after the repeal of the Corn Laws in 1846 Cobden wrote to Bright deploring 'the Palmerston system', and urging the need 'to prevent the Foreign Office from undoing the good which the Board of Trade has done to the people.'[18] Foreign policy, as conducted by the aristocratic establishment, constantly undermined the pacifying influence of commerce. Hence the slogan: 'As little intercourse as possible betwixt the *Governments*, as much connexion as possible between the *nations* of the world!' Cobden explained:

> . . . the progress of freedom depends more upon the maintenance of peace, the spread of commerce, and the

diffusion of education, than upon the labours of cabinets and foreign offices.[19]

However, 'no foreign politics' – Cobden's favourite toast[20] – implied an abstentionist spirit which sat uneasily with the righteous tone of middle-class politics. When the Victorian public became excited about foreign affairs, the issue was not *whether* the British state should intervene but *how*, and on whose side.

Popular politics in mid-Victorian Britain was inextricably bound up with religion. True, most of the urban poor were cynical about the churches: but they were equally indifferent to political agitation. And, despite the moralizing impact of the evangelical movement, the ruling aristocracy wore its Christianity lightly, or at least kept it at one remove from the serious business of politics. But religion suffused the lives of the provincial middle class. Theirs was an activist Protestant-ism that preached salvation through works, not detachment from the workaday world. There was, as Cobden had understood, no clear dividing line between their religious and their political enthusiasms:

> Henceforth we will grapple with the religious feelings of the people. Their veneration for God shall be our leverage to upset their reverence for the aristocracy.[21]

It was as the party of Christ that middle-class England made its mark on Victorian politics, seeking always to impose the dictates of morality on the conduct of public affairs. The churches provided the major organizing base for the great middle-class agitations – the Anti Corn Law League of the 1840s, and the many-sided campaigning activity of extra-Parliamentary Liberalism in the 1860s and 70s.

Rooted in this moralizing soil, public concern with foreign policy had little time for *raison d'État* and pragmatic arguments about the balance of power. But neither did it embody the quietist implications of Cobden's non-interventionism. Rather, the characteristic middle-class agitation over foreign affairs sprang from identification with small peoples struggling to be free. There was, in what Gladstone once called 'the virtuous passion'[22] of such movements, a heady combination of moral earnestness and national pride. In 1851 the leader of Hungarian nationalism, Lajos Kossuth, toured English cities speaking to gigantic crowds. In the face of Tsarist tyranny, he exclaimed, 'humanity expects Britannia to shake her mighty trident and shout a mighty Stop.'[23] Such an appeal from the leader of a popular revolution was irresistible, and the crowd's response helped pave the way for British entry into the Crimean War three years later. It is little wonder that Cobden lamented the weakness for good causes which made his middle-class public putty in the hands of aristocratic war-mongers.[24]

Nevertheless, the 'virtuous passion' did not always go along with balance-of-power politics. Popular enthusiasm for Abraham Lincoln in the 1860s clashed with Palmerston's support for the South in the American Civil War.[25] And, in 1876, Disraeli's Near Eastern diplomacy ran into a tidal wave of protest against British support for a Turkish regime responsible for the massacre of Bulgarian Christians. It was to this same tradition of sympathy with oppressed nationalities that radicals appealed during the Boer War, eagerly embracing the label 'pro-Boer'. British annexation of the Boer republics was denounced as 'a crime against the principle of nationality unparalleled since the Partition of Poland'.[26] John Burns, once a socialist and now the leading working-class Liberal, opposed the war in the name of a patriotic, if selective, rendering of British history:

> I remember reading, as a schoolboy, with pride and pleasure, how Old England, from King Alfred's time, has been the protector of liberty and freedom. That is the quality that differentiates us from all other countries in the world. Except Ireland [he had to admit!], Britain has been through the centuries the knight-errant of the smaller peoples. Who set Belgium on its legs, gave Greece its independence, helped united [unite?] Italy, and stood by Switzerland from time to time? England. In this war England is not fulfilling her traditional task, the protector of the smaller nations. . . .[27]

'A Liberal', quipped Bernard Shaw, 'has three duties: a duty to

Ireland; a duty to Finland; and a duty to Macedonia.'[28]

It was Gladstone who built the most significant bridge between the 'virtuous passion' of the Victorian middle class and the *raison d'État* of the governing élite.[29] In particular his conception of the 'Concert of Europe' became an important point of reference for British pacifists. Gladstone shared Cobden's belief in the pacifying and civilizing influence of commerce. But, as a member of the ruling élite, he also believed in foreign policy – so long as this was conducted in accordance with 'the public law of Europe'. History for Gladstone was primarily a European drama. European civilization, resting on the twin pillars of Jewish spirituality and the Greek intellect, held the Great Powers together in a moral order, a community of nations.[30] Gladstone's 'European sense' provided moral rationalizations for traditional Foreign Office practices: it did not seek to overturn and transform them. Through the rhetoric of 'the concert of Europe' he aspired to harness the godly passions of the masses to the mundane pragmatism of their rulers. An offshore naval power with no territorial ambitions in Europe, Britain had long seen its role on the Continent as essentially a stabilizing one: its interventions designed to prevent any one power or group of powers from achieving overall hegemony. This was the traditional doctrine of the Balance of Power as laid down by William Pitt. And it was to this doctrine that Gladstone lent his moral weight:

> The high office of bringing Europe into concert, and keeping Europe in concert, is an office specially pointed out for your country to perform. . . . That happy condition, so long as we are believed to be disinterested in Europe, secures for us the noblest part that any Power was ever called upon to play . . . for it is the work of peace and the work of good will among men.[31]

It would be wrong to see this merely as a more elegant version of John Burns's 'knight errant' conception of British history. When crisis threatened, argued Gladstone, it was the task of a British government to persuade the Powers to act in concert, not to arrogate to itself the right to impose a solution of its own devising. Britain, in Gladstone's view, was first among equals, not a superpower. This did not mean, however, that Gladstone was prepared to surrender British sovereignty to the judgement of her peers. In the last resort, when the Powers could not be persuaded to fulfil their duty to the civilized world, he reserved the right of unilateral action. When Gladstone invoked that right, authorizing the British occupation of Egypt in 1882, John Bright resigned from the Liberal Cabinet. Since Gladstone had won a general election two years earlier proclaiming his opposition to Disraelian imperialism in general, and the occupation of Egypt in particular, this betrayal was long remembered in radical circles: 'Henceforward Liberalism had a lie in its soul'.[32] Nevertheless, such incongruities between theory and practice did not prevent Gladstone's 'European sense' – reworked as 'the League of Nations sense' – from playing a major role in the thinking of early twentieth-century liberal intellectuals.[33]

Free-trade pacifism, a penchant to crusade for the rights of oppressed nationalities, and aspirations to membership of a common European polity – these were the leading moral ideas which, to varying degrees, informed the spasmodic agitations of mid-Victorian public opinion about foreign affairs. Whatever the contradictions between them, all bore the mark of their origin in the era of Pax Britannica – a firm belief that Britain's destiny was to serve the universal interests of mankind. It was a comforting illusion, and one that continued to be fostered by twentieth-century pacifists long after the Establishment had abandoned it.

2

Victorian Protests: Organizing the Virtuous Passion

Alongside this inheritance of pacifist ideas, Britain's twentieth-century peace movements drew upon sophisticated traditions of public agitation over foreign affairs. The Peace Society, founded by Quakers in 1816, had developed a non-sectarian style of work in which absolute pacifists of all Christian denominations could co-operate effectively with much wider currents of pacifist opinion. During the late 1840s and early 1850s, the Society played an important role in organizing pacifist pressure on Governments, often in co-operation with Cobden and Bright. In the later decades of the nineteenth century, however, it became a rather conservative body, and contributed little to pacifist agitation before or during the First World War.[1] When pacifists sought to channel public outrage into effective political action they turned not to the Peace Society, but to the agitational traditions of extra-Parliamentary Liberalism.

In 1858, at a banquet in Birmingham Town Hall, John Bright declared his faith in the irresistible power – as well as the untarnished virtue – of enlightened public opinion:

> It is not from statesmen that these things come [the abolition of slavery, free trade, etc]. . . . It was from public meetings such as these, from the intelligence and conscience of the great body of the people who have no interest in wrong. . . .[2]

While this kind of talk might be good for morale, especially after a good meal, it offered little guidance to political strategy. In fact the leaders of nineteenth-century popular movements faced formidable obstacles in their efforts to bring the virtuous passions of the moral nation to bear on the operations of the aristocratic Foreign Office. Manufacturing public opinion was one thing: making it politically effective was quite another.

Rather more considered was Cobden's remark, in the course of the campaign against the Corn Laws, that: 'Ultimate victory depends upon accident. . . .' Without 'further political changes', which were not [in 1840] immediately on the agenda, the popular movement was unlikely to get its hands on the levers of power. Its only hope of success, therefore, was that events outside its control would eventually force the Government to face up to the issue. In the meantime the movement's task was 'the enlightenment of the public mind, so as to prepare it to take advantage of such accident when it arises.'[3] This was indeed how the Anti Corn Law League succeeded. Its years of educational campaigning prepared the way for winning the argument when the Irish potato famine of 1845–46 finally forced the Prime Minster, Peel, to face the issue. A similar lesson could be drawn from the experience of the anti-slave trade campaign a generation earlier. In the 1770s and 1780s Wilberforce and his fellow campaigners had developed many of the abiding techniques for arousing the conscience of the nation, but it was the unpredictable fortunes – and calculus – of war that, in 1807, created the circumstances in which arguments of economic and strategic interest could be mobilized by reformers to finally persuade politicians to take the step long demanded by enlightened public opinion.[4]

If 'waiting for something to turn up' was central to the strategic thinking of movements which had the support of the mass of articulate opinion in the country, it was all the more important to movements whose enlightened demands failed to gain mass support. Cobden and Bright stated their opposition to the Crimean War clearly, but they made no attempt to get up an agitation against so popular an enterprise: 'You might as well reason with mad dogs as with men when they have begun to spill one another's blood.'[5] Half a century later the pro-Boer movement similarly accepted the inevitability of its minority status, though not with quite the same degree of resignation.

The first major initiative after the war broke out in October 1899 was an unobtrusive 'watching committee' of Liberal politicians. Seeing no basis for an agitation, they confined themselves to keeping alive the voice of reason by writing letters to quality newspapers. After a more militant Stop the War campaign was launched in January 1900, the committee came out openly to uphold the voice of moderation and responsibility in the anti-war movement:

> It behoves us, though the minority, to press the truth as we see it with zeal and courage but without temper or exaggeration.[6]

Stop the War, the target of this remark, certainly went in for extravagant language, but they were equally reconciled to their minority position. Neither organization found it easy to hold public meetings without attracting the often violent attentions of jingo mobs incited by the popular press. In such a climate they made few attempts at open-air rallies. Radicals were shocked both by popular jingoism and by the failure of the authorities to uphold their rights of free speech:

> . . . the friends of Peace have been most pacific. They have been most considerate of the authorities in a season of popular delirium. They have held no processions. They have, to a great extent, abstained from public meetings. And now, as their reward, they are lectured . . . as if they were the real criminals when they venture meekly to suggest that in free England private meetings ought not to be broken up by ruffianly mobs and that private citizens ought to be protected from being rabbled by Hooligans because of the unpopularity of their political opinions.[7]

Keeping the voice of reason alive during a 'season of popular delirium' has been a common position for peace movements to find themselves in – the heroic, embattled minority, keeping up morale by swapping stories of near scrapes with the unreasoning fury of the mob, while waiting for the return of peace, or for one of Cobden's unpredictable 'accidents', to rescue them from impotence and isolation. For the pro-Boer movement just such an 'accident' was waiting in the wings. To fully appreciate its significance, however, it will be necessary to look back for a moment to the Bulgarian atrocities agitation of 1876 – 'the greatest storm over foreign policy in our history.'[8]

Responding to a nationalist rising in the summer of 1876, Turkish forces pillaged and burned seventy Bulgarian villages. 15,000 Christians – men, women and children – were killed by the Bashi-Bazouks, mercenary troops, often in the most atrocious ways. These distant horrors would probably have caused little stir in Britain had it not been for the fact that Disraeli's Government was engaged at the time in strenuous diplomatic efforts to protect Turkish rule against Russian-backed Bulgarian nationalism. In diplomatic circles the massacres were seen as an unfortunate embarrassment, but certainly not as a reason to abandon the Great Game of propping up a decadent Islamic empire to prevent Russian expansion towards Britain's imperial lifelines to the East. But outside Whitehall 'the heart of the country thrilled with horror at these infamies'.[9] The Bulgarian atrocities had touched a raw nerve in the psychology of British nationalism. The local leaders of every fair-sized town in Northern England, and many in the South, held meetings. In the space of six weeks nearly 500 such gatherings – convened by mayors, addressed by ministers and magistrates – had bombarded the Foreign Office with their protests. As the waves of moral outrage broke against the walls of the Establishment, popular fury was immeasurably increased by the obvious contempt of the ruling élite – in the word of one leaked ambassadorial telegram – for 'those shallow . . . persons who have allowed their feelings of revolted humanity to make them forget the capital interests involved in the question.'[10] W. T. Stead, a Northern Non-Conformist journalist who played a leading part in the agitation, called on Queen Victoria to declare a 'Bulgarian Sunday' – 'a solemn day of humiliation' and 'national repentance' – on which Churches and Chapels would join together to mourn the victims and collect funds for the relief of 'the sufferers whom we have been the unwitting means of destroying'.[11] Stead's plea embodied much of the psychology of the movement: guilt, shame and the need to atone for belonging to a nation that could, in the amoral pursuit of power politics, become complicit in such outrages.

Twenty-five years later, in a pamphlet issued by the Stop The War Committee for the 1900 'Khaki' Election, Stead deployed the same rhetoric. The election, he explained, was 'a Day of Judgement', on which the nation had the opportunity to repudiate the murder being committed in its name in South Africa: 'we must cleanse our own souls from blood-guiltiness.'[12] What transformed such vapid moralizing into an effective weapon against popular support for the war was the British Army's attempts to counter the guerilla tactics of the Afrikaners by burning down their farmsteads and herding the women and children into disease-ridden 'concentration camps' where large numbers of them died.

Instead of denouncing the war in isolation, the pro-Boer movement could now position itself at the head of a broad tide of public concern about the way in which the war was being fought. When news of farm-burning first reached England it was Emily Hobhouse, a well-connected and determined woman drawn into politics by the war, who saw how to seize the opportunity it provided. After setting up a relief fund for women and children evicted from their farms, Emily Hobhouse travelled to the war zone to distribute the cash. On her return to England in May 1901 she published a moving personal account of what she had witnessed in the camps. Her revelations gave new impetus to the peace movement. Stop the War drew an explicit parallel with the earlier agitation: 'this war . . . has now degenerated into a campaign of extermination, carried out by a policy of systematic devastation, the like of which for atrocity can only be paralleled in our time by the operations of the Turks in Armenia and Bulgaria.'[13] More important, Campbell–Bannerman, the Liberal leader, used Hobhouse's revelations to unite his Party against the Government's 'methods of barbarism' without the necessity of courting disgrace by unpatriotically opposing the war itself.

In 1900–01, as in 1876, the horror expressed at outrages committed – or condoned – by Britain owed much to the creed and colour of the victims. 'The Boers are the Dutch of South Africa', wrote Stead, 'white men, and Protestant christians like ourselves. They read the same Bible, keep the same Sabbath, and pray to the same God as ourselves.'[14] Much of the propaganda against the mineowners and financiers held responsible for the war had a strongly anti-semitic flavour, while anxiety that this civil war amongst the whites might encourage black revolt was expressed by leading opponents of the war. Emily Hobhouse's humanitarian concern for the internees was not uninfluenced by her alarm at 'the growing impertinence of the Kaffirs' who witnessed the humiliation of white women in the camps.[15] The feelings of national guilt and shame tapped by these agitations were cast in a deeply racist mould. As with so much of the legacy left by the virtuous passion of the Victorian middle-class, there was poison in the chalice handed down to twentieth-century peace movements by the agitations of 1876 and 1901.

Cobden's strategic doctrine of waiting for 'accidents' reflected an assumption that, in the short term, nothing could be done to break the aristocratic hold on the House of Commons and place middle class opinion more directly in control of Government. With the extension of the franchise in the Reform Acts of 1867 and 1884, and the consequent growth of mass extra-Parliamentary parties, the possibility of gaining direct influence over the actual or potential Government came to play a central role in the strategic calculations of the leaders of popular movements. At the same time Liberal politicians, having now to concern themselves with the mobilization and management of a mass extra-Parliamentary party as well as with manoeuvring in Parliament, took a keen interest in any agitation that might be turned to party advantage or used to promote their own advancement. Much the same was true of the Labour Party when it emerged, at the turn of the century. Negotiating the frontier with party politics became a leading concern of every upsurge of public agitation from the Bulgarian atrocities in 1876 to the anti-nuclear movement of the last thirty years.

The upsurge of 1876 did not begin as a Liberal Party affair. W. T. Stead, with memories of the Chartist Convention at the back of his mind, wanted to turn the movement into a full-blown 'anti-parliament' with a Convention of delegates elected from every constituency challenging Disraeli's right to pursue such an unpopular policy while Parliament was not sitting. The efforts of Liberal politicians to turn the affair to Party advantage, however, proved more important than Stead's quasi-revolutionary fantasies. At first Gladstone, who had been in semi-retirement since the defeat of his second administration in 1874, hung back from involving himself in the agitation. It is significant that his decision to come in was triggered by evidence of working-class enthusiasm for the cause. It was as an opportunity to rebuild his rapport with the masses that the Bulgarian atrocities issue mattered most to Gladstone, and the agitation helped to give him a lasting place in the affections of the radical rank and file of the Liberal Party. As such it played an important part in his battle to prevent his ambitious younger rival – Joseph Chamberlain – from destroying the class alliance at the base of popular liberalism by focusing political attention on divisive social questions rather than on the great moral issues of foreign affairs.[16] Not for the last time, agitation over foreign policy served to sustain alliances between middle-class and working-class activists on the left of British politics.

The pro-Boer movement again placed a premium on the politics of class alliance, tending to subordinate socialism and independent working-class politics to the overriding need to sustain a common anti-imperialist front. Until Campbell-Bannerman's 'methods of barbarism' speech in June 1901, the Liberal Party was hopelessly split in its attitude to the war. While this situation provided an opportunity for socialists to make a bid for the leadership of the anti-imperialist cause, the absence of any mass working-class opposition to the war held them back from attempting to use the newly formed Labour Representation Committee – forerunner of the Labour Party – as a focus for anti-war politics. Instead the two main socialist parties – the Independent Labour Party (ILP) and the Social Democratic Federation – worked closely with the largely middle-class peace committees.[17] Despite his previous commitment to the political independence of Labour, Keir Hardie tried hard to persuade Liberals to take the lead in expanding the anti-war agitation, and was keen to develop an electoral understanding to prevent clashes at the polls between

Liberal and Socialist opponents of the war. In the General Election of October 1900 he was returned for Merthyr, running in tandem with a Liberal mineowner, and claiming Liberal votes as the natural successor to the Rev. Henry Richards, President of the Peace Society, who had held the constituency between 1868–88. Speaking elsewhere in the election campaign, Bruce Glasier – another leading ILP politician – found his Liberal audience 'much touched by my references to Gladstone and Bright.'[18]

The readiness of Socialists and Liberals to suspend their electoral competition in the name of peace anticipated developments during the First World War and the later 1930s. Whether, as Hardie optimistically forecast, such alliances opened the way for socialism, or whether they subordinated it to traditional radical liberalism, remained a hotly contested question.[19] In the case of the Boer War, there seems little doubt that the agitation served mainly to ensure the continuing vitality of radicalism. The general indifference of organized labour to the issue indicated how very difficult it was going to be to persuade the new Labour Party to take any interest in foreign affairs.[20] And, when it came to analysing the causes of the war, most socialists were content to accept the rather conspiratorial explanation offered by the leading radical theorist of imperialism, J. A. Hobson.[21] The incapacity of socialists to develop an independent position in foreign policy reflected both theoretical weaknesses and the lack of interest in foreign affairs shown by their predominantly working-class constituency.

3

Hobson and Angell

Cobden's liberal pacifism was, as we have seen, more than an ideology of protest. It was frequently used by statesmen – Palmerston, Gladstone – to provide a moral gloss to a foreign policy that actually owed little to principle and much to the pragmatic calculus of the balance of power. So long as Britain remained the leading industrial force, it was relatively easy to reconcile moral purpose with the defence of British power. As that power declined, however, the gap between Cobdenite principle and Government practice tended to widen. Under pressure of emerging economic and imperial rivalries during the last quarter of the nineteenth century, many of the underlying assumptions of Cobdenism were called into question. But the theory did not, as might be expected, simply disappear. Latter-day Cobdenites faced the future by returning to the subversive roots of their creed. Increasingly it was the critical functions of Cobdenism that mattered, not its capacity to lend high moral tone to the self-interested actions of the British state.

Mid-Victorian liberals had supposed that, as the beneficent influence of commerce penetrated the decadent societies of the East, ancient tyrannies would give way more or less peacefully to new principles of social order mirroring the civilization of bourgeois England. As this occurred, the existing mechanisms of formal and informal imperial control would dissolve into bonds of friendship between equal trading partners.[1] These rosy expectations were not fulfilled. Instead, during the last quarter of the nineteenth century, Britain embarked on a major expansion of formal imperial control. The impact of European economic expansion in Asia and Africa tended to produce, not thriving bourgeois communities, but anarchy and chaos. The Indian Mutiny of 1857 was the first of many rebellions which gradually transformed British attitudes to the

non-white world. The people once optimistically seen as
potential partners in commerce and civilization, were re-
defined as 'lesser breeds without the law'. No longer was it
England's mission to lead willing peoples towards enlightenment. In place of that delightful task was a heavy burden of
paternalistic duty:

> Take up the White Man's burden –
> Send Forth the best ye breed –
> Go bind your sons to exile
> To serve your captive's need;
> To wait in heavy harness
> On fluttered folk and wild –
> Your new-caught, sullen peoples,
> Half devil and half child.

Such attitudes were reinforced by the increased contact with
more remote societies as tropical Africa was opened up during
the later decades of the nineteenth century.[2]

The replacement of the merchant venturer by the imperial
bureaucrat as the chief agent of expansion, represented a
fundamental challenge to the values of Cobden's England. As
the apparatus of imperial rule expanded in Asia and Africa, the
aristocratic militarism that Bright had decried gained a new
lease of life. Among the upper classes the public schools
laboured to subvert the principles of liberalism, inculcating
future imperial governors – 'Head Prefects of the World' –
with élitist and anti-democratic values.[3] Simultaneously,
imperialist sentiment among the masses was nurtured by the
new mass-circulation press which used sensationalized
accounts of the dramas of imperial expansion as a way of
establishing the habit of newspaper reading among a large and
ill-educated public. Small wonder that, by the time of the Boer
War, the pacifists felt like a small and beleaguered minority.
Following the great betrayal of 1882, when Gladstone
presided over the annexation of Egypt, they could not even
rely on the Liberal Party to resist the imperialist tide.

Imperial expansion was driven forward not only by the
collapse of order in extra-European societies, but also by
intensifying competition from Britain's European rivals for 'a
place in the sun'. British Governments staked their claim to

disputed areas by formalizing imperial control. As British diplomats manœuvred to protect extra-European spheres of influence against foreign rivals, they found themselves inexorably drawn into taking sides in the hardening alliance system on the European continent. Early in the new century, agreements to resolve imperial clashes with the old rivals, France and Russia, drew Britain into close association with the anti-German Dual Entente. Imperial competition with Germany, embodied in an escalating naval race, became interlocked with the enmities between the continental powers.[4] During the first decade of the twentieth century it became apparent that Britain could no longer sustain its role as an independent makeweight in the European balance of power. Unable to police the world unaided, Britain was losing its freedom of manœuvre – including its freedom to avoid involvement in future European wars.

The wave of imperial annexations and Britain's entry into the European alliance system, did much to sap the foundations of pacifist optimism. But the frontal assault on Cobdenite assumptions was the challenge to free trade itself. When, in 1860, Cobden, a private citizen acting on behalf of the Government, negotiated a commercial treaty with France, it seemed that the era of universal free trade was well on its way. But from the 1870s, as European and American industrialization intensified completion in international markets, the trend reversed. By 1900 most of Britain's industrial rivals had substantial tariffs in place. This included Britain's own semi-independent white dominions – Australia, New Zealand, Canada and South Africa. Their resistance to throwing their home markets open to British manufacturing industry was symptomatic of the loosening of imperial bonds.

Those imperialists who took the full measure of Britain's declining ability to dominate the world either economically or militarily, moved towards a strategy of imperial consolidation. Rather than continuing to attempt to police the whole world, they looked for a tighter unity of the formal Empire. Only in this way, they believed, could Britain hope to count in the twentieth-century world, alongside the emerging superpowers of America, Russia and Germany. The first step towards the consolidation of the Empire as a coherent military and political bloc, was the establishment of an imperial customs union. In 1902 Joseph Chamberlain, Colonial Secretary in the Conservative Government, resigned from the Cabinet in order to campaign for Tariff Reform. By imposing a general tariff on foreign imports, Britain would be able to open negotiations with the White Dominions for a mutual removal of tariff barriers, drawing them into closer economic ties with the homeland as a first step towards final political federation of the Empire as a whole and the establishment of a supreme representative Imperial Parliament in London. The primary purpose of Chamberlain's Tariff Reform programme was imperial consolidation. But it also offered other advantages – protection of British jobs against cheap foreign imports, and an inflow of customs duties to the Treasury which could be used to pay for the escalating costs of both armaments and social reforms.[5] As Chamberlain's doctrines swept the Tory rank and file, liberal pacifists feared that Tariff Reform would provide the new imperialism with a level of popular appeal that would make it unstoppable.

It was J. A. Hobson who made the most influential and original attempt to come to grips with the nature of the new imperialism. Born into a provincial Liberal family in 1858, Hobson developed unorthodox views which prevented him from securing an academic career in his chosen field of economics. His sin, anticipating Keynes, was to question the value of limitless saving. Over-saving, he argued, was a product of inequality. Unless the proceeds of industry were more equally distributed – putting cash in the hands of working-class people who would spend it not save it – the market for the products of industry would tend to dry up, leading to recurrent crises of over-production or, as he preferred to describe it, under-consumption. He worked as a journalist in the 1890s, and took an active role in discussions among liberal and socialist intellectuals. In 1899 he went to South Africa to report on the tensions in the Transvaal. His book on the South African War – which placed the blame squarely on the shoulders of the Johannesburg mineowners and their cosmopolitan financial backers – was widely distributed by the pro-Boer movement. *Imperialism*, which was published in 1902, represented a fusion of his South African experience with his earlier ideas on under-consumptionist economics.[6] Hobson's work is mainly remembered because Lenin used it to construct his own, quite distinct, theory of imperialism. Hobson's *Imperialism* is important in our context not because of its impact on the development of Marxist theories of 'the last stage of capitalism', but as an attempt to restate for the new century the fundamental principles of Cobdenite free trade. It was the 'liberal socialism' espoused by Hobson, not Lenin's Marxism, that played the dominant part in British peace politics well into the inter-war years.

For Cobden, capitalism had been the chief agency of peace between nations. Hobson, while proclaiming the validity of Cobden's analysis, nevertheless gives capitalists the central role in promoting the new aggressive imperialism. The key to this paradox is that they were talking about different kinds of capitalists. Cobden's hero was the trader, who had no use for protective tariffs which impeded the expansion of commerce between nations. Hobson agreed. The merchant had no particular interest in which Great Power established law and order in the regions with which he traded, so long as somebody did. And even if a protectionist Power were to exclude British goods from some newly developing market, it was 'mercantilist superstition'[7] to believe that this would do permanent damage:

> The intricate and ever-growing industrial co-operation of the civilised nations through trade does not permit any nation to keep to herself the gain of any market she may hold.[8]

Had it been only the interests of traders that were being considered, there would have been no need for Britain to have responded to the competitive challenge of other European states by formalizing and expanding her own empire, with all that this entailed in provoking international tensions, arms expenditures, and general insecurity.[9]

Though Hobson argued that the new imperialism was irrational from the standpoint of the peaceful commercial nation, he did not believe that its source was to be found

merely in an irrational aggressiveness on the part of peoples or
Governments. Rather: 'The business interests of the nation as
a whole are subordinated to those of certain sectional interests
that usurp control of the national resources and use them for
their private gain.'[10] Behind the policy of imperial expansion
stood the sinister figure of the financier engaged not in honest
trade but in channelling the surplus product of British industry
into overseas investment. Unlike the provincial businessmen
represented by Cobden, the financiers of the City of London
had long been intimate in the aristocratic circles that
dominated Westminster and Whitehall. To safeguard and
expand their overseas investments, they used their political
influence to suborn the 'the public policy, the public purse,
and the public force' to the promotion of their private
interests. In this they were supported by a number of other
vested interests: arms manufacturers, imperial bureaucrats,
admirals and generals. The high-minded imperialist rhetoric
of politicians like Joseph Chamberlain served, wittingly or
unwittingly, simply as a cover for the selfish profiteering of
the vested interests. 'This', wrote Hobson, 'is, perhaps, the
most important fact in modern politics, and the obscurity in
which it is wrapped constitutes the gravest danger to our
State.'[11] The secretive greed of the bankers had replaced the
open belligerence of the aristocrats as the main threat to peace.
Sinister though their role was, Hobson did not believe that the
financiers were out to provoke war between the European
powers. Certainly the struggle for overseas investment
opportunities provoked tensions; and small colonial wars
could yield large profits. The competition in armaments was
good for business and great bankers knew how to use their
inside political knowledge to make money out of fluctuations
in the currency markets caused by international disputes. But,
knowing that a great war would kill the goose that laid the
golden eggs, the bankers could probably be relied upon to use
their enormous influence to prevent it:

> The modern science of militarism renders wars between
> 'civilised' Powers too costly, and the rapid growth of
> effective internationalism in the financial and great
> industrial magnates [sic], who seem destined more and

more to control national politics, may in future render
such wars impossible .[12]

The bankers' peace, however, was not a genuine one, but a
rampant militarism which threatened to destroy the foundations of
civilized life as surely as, if less quickly than, war itself. Just before
the outbreak of the First World War, H. N. Brailsford, a liberal
socialist who did much to popularize Hobson's ideas, coined the
phrase 'dry war' to describe relations between the European powers:

> Modern conditions have involved us in rivalry of
> armaments which is now a conscious struggle to achieve
> by expenditure and science, by diplomacy and alliances,
> a balance of power which always eludes us, and because it
> is always variable and unstable condemns us to a
> bloodless battle, a dry warfare of steel and gold.[13]

In Europe international tensions would be kept artificially
alive in order to justify massive expenditure on armaments
and the construction of centralized bureaucracies and armies
capable of suppressing any democratic movement attempting
to challenge the power and wealth of the bankers and their
hangers on. Outside Europe international finance would pool
its resources to open up the biggest prize of all – the vast
reservoir of cheap labour awaiting Western exploitation in
China. An England grown fat on imperial tribute, its manufacturing industry relocated in the East, and its proletariat
reduced to servicing the conspicuous consumption of idle
rentiers, would provide little basis for democratic resistance to
the power of the financial oligarchy. In Hobson's bleak vision,
European civilization, for all its nineteenth-century promise,
was heading for the fate of the Roman Empire.[14]

Hobson and Brailsford's belief in the improbability of war
in Europe was shared by most pre-1914 pacifists. Many,
however, were less pessimistic about the malevolent desire of
powerful vested interests to obstruct the progress of
democracy and genuine peace. The imperialist politicians
who, at the turn of the century, seemed to be carrying all
before them, turned out to be far less powerful than Hobson
and others had feared. The long drawn out war in South Africa
did much to discredit imperial adventuring. Popular responses

to military emergencies – like celebrations that followed the relief of Mafeking – might depress the radicals. But imperialists were equally dispirited by their inability to turn such moments of excitement into a sustained popular identification with their long-term goals.[15] Despite intensive efforts to reinvent the national identity along imperial lines – including the rebuilding of central London as a theatre for imperial parades[16] – the English remained obstinately English, refusing to think of themselves even as 'Britishers', let alone as members of the Greater Britain projected by imperialist dreamers. 'We have not even a name, with any emotional associations, for the UK itself', remarked one political theorist. 'No Englishman is stirred by the name "British", the name "English" irritates all Scotchmen, and the Irish are irritated by both alike.'[17]

Hobson's belief that protectionism was the logical next step for imperialist politics was reinforced by the launching of Joseph Chamberlain's Tariff Reform campaign in 1902. But the voters were unresponsive to Chamberlain's vision. They measured Tariff Reform on strictly financial grounds and found it wanting. In 1906 the Liberals came romping back to power on an electoral landslide caused, above all, by their success in branding the Tories as the party of bread taxes.

The electoral unpopularity of Tariff Reform might not have been decisive in defeating Chamberlain's programme had it not been for the fact that the most powerful sections of Britain's business élite – and in particular the bankers of the City of London – agreed with the voters. Whatever windfall profits might be earned from minor wars and international tensions, there was little doubt in the City that their interests lay in sustaining Britain as the free trading capital of a worldwide empire of finance, rather than retreating into the protectionist bloc envisaged by proponents of Imperial Federation.[18] This was good news for pacifists, but bad news for Hobson's theory, and it opened the way to a more optimistic interpretation of the role of finance in international relations.

No single book ever had a greater impact on pacifist thinking in Britain than Norman Angell's *The Great Illusion*. First published (under a different title) in 1909, it eventually sold over a million copies and was translated into 25 languages. Angell's central argument was a simple restatement of the interdependence of modern capitalist economies. The 'great illusion' was the belief that a modern European state could increase its wealth by seizing the territory of its competitors:

> As between economically highly organised nations a customer must also be a competitor, a fact which bayonets cannot alter. To the extent that they destroy him as a competitor, they destroy him, speaking generally and largely, as a customer.[19]

A. J. P. Taylor's grandfather, a businessman who had no doubt read the book, put the point more succinctly in the early months of the First World War: 'Can't they see as every time they kills a German, they kills a customer?'[20] For Angell the key evidence of the irrationality of war lay in the very delicacy of the newly evolved mechanisms of international finance. 'The [financier], wrote Angell, 'has no country, and he knows, if he be of the modern type, that arms and conquests and jugglery with frontiers serve no ends of his. . . .'.[21] Attempts by an aggressor power to exact indemnities or to confiscate the wealth of private individuals in a conquered state would cause chaos in the international money markets, undermining the basis of the conqueror's own prosperity.

Angell shared none of Hobson's anxieties about the long-term consequences of the export of capital from Europe. It was, he believed, the job of civilized nations to impose – by force if necessary – law, order and the virtues of capitalism on less developed peoples. The problem was how to prevent the necessary use of force outside Europe from precipitating war in Europe itself. However necessary it might sometimes be to put down rebellious non-Europeans, there was no good reason why Europeans should fight among themselves over spheres of influence. Following Hobson, Angell explained that no advanced nation could hope to keep the economic advantages of colonial expansion to itself, not even by imposing tariff barriers. It really didn't matter to Britain if it was the Germans who brought efficiency to the Turkish economy – so long as someone did. Indeed the nations that stood to gain most from European expansion were those which burdened their economies least with the unproductive business of armies and bureaucracies.

Angell's analysis reflected a Eurocentric racism widespread in pacifist thinking. Quakers had long distinguished between the policeman and the soldier,[22] and the suppression of disorder among heathens was seen as legitimate in a way that prosecuting war between civilized Christian peoples could never be. As George Dangerfield remarked in 1935: 'the Englishman of the seventies and eighties . . . was strongly in favour of peace – that is to say, he liked his wars to be fought at a distance and, if possible, in the name of God.'[23] Such attitudes enabled Angell to compile a list of war-mongering nations with Britain coming last: colonial wars didn't count![24] Peace was a stage of civilization not yet reached by non-Europeans. Reforming the British Army to operate as a potential expeditionary force on the Continent was anathema to pacifist opinion. Consequently, Lord Haldane was careful to present his Army reforms as designed to create 'an Imperial police force which can be sent on small expeditions, on short notice' – a rationale which, he calculated, would be acceptable to most pacifists.[25]

One obvious way to reduce the risks of conflict between the powers was to encourage the formation of an 'ultra-imperialist' consortium of powers to open up new territories like China. Angell endorsed such proposals enthusiastically. Some radical writers, like Brailsford, were more circumspect:

> We have found, so far, no solution which is satisfactory from the standpoint of the debtor nation. The inroad of foreign capital always means for it some loss of independence, and it has nothing to gain by agreement among competing Empires . . . The pacifist and the nationalist are here divided in their sympathies. The former, thinking only of European peace, rejoices when Russia and Britain end their differences by the partition of Persia. The latter seeing only that a nation has been destroyed, regards the agreement as a peculiarly evil development of Imperialism. . . . The ideal expedient would preserve European peace without destroying the

victim nationality. To propose that expedient requires an
excursion into the realms of Utopian construction. We
can propose nothing which seems feasible today. . . .[26]

It was only after the collapse of peace in Europe that radicals
could begin to envisage 'such a weakening of all the Great
Powers of Europe as shall enable the more backward nations
to throw off the yoke fastened on them by the Cabinets and
financiers of "civilised" States.'[27]

Where Hobson and Angell really diverged was in their
assessment of the attitudes of the rich towards international
conflict short of war itself. Angell said little about the vested
interest of arms manufacturers in war scares, or of financial
speculators in international instability. Militarism was kept
alive not by vested interest but by pure superstition. This did
not mean that there was no danger of war. It was what people
believed their interests to be, not what they actually were, that
determined their actions. Angell was not complacent. He
stressed the urgency of the pacifist work of enlightenment:
'. . . the only solution will be found in the reform of
opinion. . .'.[28] But he believed that pacifism could expect
support from all the major vested interests in a modern
capitalist society.

Perhaps because Angell's analysis did not attack the
Establishment, he was never short of friends in high places.
Before 1914 he numbered among his acquaintances the
Chairman of the Committee of Imperial Defence, the leader of
the Tory party and the Liberal foreign secretary.[29] A wealthy
industrialist established a foundation to promote his ideas
among the rich and powerful. In response to the book, Angell
clubs sprang up not only in Britain but also on the Continent,[30] one more link in the vast variety of international
organizations that networked Europe, promoting peace and
international understanding. In 1910 representatives from
over 100 international organizations – religious, cultural,
professional and political – had met in Brussels to establish a
Union of International Associations. Women were organized
internationally in the International Women's Suffrage
Alliance. Most important of all, the two greatest social forces
of the epoch – capital and labour – were themselves organizing

on international lines. All these developments appeared to confirm Angell's view that the boundaries of the real communities in Europe had long since ceased to be represented by state frontiers.

The publication of Angell's book coincided with the triumph of a campaign to abolish slavery in the Congo. This agitation is worth mentioning at this point, both because it perfectly exemplified the continuing strengths of liberal pacifism, and because its leader and organizer, E. D. Morel, was later to play a key role in sustaining British pacifism after the outbreak of war in 1914. Morel, a shipping clerk who had taken up campaigning journalism on behalf of Liverpool's African merchant interests, set up the Congo Reform Association in 1903, following his success in persuading the Government to issue a formal protest about the brutal regime of forced labour exercised by the Belgian King, Leopold, in the Congo. Six years of intense agitation followed, until Leopold's death finally opened the way for reforms in the Belgian Congo, and the opening of the colony to free trade. Throughout this agitation Morel's appeal to the presumed interests of Liverpool merchants was quite open and unashamed: the liberation of Africans enslaved by Leopold and his monopolistic ring of financiers, and the interests of genuine traders in free trade, went hand in hand.

Just as in 1876 – Morel frequently compared his efforts with the outburst against the Bulgarian atrocities – the campaigners were outraged by Foreign Office insistence that wider considerations of the balance of power should be taken into account when deciding how far to push their humanitarian crusade. Impatient with the intricacies – and amorality – of international diplomacy, Morel demanded unilateral action by the British Navy. A blockade of the rubber ships would soon bring Leopold to his knees. 'I am convinced', he wrote in 1905, 'that . . . at the present stage of world politics, the British people can get anything they want if they put their backs into it.'[31] It was the Foreign Office's reluctance to upset the *entente* with France by pressing too hard on the Congo issue which first convinced Morel of the baneful effects of traditional diplomacy, and provoked him to develop a coherent critique of what he later called 'the intrigues and

imbecilities of professional diplomats.'[32] Morel's attack on
'secret diplomacy' was to have immense influence after war
broke out in 1914. It is not without significance that it had its
source in a campaign which effectively combined Cobdenite
principles of free trade with a 'bellicose philanthropy'[33]
worthy of the most self-righteous of Victorian imperialists.

4

Socialism, Liberalism and Peace before 1914

Socialism, as it developed in Britain, had little distinctive contribution to make to the formulation of foreign policy. Most socialists, if they were interested at all, took their foreign policy from middle-class radicals, and pacifist politics continued to be dominated by essentially Cobdenite assumptions about the relationship between capitalism and peace.[1] The major challenge to the dominance of such assumptions in progressive politics came, not from the mainstream Labour and socialist movements, but from a minority of socialists who anticipated post-1914 developments by seeking an accommodation with nationalist and imperialist ideas.

Nationalist responses to the crisis of the international order were, of course, most apparent on the Right. But, although they defended free trade against Joseph Chamberlain and the Tariff Reformers, most of the leading Liberal politicians and an influential minority of socialists accommodated themselves to the underlying assumptions of the new imperialism. The appalling health of the population, revealed by Boer War recruitment, did much to persuade the Establishment of the need for an extensive programme of social reform to improve the condition of the working class. If Britain was to survive in the new world of rival empires she must look to the fitness of her population, both for the military and for the economic struggle. Some left-wing reformers – notably the leaders of Fabian socialism, Sidney and Beatrice Webb – were quick to take up 'national efficiency' as an argument for social reform. The Webbs, who had little sympathy with Liberal cosmopolitanism, were happy to come to terms with the imperialist agenda in order to promote their own brand of statist socialism.[2]

The argument for 'national efficiency' helped to win the Liberal Party leadership to the case for social reform after they gained office in 1905. For the new Liberal Government, the introduction of medical inspection in schools and the construction of Dreadnoughts were not contradictory undertakings, but complementary facets of Britain's rivalry with Imperial Germany. Lloyd George began his governmental career after 1906 as leader of the social reformist left in the Liberal Party. With his background in the pro-Boer agitation, he initially followed the pacifist line of counterposing social reform to spending on armaments. But he was quick to perceive that there was little future in such arguments, at least for a Government Minister. His subsequent rise to power as the charismatic leader of Britain's 'war socialism' provides the best illustration of the tendency for left and right-wing collectivism to converge around a nationalist economics utterly alien to the Cobdenite traditions of the pacifists.[3] But some of Britain's leading socialists were ready to follow a similar trajectory.

H. M. Hyndman, the ex-Tory founding father of British Marxism, saw the defence of bad states against worse ones as a legitimate socialist position. The humiliation of Tsarist power in the Russo–Japanese war of 1904–05, led him to substitute the Kaiser for the Tsar as the main threat to democratic and socialist progress in Europe. He saw no evidence that the German Socialists were either willing or able to restrain Prussian ambitions, nor did he place any faith in bourgeois internationalism. Hyndman drew the pessimistic conclusion that it was British power, rather than any kind of pacifism, which held the key to peace. In 1910 he followed the logic of the 'German threat' into support for naval expansion.[4] Robert Blatchford, Britain's most popular socialist writer, came to the same conclusion, but went further, writing enthusiastic articles for the *Daily Mail* in support of military conscription.[5] Like Hyndman, and the Webbs, Blatchford had always looked to the state as the main agency of social change.[6]

This 'realist' attitude towards international affairs was partly a product of unqualified support for the expansion of state intervention in the domestic economy. If the state was everything, and civil society nothing, then pacifist faith in the power of the international community to restrain the war-making proclivities of nation states was merely wishful thinking. The single-minded pursuit of 'national efficiency' was not compatible with a pacifist orientation in international affairs. Rising international tension left these statist socialists no option but to support the British state against its less democratic German rival. The full implications of this convergence between state socialism and nationalism only became apparent after war broke out in 1914. It paved the way for a national socialism which was to play an important – if frequently neglected – part in the evolution of British Labour politics.

In proposing a rupture between liberal internationalism and nationalist socialism, Hyndman and Blatchford were ahead of their time. Such views were to move into the mainstream of Labour politics only when liberal capitalism collapsed under the strains of the First World War. Meanwhile the frontier between liberalism and socialism remained open, both ideologically and organizationally. The Labour Party, which had forty MPs by 1914, had established itself since the turn of the century largely on the basis of an electoral pact with the Liberals. It acted in Parliament as the representative of Labour interests within a broader alliance of progressive forces.[7] This was not an unnatural alliance. The social reforms promoted by post-Gladstonian liberals had much to offer the workers, while, in their commitment to self-help and autonomy from state controls, the major institutions of the British working class – trade unions, the co-operative movement – had a genuine affinity with Liberal suspicion of unrestrained collectivism. William Morris, drawn into politics by the Bulgarian Atrocities agitation, had originated the trend for middle-class intellectuals disillusioned with liberal foreign policy to place their faith in the workers. After becoming a socialist in the early 1880s he retained what he called 'an Englishman's wholesome horror of government interference and centralisation.'[8] Leaders of the main pre-war socialist party, the ILP, had long cultivated friendly relations with Liberal intellectuals. In the late 1890s, for example, Ramsay MacDonald worked closely with J. A. Hobson on the *Progressive Review*, a liberal socialist journal which attacked 'Manchesterism' in the

name of domestic social reform, while remaining 'keenly alive
to the dangers of a powerful State, taken as an instrument of
absolute control and adducing "reasons of State" as an over-
ruling principle of policy.'[9] Many social reformers, both
liberal and socialist, shared Hobson's distrust of the big state;
and, in pacifist campaigns against militarism, they maintained
the links between liberal socialism at home and a revised and
updated Cobdenism abroad.

The pre-war career of H. N. Brailsford illustrates the easy
co-operation of liberal and socialist internationalism before
1914.[10] As a young man Brailsford abandoned an academic
career to fight Turkish oppression alongside the Greek army
in 1897. When he returned he took up journalism. Thereafter,
he devoted most of his energies to the attempt to develop
debate about alternative foreign policy in pacifist, liberal and
socialist circles. Despite joining the ILP in 1907, he continued
for a long time to write leaders for Liberal journals. He did not
anticipate an open struggle for power between the Liberal and
Labour Parties, but looked for proportional representation to
resolve the tensions over distribution of seats between the two
parties within an ongoing alliance of progressive forces.[11] The
immediate task, as he saw it, was to open foreign policy up to
democratic pressure, so that both the disinterested masses and
the interested merchants and manufacturers could concert
their influence for peace against the machinations of militar-
istic bureaucrats and their allies in the aristocracy of finance.[12]

Brailsford deplored the incapacity of pacifists to get to grips
with the larger drift of British foreign policy – the effective
entry of Britain into the European alliance system. To those –
like C. P. Scott, editor of the *Manchester Guardian* – who
opposed all alliances in the name of the Cobdenite principle of
non-intervention,[13] he replied that non-intervention was a
sterile doctrine that would cut Britain off from its rightful
place within the emerging community of European nations.
The alternative to the balance of power politics pursued by the
British Foreign Office was not isolation, but the Concert of
Europe. 'When we think of peace,' he wrote, 'we must learn to
think as Europeans.'[14] He looked to 'a natural grouping of the
more advanced Western powers'[15] – Britain, France and
Germany – to lay the foundations for a genuine Concert of

Europe which would mediate the conflicts between the powers and, through the systematic regulation of its activities, turn the potentially disruptive operations of international finance into a force for peace and tranquillity.

Brailsford was no utopian. He combined largeness of vision with a restless search for immediately practicable steps. As a first step to bringing democratic pressure to bear on foreign policy he advocated the establishment of a select committee of MPs to shadow the operations of the Foreign Office. In 1911 Liberal backbenchers did establish their own unofficial committee. But it was not until war actually broke out that any concerted attempt was made to organize an informed public opinion outside Parliament that would be capable of mounting detailed criticism of and pressure on the Foreign Office. Before the war the attitude of the typical radical remained one of 'semi-indifference. . . . The conception of conflict between nations, on which foreign policy was based, was distasteful to him; he had no wish to acknowledge it. He was internationally minded; he believed in concord between nations, and so ardently that he did not question over much whether concord between nations actually existed.'[16] Meanwhile pacifists were generally content with the abstract moralizing suggested by the *Manchester Guardian*'s opposition to the formation of a Liberal Foreign Affairs Committee on the grounds that the 'success or failure [of foreign policy] depends on the application of a few simple principles to facts which as a rule are not very numerous nor very complicated.'[17]

While such wilful ignorance prevailed it is not surprising that pacifist opposition to Sir Edward Grey's foreign policy tended to be episodic and dominated by side issues. The greatest stir was caused by Britain's growing friendship with Russia, culminating in an Anglo-Russian Convention in 1907 and an official visit to Britain by the Tsar two years later. Most radical opinion was outraged by the fact that Britain should be reversing its traditional hostility to Russia just at the moment when defeat by the Japanese in 1904–5, and the revolutionary upheavals which followed, had rocked the foundations of Tsarist tyranny. The loans and diplomatic favours that paved the way for the *entente* with Russia helped to prop up a regime seen by radicals as the major threat to freedom – and to peace – in Europe.[18] This was the one international issue between the Boer War and 1914 which mobilized large public demonstrations. Solidarity with the Russian democracy even engaged the sympathies of trade unions, normally quite indifferent to foreign affairs.[19]

The main focus of pacifist activity in the immediate pre-war years was the naval race with Germany. The apparent success of the Admiralty and the arms firms in 1908–9 in bouncing the Cabinet into a major escalation of naval building, alerted radicals to the dangers of militarism. Their concern was not only with 'the danger that the guns may suddenly go off, as it were.'[20] Indeed, some pacifists even drew comfort from the idea that modern weapons had become so destructive that no one was likely to contemplate actually using them;[21] others were reassured by the apparent improvement in Anglo-German relations after the upheavals of the Balkan Wars of 1912. But whatever happened on the diplomatic front, it seemed, arms expenditure rose. 'With nothing left to fight about', wrote Brailsford in 1914, 'our chief concern is that we may have something to fight with.'[22] What concerned the radicals was militarization itself, and the corruption of democratic process involved. Although the socialist ILP played a leading role in agitations against the 'arms ring', exposure of the close links between naval officers, Admiralty bureaucrats and their private industrial suppliers did not necessarily lead pacifists to draw socialist conclusions. The favoured solution, the nationalization of the arms firms, was generally presented as an anti-monopoly measure quite acceptable to liberals, not as (what actually it would have been) the state taking over the commanding heights of the economy. It was the vested interests of arms manufacturers, not capitalism as such, which they were trying to break. And even those, like Brailsford, who insisted that the arms manufacturers were only junior partners to the financiers, took care to distinguish these malign features of capitalism from the equally selfish but nevertheless socially beneficial activities of ordinary manufacturers and traders.[23] The search for middle-class allies still inhibited most socialists from attributing militarism, imperialism and the war danger to capitalism as such.

In one respect the pre-war pacifists probably under-estimated the importance of the emerging military industrial complex. Committed to the cult of the workers as 'dis-interested' opponents of militarism, they generally remained silent about the degree to which workers themselves had come to have a vested interest in the arms race. The Labour Party wrestled with the problem by linking demands for dis-armament with plans for legislation guaranteeing the Right to Work. But it was unable to impose the Party line of opposition to the annual defence estimates on MPs representing con-stituencies with large defence contracts.[24] Nor was this a marginal problem. It was estimated in 1913 that as many as 1.5 million people had a vested interest, directly or indirectly, in defence spending.[25]

During the last years of peace Keir Hardie, the leader of British socialism, played a central role in committing the Socialist International to a policy of the general strike against war. In 1912 the Labour Party overcame its caution sufficient-ly to agree at least to inquire into the feasibility of such a strike. But the new interest shown by socialists in the old anarchist nostrum of 'the general strike against war' did not rest on an acceptance that only the proletarian revolution could prevent war. Neither British nor continental socialists saw any contradiction between endorsement of the strike weapon and the pursuit of co-operation with middle-class pacifism. Indeed, at the same time as they debated the general strike, leaders of the Second International became increasingly interested in the implications of modern capitalist develop-ments for the elimination of war. Most of them moved towards a similar view of the pacifist tendencies of modern capitalism to that expounded by Norman Angell. In 1911 Bebel, the German socialist, declared:

> I say openly that the greatest guarantee for the preserv-ation of world peace today is found in the international investments of capitalism. These investments make war so dangerous for both sides that it would be pure madness for any government to push things to the brink over Morocco.[26]

Keir Hardie favoured the general strike, not as an instrument of class struggle and revolution, but because he believed it could make a valuable contribution to maintaining the peace of bourgeois Europe. Well aware that most workers were indifferent to foreign affairs, he fully expected the majority of them to be swept into fratricide by patriotic propaganda if war actually came. He did not believe a strike would be easy – or even, necessarily, possible – to arrange. Rather, the socialist leaders were trying to intervene in the high politics of Europe by means of a deliberately constructed myth. They hoped that the very talk of a general strike would act as a restraining influence on militarism. If the élites could be persuaded that war might trigger revolution, then they would think twice before unleashing it. Hardie said in 1910 that:

> It was too late to begin to take action when the war fever had maddened the blood of the people, but if the warmongers in Germany and in this country knew beforehand that the working class of the two countries had come to an understanding, and would stand by it, the influence of that knowledge upon their counsels would be such as to compel them to submit to arbitration the points which would otherwise have been submitted to war.[27]

The 'international strike against war', as espoused by Hardie and other Second International leaders, represented a sophisticated politics of bluff, quite compatible with their attempts to form class alliances against the war danger. When the bluff failed, it is hardly surprising that no-one seriously considered attempting to implement the general strike against war. The coming of war in 1914 unleashed forces which pre-1914 pacifists – liberal or socialist – did not begin to understand. Without substantially re-thinking their politics, there was little they could do to resist these forces.

5

Sustaining Pacifism, 1914–15

> Trade, travel and intellectual intercourse bring [states] constantly closer together. They copy each other's institutions; and, to strengthen their common interests, they have built up a series of common institutions – international unions to govern postal, railway and telegraphic communication, conferences and conventions to regulate affairs both of property (such as copyright) and labour; international law courts (at the Hague and elsewhere) supported by a network of Arbitration and other treaties; a sort of World-Duma, in the periodical Peace Conferences at the Hague; and last but not least, the growing international organisation of the Labour and Socialist movements. That is one picture; national peace and the beginning of a Union of nations: in a rudimentary form, the United States of Europe is an accomplished fact.[1]

Pre-war Europe was a community networked by transnational institutions. Rooted in civil society and operating with some independence from inter-state relations, such institutions provided a potential check and counter-balance to the tendency towards anarchy inherent in a system of rival nation states. The hopes of both liberal and socialist pacifists in pre-war Britain were, as we have seen, very largely invested in this emergent transnational community.

The crisis posed for such a pacifism by the Great War was twofold. Transnational links were shattered by closing frontiers and the tide of nationalist sentiment sweeping through society. Pacifists struggled to keep alive some remnant of the pre-war networks, and their modest successes laid a basis for the eventual revival of internationalism as the passions of war cooled. The deeper crisis of pacifism, however, emerged more gradually. As the state mobilized the population for war, the very basis of transnationalism – a civil society autonomous from the state – was drastically undermined. Individual liberties, voluntary organizations, political parties and the whole apparatus of economic life were subordinated to the war-making purposes of the state. The Great War marked the beginning of the end of the era of liberal capitalism. In the long term, the future of British pacifism lay in its capacity to adapt to the demise of the world order from which, often unconsciously, its most fundamental assumptions were derived.

On August 2nd, 1914 British Labour mobilized its biggest demonstration for many years. The crowds assembled in Trafalgar Square cheered demands for Britain to keep out of the spreading European crisis. Liberals and Socialists agreed that the only purpose served by an Anglo–German war would be to place Europe at the mercy of the Russian autocracy. Within hours, however, the German invasion of Belgium overshadowed the Russian menace, and put a sudden end to pacifist resistance. The Liberal Cabinet united, shedding two unrepentant pacifists – Gladstone's biographer, John Morley and the ex-socialist leader John Burns. Another minister, Edward Pease, who was also Chairman of the Peace Society, decided to stay on.[2] The Labour Party, after some initial ambivalence, had moved by the end of August to outright support of the war effort, accepting an electoral truce and joining with other parties to lend support to the recruiting drive. Earlier, the TUC had declared an industrial truce for the duration of the war. Serious efforts to sustain pre-war international networks were confined to the socialists of the ILP and a section of the women's suffrage movement.

On August 11th the ILP sent greetings – 'across the roar of the guns' – to their German comrades. The statement, however, contained no demand for an immediate armistice, and until 1916 few ILP leaders saw any prospect of public agitation to stop the war. Internationally some attempt was made to sustain the networks. The International Socialist Bureau, the office of the Second International, moved from Belgium to neutral Holland. In May 1915 the Italian and Swiss Socialist Parties called for a conference of socialists who had 'remained true to the old principles of the International . . .

and were ready to fight for the mobilization of Socialists in all countries against war.' Delegates from most of the belligerent countries managed to get to the Zimmerwald Conference in the autumn, but representatives from Britain, appointed by the ILP and the British Socialist Party, were denied passports. Lenin wanted to use the conference to launch an international struggle to turn the war into the revolution. Most other delegates dismissed this as quite unrealistic and agreed merely to encourage the International Socialist Bureau to continue seeking opportunities for a peaceful settlement, 'without annexations or indemnities'. No such opportunities, however, were in sight.[3]

The feminists had rather more success. When war broke out the best known suffragettes turned overnight from militant confrontation with the male establishment to enthusiastic participation in the crusade against Prussianism. But members of the largest suffrage organization – the non-militant National Union of Women's Suffrage Societies – were deeply divided on the merits of the war. Early in 1915 most of the younger activists resigned in order to devote their energies to developing a women's peace movement. In the autumn they established a Women's International League based on a joint platform of women's rights and pacifism: 'only free women can build up the peace which is to be.'[4] After the war this became the British section of the Women's International League for Peace and Freedom, a transnational organization which exists to this day.

The occasion for the split in the National Union was a call from women involved in the International Women's Suffrage Alliance for delegates to attend a Women's Congress in The Hague in April 1915, the first major international meeting of any kind since the outbreak of war. The Congress endorsed a call for neutral countries to mediate between the belligerents. More ambitiously, it appointed envoys to present their views directly to the politicians. Over the summer of 1915 these women were remarkably successful in gaining audiences with the powerful throughout Europe and in the United States. Underlying this exercise in unofficial shuttle diplomacy was an assertion that, denied the elementary rights of citizenship in most of the war-making nations, women could stand above the battle 'providing the motive power' for peace. Catherine Marshall, a leading feminist pacifist, wrote:

> War is pre-eminently an outrage on motherhood and all that motherhood means; the destruction of life and the breaking-up of homes is the undoing of women's work as life-givers and home-makers.[5]

The diplomacy came to nothing, but the Hague Congress did much to crystallize the belief that women had a spcial role to play in the politics of peace. Feminism, particularly the maternalist feminism expressed by Catherine Marshall, long remained a powerful source of pacifist activism.[6]

The substantial minority at The Hague who opposed the plan to send envoys believed that the time was not yet ripe for direct public agitation to stop the war. The need of the moment, they argued, was not dramatic gestures, but hard thinking and patient propaganda about the conditions required for a lasting abolition of international anarchy. Such views echoed the standpoint of Britain's major wartime peace organization, the Union of Democratic Control (UDC).[7] The initiative which led to the formation of the UDC was taken by Charles Trevelyan on August 5th, the day after he resigned from a junior ministerial post at the Board of Education. What was now essential, he believed, was the development and promotion of the principles which would enable democratic forces throughout Europe to ensure that when peace returned it was built on secure foundations. He contacted E. D. Morel, whose Congo Association had been a model of effective agitation; Normal Angell, the best known public advocate of pacifism; and Ramsay MacDonald, who had resigned the leadership of the Labour Party when it agreed to vote for the war credits. This was not a powerful cabal, and they had little expectation of early success. 'They talked of starting a new party,' commented Bertrand Russell who was involved in the early stages: '. . . it seemed like eight fleas talking of building a pyramid.'[8] At first Trevelyan attempted to prevent a public launch, in the hope of winning support from some rather more substantial Liberals. But Morel and MacDonald saw no advantage in delay and by September 1914, the UDC's Four Points were public property:

1. There should be no annexation of territory without the consent of the population involved.

2. Parliament must exercise democratic control over the conduct of foreign policy. Secret diplomacy must be abolished.

3. International disputes should be resolved through the methods of conference and arbitration. A permanent International Council, deliberating in public, should replace balance-of-power diplomacy.

4. National armaments should be limited by mutual agreement, and the pressures of the military-industrial complex regulated by nationalization of armaments firms and control over the arms trade.[9]

This programme focused on the construction of a better international order after the war, rather than attempting to elaborate detailed terms for an immediate negotiated settlement. The UDC was not established as a stop-the-war organization. While it published scorching critiques of the diplomacy that had led Britain into war, MacDonald insisted that 'whatever our views may be on the origins of the war, we must go through with it.'[10] The UDC's first pamphlet, written by Morel, was unequivocal in asserting the necessity of military victory over Germany if Belgian sovereignty was to be restored. It took the military stalemate of 1915 to persuade the UDC that the time was ripe to talk about peace without victory. Meanwhile, they argued, pacifists should set themselves the more modest task of sustaining the voice of reason amidst the dementia of war.

With single-minded purpose and consummate skill, Morel set about organizing a movement. Within two weeks of the outbreak of war, he had drawn up a 'Plan of Campaign for Distribution of Literature, Organisation of Meetings, etc.' Cash was solicited from wealthy sympathisers, notably Quakers with whom Morel had worked closely in the Congo Association. An impressive range of intellectuals were persuaded to write for the UDC. Within a year half a million pamphlets had been sold. Local branches were systematically established – fifty in the first twelve months, 100 at the peak of UDC influence in late 1917, at which time there were around 10,000 individual members. These branches became centres of propaganda, organizing public meetings, canvassing influential figures, co-ordinating letter writing to the local press, distributing literature, and sending speakers to other organizations. A wide range of such organizations were affiliated to the UDC during the war years, with a collective membership of 650,000.

Beyond the disaffected Liberals who were Morel's first point of contact in most localities, the UDC found supporters in the ranks of defunct local Peace Societies, and other pacifist groups like those established in 1913 to promote 'Angellism'. In sharp contrast to previous pacifist agitations, the Nonconformist churches played only a minor role. Few church bodies were affiliated, and no churchmen joined the UDC Executive. By and large the Nonconformist churches supported the war, destroying themselves as a significant political force in the process. In 1918 the Liberal journalist H. W. Massingham remarked that the Labour Party had become 'the natural home . . . of the younger Nonconformists and of the younger clergy'. The new recruits to Labour did not, however, bring with them the institutional structures of Nonconformity which played so important a part in both Liberal and peace politics before 1914.[11] A different Christian response to the war was represented by the formation of the non-denominational Fellowship of Reconciliation by a small group of non-resisters. In September 1915, the UDC refused to accept their affiliation on the grounds that the UDC had less to gain from any activity the Fellowship might undertake on its behalf than it had to lose from being associated with the doctrine of non-resistance.[12] This was understandable since the Fellowship cultivated a quietist spirit remote from active engagement in politics.[13] Not all Christian pacifists adopted this quietist approach. Many Quakers and, as we shall see, large numbers of Christian socialists in the ILP played an active role in resisting the war.

While the churches had little to offer to the UDC, the women's movement was important from the outset. Helena Swanwick, a leading figure in the National Union of Women's Suffrage Societies, was invited to join the Executive. Morel directed the local branches to look to the (non-militant) suffrage societies for support. Women's Co-

operative Guilds and other working class women's organizations were affiliated, and the UDC was closely involved in
preparations for the Hague Congress.[14]

The primary basis of UDC support, however, was what
Morel described as the 'enthusiasm and spiritual driving
power' of the ILP, together with the local structures of the
trade union movement. In March 1915 a significant step was
taken with the appointment of Egerton Wake to spearhead a
UDC campaign in the Trades Councils and local Labour
Parties. Before the war, Wake had been a respected Labour
Party organizer, and by the autumn of 1917 he was again
working closely with Arthur Henderson.[15] His sojourn with
the UDC is suggestive of the role played by that organization
in maintaining a basis of grass roots campaigning activity at a
time when the official Labour Party had abandoned election-
eering for the patriotic excesses of all-party recruiting
platforms.

From the start, the formation of the UDC represented a
conscious attempt to unite the fortunes of radical liberalism
with those of the pacifist section of labour movement. Hence
Trevelyan's invitation to MacDonald to chair the new
organization. As in the Boer War, the issue of peace cut across
class lines, opening the way to a political realignment. The
City of London branch of the ILP, which had long cultivated a
middle-class membership well informed about international
affairs, developed close links with many of the leading figures
in the UDC. The leading ex-Liberals, however, not wishing
to cut themselves off from potential new Liberal recruits, held
back from actually joining the ILP.

However closely it cultivated its links with the labour
movement, the UDC was not simply a device for maintaining
Labour politics during the wartime political truce or for
bringing individual ex-Liberals into the labour movement. Its
leaders were determined to maintain an independent and
non-partisan identity. In the eyes of pacifists, after all, the
Labour Party was no less discredited than the Liberals,
especially after Labour joined a coalition Government in May
1915. Until the final stages of the war the future form of radical
and socialist politics in Britain remained obscure. With the
whole political system in a state of flux, UDC leaders, like

other members of the political classes, speculated endlessly about the coming realignments. But the only wisdom was patience. 'We cannot tell at all how the pol[itica]l situation will develop,' wrote Trevelyan to Morel in July 1915, adding: 'There is no hurry.'[16]

The UDC's contribution to the politics of progress had more to do with the transmission of old values than with any radical new thinking. Its founders were clinging to the wreckage, not setting out on a brave new voyage. Established within days of the outbreak of war, the UDC represented the most ambitious attempt to sustain the mental world of pre-1914 pacifism. In *The Morrow of the War*, the UDC's first pamphlet, Morel condemned pre-war diplomacy for its artistocratic neglect of the 'business interests of the nation':

> The connection between politics and business – and by business we mean the entire framework of peaceful commerce upon which the prosperity of this country depends – appears to be ignored, or, at least, treated with indifference and something like contempt.[17]

And his appeal to 'the democracy' to assert its pacifist instincts was explicitly aimed at capital as well as at labour:

> . . . peace will be permanently preserved only if our artisans and industrialists keep up with the artisans and industrialists of other countries a constant and deliberate communication through their political parties and other organisations. . . .[18]

Other UDC leaders, like J. A. Hobson, had long taken a more critical view of 'the relations between business and politics'. But even the most socialist of them shared the view, articulated by Brailsford before the war, that the first task of the pacifist was not to overthrow capitalism but to 'check the worst consequences of a capitalistic foreign policy, and, if possible, turn it to some partial good.'[19] While revolutionaries may condemn such temporizing, this was an orientation which continued to inform the approach of most peace activists, including socialist ones, down to the present day.

In the early years of the Great War, however, Morel soon

discovered that, outside a handful of Quakers, capitalists had little to offer the pacifist cause. Norman Angell, the leading spokesman of a strictly bourgeois pacifism, took no active role in UDC affairs. By and large, capital had come to terms with war – an alliance given prominence in 1916 by press agitation for Allied plans to translate the wartime economic blockade of Germany into a post-war policy of concerted discrimination against German exports – the so-called 'War After the War'. Morel's even-handed appeal to 'artisans' and 'industrialists' quickly gave way to the belief that 'if any radical changes were to come in the system of intercourse between states . . . the driving force must come from the organisations of labour.'[20] Neither Morel, nor any of the other ex-Liberals involved in the UDC, underwent a *conversion* to socialism. Even when, towards the end of the war, they decided to join the ILP, they embraced socialism, not as a radical break with previous assumptions, but as a natural extension of their pre-war New Liberal commitment to social reform and co-operation with labour. However much specific capitalist abuses figured in their thinking about the causes of war, the principal enemies remained secret diplomacy, militarism and the delusions of economic nationalism, not capitalism as such. Reacting against the economic nationalism of 1916, Morel attacked (in capital letters!) those who sought 'TO PREVENT THE BRITISH WORKING CLASSES FROM TRADING WITH THE GERMAN WORKING CLASSES WHEN THE WAR IS OVER.'[21] The curious absence of the traders themselves from this formulation reflects Morel's concentration on winning labour to the pacifist cause. But the essential con-servatism of UDC thinking is revealed in the fact that, apart from a footnote on women's suffrage, the only addition made to a platform written within weeks of the outbreak of war was a commitment to the defence of free trade. The experience of total war, and the construction of a war economy which transformed relationships between economic and political life, required, it seemed, no adaptation of the UDC's original response to August 1914 – except a reaffirmation of the central panacea of Cobdenite pacifism: Free Trade.

6

Resisting War and Militarism, 1916–17

During 1915 mounting pressure from the pro-conscription lobby threatened to precipitate a crisis in the popular legitimacy of the war. Many Liberals were deeply unhappy that, in the name of fighting 'Prussianism', Britain should adopt precisely the system of compulsory military service whose absence had for so long distinguished the 'freeborn Englishman' from the less fortunate citizens of continental states.[1] For the labour movement there was an added anxiety: that military compulsion would be used to discipline and control the workers, introducing full-scale industrial conscription by the back door.[2] In September 1915 the TUC unanimously opposed conscription, despite its overwhelming support for the war.

The UDC decided against taking up the issue, judging that, despite the breadth of opposition, when the Government made up its mind that conscription was necessary, the defence of civil liberties would crumble before the appeals of patriotism.[3] They were right. When the Military Service Act was introduced in January 1916, the Labour Party Conference, while dissenting, agreed not to campaign for its reappeal, thus enabling the Party leader, Arthur Henderson, to remain in the Coalition Government.[4] From then on, the labour movement offered no serious opposition to conscription as such. Skilled munitions workers, in the Amalgamated Society of Engineers (ASE) were militant in defence of their own exemption. But the defence of sectional privilege was easily mocked:

> Don't send me in the Army, George,
>   I'm in the ASE,
> Take all the bloody labourers,
> But for God's sake don't take me![5]

Later in the war, as we shall see, the engineers' struggle came close to merging with the larger pacifist cause. In 1916, however, the brunt of resistance to the Military Service Act fell on those who were prepared to resist it directly – the conscientious objectors.

Within months of the outbreak of war a group of young men, most of them in the ILP, had established the No-Conscription Fellowship (NCF).[6] Clifford Allen, who quickly emerged as the political and spiritual leader of the movement, saw in the collapse of the Second International:

> . . . the great purging by fire of the half-formed socialist character. . . . We have perhaps learned one great lesson – that Socialism must be something of a religion to us before it can have any meaning in times of real stress.[7]

The primary object of the new organization was neither to mount a conventional political campaign against the intro-duction of conscription, nor to use the unpopularity of conscription to begin an agitation against the war itself. Rather, it existed to provide organized support for young men of military age determined to resist conscription if and when it was introduced. The NCF established close relations with like-minded Quaker pacifists and the Fellowship of Reconcili-ation. Clifford Allen's new 'religion of socialism' drew on Christian as well as secular sources. Above all, it was Allen's identification of socialism with a belief in the 'sanctity of human life' which distinguished the NCF from any previous expression of socialist pacifism. For the absolute pacifist, Christian or secular, conscription had transformed the refusal to kill from a matter of private conviction into an issue of public controversy. 'It is a privilege', wrote Allen, 'that the young men of our generation should have such an opportunity of bearing witness to the faith that is in them.'[8] For Allen it was the anticipated testing of conscientious objectors by state persecution that offered the prime source for a renewal of socialism after the castastrophe of 1914. He also, at first, saw conscientious objection as a key to mobilizing opposition to the war itself. The readiness of individual pacifists to suffer for their faith would be 'a far more powerful propaganda than countless meetings. . . . Just in so far as we cause the Government to persecute those who believe in peace, so we may be doing the greatest service . . . to stimulate the national consciousness in [the] direction [of peace].'[9]

From the outset, this project was seriously flawed. The Government, responsive to its own Liberal supporters, was more concerned to accommodate than to confront conscientious objectors.[10] Under the Military Service Act provision was made for exemption from military service on grounds of conscience. Problems arose mainly because the Tribunals of local worthies charged with enforcing the Act usually disagreed with Parliament's intentions, and sent men who were obviously conscientious objectors into the Army. There, if they maintained their resistance, they were frequently treated with great brutality and, in a few cases, threatened with posting to the front, where they could be summarily shot. Alerted to these abuses, the Government intervened to stop them. Resisters were court martialed and sent to civil jails. From July 1916 a system of alternative service was introduced, enabling objectors to choose civilian work under Home Office control instead of going to jail.

The NCF opposed the Home Office scheme on the grounds that, by performing work of national importance, objectors would merely be releasing someone else for military service – 'killing by proxy'.[11] Only by refusing all compromise and inviting martyrdom could the NCF hope to sabotage the workings of the Military Service Act and shock the public into reconsidering its support for the war. Writing from Maidstone Prison in April 1917, Allen repeated his refusal to exchange the physically destructive conditions of hard labour in prison for 'spiritual death in safe civil work.'[12] Nine out of ten of the 16,500 conscientious objectors, however, rejected this absolutist stand and accepted alternative service. This was predictable, not only because of natural human frailty, but also because, despite Allen's initial hopes, there was in fact little political purpose to be served by adopting the absolutist position.

As the NCF tried to come to terms with the fact that most of its supporters were opting for the Home Office scheme, bitter arguments broke out. Catherine Marshall, who did much of the day-to-day work of the NCF, placed humanity before principle, intervening with the authorities to secure improvements in the treatment of absolutists and 'alternativists' alike. She was attacked by some of the more irreconcilable young Quakers for betraying the spirit of absolutism by helping the authorities in the administration of the Military Service Act and turning the NCF into 'a society for the prevention of cruelty to conscientious objectors.'[13] The accusation had force. Marshall's skilful lobbying, which relieved the suffering of many an objector, did much to prepare the way for the relatively unproblematic acceptance of the right to conscientious objection and alternative service in the Second World War. What had begun as a movement of resistance to the new apparatus of militarism, became itself a tolerated part of that apparatus. The political sting had been drawn from pacifist witness.

It is difficult to see how this could have been avoided. A propaganda of peace based on the readiness of objectors to undergo hard labour was likely to meet with derision, if not anger, at a time when hundreds of thousands of young men were fighting and dying for their country in far more appalling conditions. While the NCF was, of course, sensitive to this point, it did rather undermine its initial political strategy. By the end of 1916, Allen was acknowledging from his prison cell that any propaganda effect of conscientious objection would occur, if at all, after the war.[14]

About the same time, Brailsford, who had toyed with the idea of working for the NCF, judged it more harshly: 'a blind alley which won't bring us even infinitesimally nearer to peace.'[15] To many pacifists, the conscientious objectors appeared to be substituting self-righteousness for any coherent thinking about the likely consequences of their actions. Bertrand Russell, who took over the chairmanship of the NCF when Allen was jailed, later remarked: 'In some men the habit of standing out against the herd had become so ingrained that they could not co-operate with anybody about anything.'[16] By 1919 Allen himself recognized that, in their often fanatical pursuit of principle, the absolutists had 'repelled' and 'muddled' public opinion, rather than opened the way for a broader peace politics.

> We seemed to wrap ourselves in coil after coil of finely
> spun logic, to raise our pedestal upon a mountain of
> phrases and formulas and to be unresponsive to the
> altered mood of those whose opinions we sought to
> change.[17]

All this was understandable, given 'the strained and anxious psychology of young men . . . aggressively on their defence in a world of enemies.' But Allen insisted that the record of the NCF could hardly stand as a model for spreading the pacifist word in years to come.[18] This did not prevent later generations of pacifists from taking the NCF as precisely such a model.

From the early summer of 1916, the growth point of pacifist protest was not resistance to conscription, but the demand for a negotiated peace. As the death toll mounted, and the futility of the war of attrition on the Western Front seeped into public consciousness, the pacifists moved onto the offensive. In May 1916 all the main peace organizations joined together to launch a petition calling for peace by negotiation. Over the summer, for the first time since the outbreak of war, peace rallies were held in most parts of Britain and some 200,000 signatures were collected. Organizations representing some 750,000 people, mainly trade unions, also endorsed the petition.[19] From the autumn, peace organizations joined forces with the ILP to promote peace candidates in by-elections.[20] In November, Britain's two main socialist parties – the ILP and the British Socialist Party (which had settled accounts with its old guard pro-war leadership in the spring) – announced the formation of a United Socialist Council to organize joint propaganda and agitation for peace.[21] This was not yet a mass movement, but the basis for a large-scale mobilization of anti-war opinion was at last being laid.

From the autumn of 1916 the politics of the war underwent a series of rapid transformations. Tentative behind-the-scenes suggestions by a minority of Cabinet Ministers that the Government should examine the option of peace without victory were brushed aside when, in December, Lloyd George replaced Asquith as Prime Minister, and formed a new Coalition Government explicitly committed to his policy of imposing unconditional surrender on Germany – 'the knock-out blow'. Within days, the Germans launched a new peace offensive. British pacifists, painfully aware of their own marginality, looked across the Atlantic to the still-neutral United States. For a heady moment it seemed that they would not be disappointed. On 22 January 1917, President Wilson responded to the obduracy of the Allies with a passionate endorsement of the argument that *only* a peace without victory could lay the foundations for a world without war:

> Victory would mean peace forced upon the loser. . . . It would be accepted in humiliation . . . and would leave . . . a bitter memory upon which the terms of peace would rest, not permanently, but only as upon quicksand. Only a peace between equals can last. . . .[22]

Such a proposition was no more acceptable to the Germans than to the British and they put an end to further talk of peace by declaring unrestricted submarine warfare in the Atlantic. By April 1917 the United States had entered the war.

Soon after the outbreak of war, Lowes Dickinson – a Cambridge classicist who coined the term 'international anarchy' – convened a small group to discuss ways of organizing peace after the war. In May 1915 a League of Nations Society emerged. Despite the involvement of several members of the UDC, the Society took pains to disassociate itself from 'any "stop the war" programme . . . or criticism of foreign policy.'[23] Dickinson, a cautious man, advocated limited innovations – in particular an agreement among states to observe a cooling-off period in international disputes, during which mediation could proceed and public opinion could mobilize against war. Others, including Hobson and Brailsford, went further, arguing that any League would have to concern itself with economic and social, as well as purely diplomatic, matters if the deeper causes of war were to be addressed. It was generally agreed by advocates of the League that it would have to have the power to enforce its decisions, by military means if necessary. As Hobson pointed out, only a system of 'collective security', resting in the last analysis on the threat of force against an international law-breaker, could prevent a return to competitive armaments and international anarchy.[24] But how could the warring states of Europe be persuaded to abandon national sovereignty to the degree necessary to make collective security a reality?

For two years the League of Nations Society led a modest existence, discussing ideas, publishing proposals and keeping in touch with like-minded organizations in France, Holland and, significantly, the United States, where a League to Enforce Peace had been established in 1915. The role attributed to America in League of Nations thinking had much in common with Gladstone's belief in Britain's mission, as a naval power with no territorial ambitions on the Continent, to 'bring Europe into concert'.[25] When, in 1916, pacifist thinkers cast around for an alternative power which claimed to represent the universal interests of mankind, their eyes turned to the United States.

In May 1916 Woodrow Wilson, the US President, declared his support for the idea of a League of Nations. For Brailsford, who had a tendency to overstate his case, this marked a decisive turning point in world history. Schemes for arranging Perpetual Peace had a long and depressingly futile history. Wilson, however, spoke for a genuinely new international morality:

> In the profound peace of [America's] unassailable continent . . . a new human type . . . is evolving . . . without the old formative influences of nationalism and militarism. . . . The new fact in the world's history is that for the first time a great power with a formidable Navy, a population from which vast armies might be raised, and an economic and financial strength which might alone be decisive in any future conflict, is prepared to stake its own peace, not merely to guarantee its own interests, nor to further the partisan aims of its allies, but to make an end in the world of the possibility of prosperous aggression. . . . Beyond the American continent her only interests are the open door to trade, freedom of the seas, and the maintenance of peace.[26]

By announcing America's 'preparedness' to intervene in the European conflict, while maintaining her neutrality between the combatants, Wilson had emerged as the main hope for peace in Europe. 'A policy of trust, with America to back it, ceases to be an idealistic folly.'[27] The peace that the Old World could not keep would be enforced by the New World. American intervention, and that alone, made a 'peace between equals' – and thus the avoidance of another European war – a possibility.

Russell took a similar view. Despite his involvement with the NCF – and later with the Peace Pledge Union – Russell never accepted absolute pacifism.[28] There was, he believed, no route from a world of warring states to genuine peace except via the *imposition* of the rule of law in international affairs: 'a stable peace requires all disinterested nations to form a police force in any quarrel. Mere humanity is not strong enough.'[29] In December 1916, following the German peace feeler, he wrote to President Wilson:

> You have an opportunity of performing a signal service to mankind. . . . Every nation believes that its enemies were the aggressors, and may make war again in a few years unless they are utterly defeated. The United States government has the power, not only to compel the European governments to make peace, but also to reassure the populations by making itself the guarantor of the peace. Such action, even if it were resented by the governments, would be hailed with joy by the populations. . . . It is almost certain that an offer of mediation from you would give rise to an irresistible movement in favour of negotiations. . . .[30]

The people, said Russell, desired peace: but only the Americans could enforce it.

Pacifist hopes of Wilsonian liberalism receded when, in April 1917, the US came into the war, deserting the cause of peace without victory. Paradoxically it was US entry that pushed the League idea into the forefront of politics in Britain. In May 1917 the League of Nations Society held its first major public meeting, with a galaxy of Establishment speakers. The growing enthusiasm, or at least token support, for League ideas among supporters of Lloyd George's 'knock-out blow', did much to discredit the idea in pacifist circles.[31]

Most of the UDC leaders had been unimpressed from the

outset. Brailsford, Russell and those who looked to the US to enforce peace, did so partly because they could not convince themselves, in 1916, that 'a revolutionary mass movement for peace' was in the making among Europe's democracies.[32] Others were less ready to settle for second best. Trevelyan's first draft of the UDC's four points had called for negotiations with democratic movements on the continent 'to form an international understanding depending on popular parties rather than on governments'. In 1914 this was dropped in favour of a clause proposing 'setting up an International Council'.[33] But the leading members of the UDC remained deeply sceptical of the capacity of any 'international committee of the governing classes' to solve the problem of war. Writing at the same time as Russell appealed to President Wilson, MacDonald insisted that it was disarmament, democracy and international socialism that provided the key to stable peace: 'Then we shall want no League of Nations to Enforce Peace, with its dangers and surrenders to militarism.'[34] MacDonald's rhetoric did not solve the problem identified by the League's advocates – peace through democracy required a scale of popular revolt that did not appear to be on the agenda in the winter of 1916. The entry of America into the war, however, left pacifists with little alternative but to invest their hopes in democratic revolt, unaided by the trans-Atlantic *deus ex machina*.

Just when the light in the West went out, however, a new hope was rising in the East. Hopes for a liberal alliance between US power and European democracy had been dashed. But the overthrow of Tsardom in March 1917 raised the possibility of a more radically democratic alliance for peace between popular movements in Europe and the new Russian government. For the first time since the outbreak of war, the Revolution had brought to power a Government prepared to break ranks with the Allied stance of no peace without victory. Instead the Provisional Government, following the lead of the Petrograd Soviet, called for negotiations for a general peace 'without annexations or indemnities'.

7

Pacifism, Revolution and the Labour Party, 1917–18

British pacifists responded to the Russian Revolution with euphoria. At last a genuinely transnational agitation for a people's peace appeared to be on the agenda. 'The Russian Revolution', Russell wrote in March 1917, 'has stirred men's imaginations everywhere and has made things possible which would have been quite impossible a week ago.'[1] Immediately he threw himself into the organization of a monster Albert Hall rally to welcome the Revolution. 'Our people are more cocky and believe they are winning', wrote MacDonald after 7000 people had turned out to celebrate May Day in his Leicester constituency.[2] In response to the dispatch of a delegation of patriotic labour leaders to Russia, the United Socialist Council summoned a national conference designed to challenge the right of the patriots to speak for socialist and working-class opinion on the war. On June 3rd, 1100 delegates from socialist parties, trades councils, women's organizations and peace societies assembled in Leeds under the slogan 'Follow Russia!'.[3]

For the organizers of the Leeds convention, the Russian revolution opened the way to peace without victory. The invitation to the conference warned that, unless the democratic forces in the Allied nations followed the Russian example and insisted on general peace negotiations, the new Russian Government could be forced into a disastrous separate peace with Germany.[4] But if the democracies seized the opportunity then, under Russian leadership, they could build a transnational movement capable of imposing peace on Allied and German militarists alike. Moving the first resolution at Leeds, MacDonald declared:

> When this war broke out organised Labour in this
> country lost the initiative. It became a mere echo of the
> old governing classes' opinions. Now the Russian
> Revolution has once again given you the chance to take
> the initiative yourselves. Let us lay down our terms,
> make our own proclamations, establish our own
> diplomacy, see to it that we have our own international
> meetings.[5]

Two weeks later he wrote to the Petrograd Soviet sketching
out his vision of peace from below: 'a great International of the
democracies, organised as a parliament of the world and
strong in the legislatures of every nation. . . . By the destruction of your tsardom you have opened the way to this new
world.'[6]

Alongside resolutions on Russia and Peace, the Convention
called for the immediate restoration of civil liberties, and for
the establishment of all-inclusive local committees to carry
forward the agitation – provocatively named Workers' and
Soldiers' Councils. In the event, efforts to establish local
Councils quickly faltered, and the provisional committee
appointed to oversee the process wound itself up.[7] The ILP
and BSP had formed the United Socialist Council in October
1916 when the Labour Party had appeared to be irrevocably
committed to the war. At Leeds Robert Williams declared war
on the established institutions of the labour movement: 'We
want to break the influence of the industrial and political
labour "machine" – and this Convention is our attempt to do
so.'[8] But within two months of the Convention dramatic
political events were taking peace politics into the heart of the
labour 'machine' itself. This created an entirely new situation
in which few saw any purpose in pursuing the attempt to build
the structures envisaged at Leeds. By the end of the year the
UDC, which in the summer had fully backed Leeds and urged
its local branches to support the establishment of Workers' and
Soldiers Councils, had come round to full support for the
Labour Party.[9]

When the Labour Party agreed to join Lloyd George's
'knock-out blow' Coalition in December 1916, many socialists and pacifists abandoned hope that Labour would ever
recover its independent political identity. The Russian

Revolution, however, was to have a dramatic impact on the Party. Within a year Labour had drastically overhauled its structure, adopted its constitutional commitment to socialism (Clause IV), and nailed its flag to the pursuit of War Aims acceptable to the leading ILP and UDC pacifists.[10] For an exciting moment at the beginning of 1918 it seemed possible that the pacifists might push Labour into collision with a Government still adamant that nothing short of overwhelming military victory could provide the basis for peace. They failed to do so and the chance of forcing a negotiated peace was lost. However, the boost given to Labour's independent political identity by these events made an important contribution to the future shape of party politics in Britain. As had occurred before, and was to occur again, pacifist agitators had more impact on the reorganization of the party system than they did on the issues of war and peace that they were trying to affect.

Two days before the pacifists assembled in Leeds, Arthur Henderson, Labour's representative in the War Cabinet, had arrived in Petrograd intent on persuading the Russian socialists to maintain their commitment to the Allied war effort.[11] In particular he was anxious to combat moves, initiated by the Dutch socialists in April and supported by Russian Mensheviks, for a conference of socialists from all belligerent countries in neutral Stockholm. The Mensheviks, convinced that only an early peace would enable them to consolidate the new regime, looked to the Stockholm conference in much the same spirit as did Ramsay MacDonald – to mobilize democratic forces in Western Europe to impose a negotiated peace on the warring states. As Henderson gradually became aware of the fragility of the Provisional Government and its vulnerability to Bolshevik calls for peace at any price, he was forced to reconsider his position on Stockholm. The risk that the conference would enable German socialists to divert Allied socialists from their commitment to victory had to be balanced against the certainty that a refusal by Western socialists to respond to Russian calls for a new peace initiative would play into the hands of Bolshevik revolutionary defeatism. The collapse of the Provisional Government followed by a separate Russian peace would, Henderson believed, seriously undermine the very possibility of an Allied victory. By the time he returned from Russia, at the end of July, Henderson was convinced that, in the interests of Allied victory, the Labour Party should attend the Stockholm Conference.

Before Henderson went to Russia Lloyd George himself had been toying with the idea that a Stockholm conference might help to keep Russia in the war. By the time Henderson returned, however, he had concluded that, with little to be hoped for from revolutionary Russia, Britain and France would just have to hold out until American involvement became fully effective. In this situation an international socialist conference demanding peace short of victory would not be at all helpful. Despite Cabinet hostility, however, Henderson proceeded to persuade a specially summoned Labour Party Conference to support the Stockholm initiative. He explained his change of mind by pointing to the danger that if Stockholm went ahead without the Allied socialists, the case for the Allied war effort would be lost by default:

> I have not wavered in the slightest degree in my attitude to this war, nor have I changed my mind as to the need of a final and complete settlement, but I want to say that in a war in which losses of such terrible magnitude are being imposed on all the Nations it appears to me not only wise but imperative that every country should use its political weapon to supplement all its military organisation, if by so doing it can defeat the enemy.[12]

This was still a far cry from pacifist arguments for a democratic diplomacy capable of imposing peace without victory. The gap between Labour's new position and that of the Cabinet, however, was even wider. Within hours of the Conference vote endorsing Henderson's position the Cabinet's decision to refuse passports to the Labour delegation was announced. Henderson resigned from the Government the next day.

In developing a more independent stance on the war, Henderson was driven forward not only by the logic of party politics, but also by a rising tide of war-weariness and peace agitation. The failure of the Leeds Convention's call for the establishment of Workers' and Soldiers' Councils reflected the inappropriate nature of the proposed organizational structures, not the absence of popular support for peace agitation as such. One indication of the widening appeal of pacifism was an upsurge of agitation among working-class women. For a few months in the summer of 1916 a 'Women's Peace Crusade' had been active in Glasgow. The initiative was taken by Helen Crawfurd, a militant suffragette and socialist whose involvement in the 1915 Glasgow Rent Strike had awakened her to the possibilities of resistance by working-class women. Expressing some frustration with the polite middle-class tone of the dominant peace organizations, the Peace Crusade built on its links with the Glasgow Women's Housing Association to organize daytime gatherings of housewives, soap-box meetings in working-class districts and mass open-air rallies. In June 1917, shortly after the Leeds Convention, Crawfurd relaunched the Crusade, which now spread rapidly beyond Scotland. Promoted by the ILP and the Women's International League, Peace Crusade branches sprang up throughout Northern England and the Midlands, getting large numbers of women out onto the streets to demonstrate for peace negotiations, despite constant harassment from patriotic bystanders.[13] The emergence of the Women's Peace Crusade was symptomatic of a growing war-weariness among the population at large. The impact of war on ordinary lives was beginning to create the conditions for a mass peace movement.

On July 1st, 1916 – the first day of the Battle of the Somme – 20,000 men were reported dead or missing and another 35,000 wounded. The offensive gained a strip of territory one mile wide and three and a half miles long. By December, British casualties on the Somme had risen to over 400,000. The troops had advanced up to seven miles over a thirty mile front. There was no sign of a breakthrough. During 1917 the war of attrition continued. The first attack in the Battle of Passchendale, at the end of July 1917, cost 68,000 casualties: nothing was gained. By November 1917, when the battle ended, there had been nearly a quarter of a million casualties. And still no breakthrough. For each dead soldier, several civilians mourned. In the absence of any significant movement on the Western Front people were bound to start asking what their sacrifices were for, and whether, if military victory was unattainable, some other way of stopping the slaughter should be found.[14]

Meanwhile rising prices and growing food shortages stimulated growing resentment, especially since these deprivations were popularly attributed as much to profiteering as to the effects of German submarine warfare on Britain's food supplies. By the autumn of 1917, food queues had become a major grievance and demands for a more equitable distribution of food led to mass demonstrations and even strikes in many parts of the country. While letters from serving soldiers tended to play down the awfulness of the trenches[15] their wives, writing back, did not show the same restraint. Stories of hardships experienced by womenfolk at home created a fierce anger among men who faced their own appalling conditions with resignation: 'We out here won't have our wives and children starving.' The last straw for the soldiers was not so much their own suffering as the perception that the home and hearth which, ostensibly, they were fighting to defend, was itself under threat: 'You would think they would come to some terms when they see the country in that state.'[16]

It has recently been suggested that the scale and many-sidedness of working-class militancy at the end of the Great War reflects a partial shift away from the profoundly defensive characteristics of working-class culture. Local communities became less a defence against the pressures of a hostile world, more a basis for active resistance:

> It was this that accounted for [the] breadth and resiliency [of the militancy], its tendency to spill over the boundaries of normal industrial action, its unique ability to involve women as well as men, and its political dimensions.[17]

William Gallacher, looking back at the activity of the Women's Peace Crusade in Glasgow at the end of 1917, put the same point: '. . . if you have the women with you there are no heights to which you cannot rise.'[18] At the time, Gallacher

was a leading figure in the engineering shop stewards' movement, whose narrowly craft-based militancy was expanding
to embrace other issues and other grades of workers during the
autumn of 1917.[19] By January 1918 the food issue was
reaching bursting point with strikes and demonstrations
reported from all over the country, and threats of national
strike action to force fair play from the Government.[20] It was
in this tense situation that the Labour Party, the pacifists and
the Government found themselves manoeuvring for the
leadership of the growing public demand for peace.

The Russian Revolution and the continuing military stalemate were compelling arguments for the opening of peace
negotiations – for peace without victory. In November Lord
Lansdowne, an aged, distinguished and highly conservative
Tory politician, convinced that continuation of the war would
lead to the collapse of the social order, appealed publicly for a
negotiated peace. Much of the Liberal pacifist opinion which
had held aloof from the UDC rallied to Landsdowne, though
hopes of securing support from other major political figures
for a direct challenge to Lloyd George were disappointed.[21]
The Bolshevik revolution lent new urgency to Russian
demands for general peace negotiations, and, in December,
the new regime's publication of secret treaties between the
Allies laying down agreed post-war spheres of influence in
Turkey and the Middle East, appeared to lend force to claims
that the war was being fought for imperial gain. On December
28th the Labour Party and the TUC issued their own
Memorandum on War Aims. Based on the principles of no
annexations and no indemnities (except reparations for
Belgium), Labour's War Aims were broadly in line with the
thinking of the UDC. In particular the Party had been
persuaded to drop its earlier insistence on restoring Alsace-
Lorraine to France in favour of a plebiscite under League of
Nations control.[22]

The adoption of the War Aims Memorandom was a key
moment in Labour's emergence as a genuinely independent
political party, destined to replace the Liberals as the chief
alternative to Conservatism. For the first time the Labour
Party – hitherto little more than a pressure group promoting
immediate working-class interests in Parliament – was

announcing a coherent and indepedent intervention in the debate on foreign policy. Among the ex-Liberals in the UDC this initiative settled any remaining doubts about throwing in their lot with the Labour Party.[23] The favourable response to Labour's initiative in circles well removed from the Party's normal supporters helped to persuade Lloyd George that the time had come for the Government to reassert its authority. Significantly, he chose a conference of Trade Union Executives meeting on January 5th to announce the Government's commitment to war aims curiously close to those just announced by the Labour Party.[24] A few days later President Wilson proclaimed his 'Fourteen Points', his own version of the new consensus.

One reason why Lloyd George had considered it essential to narrow the gap between the Government's declared war aims and those of the Labour Party was that a crisis was looming in industry over new measures to conscript previously exempted skilled engineers into the Army. There was a real danger that industrial unrest over this 'comb-out' would precipitate the event that revolutionary pacifists had long dreamt about – a national anti-war strike in the munitions factories. The day after Lloyd George's speech to the assembled Trade Union Executives, the National Committee of the unofficial shop stewards' movement resolved to consult its members about calling a national strike linking opposition to the 'comb-out' with the demand 'that the Government should at once accept the invitation of the Russian Government to consider peace terms.'[25] Two months earlier, a Government-backed propaganda body had reported, with regret, that the limited licensing hours imposed since 1915 in munitions towns were having an unexpected outcome. Unable to get a drink, the workers were standing around in the street listening to pacifist orators. In the pubs, the report added, they would have been 'safe . . . as the pacifists are generally teetotallers who will not show themselves in these abodes of iniquity.'[26] The Cabinet, however, regretted nothing, and, when Parliament re-assembled a week later, the government announced its firm intention to proceed with the new conscription plans. The scene was set for a confrontation which, because of the simultaneous peaking of unrest over the food question, threatened to bring not only a few militant engineers, but whole working-class communities into direct action against the continuation of the war. By the middle of January 1918 the Labour leaders knew that they were sitting on a potential volcano.[27]

In this situation, the rapid incorporation of Labour's War Aims into what looked like an Allied propaganda offensive posed complex questions both for the Labour leadership and for the peace movement. To Henderson it seemed that, whatever Lloyd George's ulterior motives, the Prime Minister was being forced away from the politics of the 'knock-out blow' by the combined pressures of Labour and President Wilson.[28] Plans were being made for a meeting of Allied socialists in February to endorse Labour's War Aims. After that it would be up to the German socialists to respond, pressing their own Government to adopt positions convergent with the emergent consensus among the Allies. Meanwhile it was crucial to prevent popular unrest from spilling over into a major social and political crisis. Such a crisis, Henderson feared, would provide Lloyd George with the opportunity to play the patriotic card and crush Labour's growing appeal as the party of responsible pacifism. Even worse, a major outbreak of direct action could precipitate the kind of revolutionary chaos which, as he saw it, had reduced Russia to its abject position of surrender to Prussian militarism.

At the Labour Party Conference in late January Henderson successfully resisted pressure for the withdrawal of Labour Ministers from the Coalition. Speaking in a debate on the food question, J. R. Clynes, Minister of Food in the Coalition Government, used the apparent progress on the international front to preach patience at home:

> They had laid down their War Aims and they were waiting for Germany to speak. Meantime there was greater need for unity, greater need for national composure than ever. They might have to wait some time. . . . Were British workmen to show themselves willing to suffer in the pursuit of the Peace Terms or War Aims which Labour had laid down?[29]

Clynes's uncertainty about whether Labour was laying down War Aims or Peace Terms was significant. In appealing to conference delegates he stressed the latter. But it was the former which, as a member of the Government, he was really concerned to promote: Labour's War Aims Memorandum was to serve primarily as a reason to continue fighting the war.

For the pacifists of the ILP, however, the Memorandum was seen as a first stage in the creation of a new diplomacy from below: 'our own proclamations . . . our own diplomacy . . . our own international meetings', as MacDonald had said at the Leeds Convention.[30] Withdrawal from the Coalition Government was critical if the process was to go any further: how could Labour make genuinely independent peace overtures to the German socialists while retaining its direct involvement in the Lloyd George Government? The decision of the Conference, by a margin of nearly three to one, to stay in the Government, fed MacDonald's fears that the newly adopted War Aims would become a mere 'plaything of Governments. . . . If the Labour Party, having made its pronouncement, lapses back into the acquiesence which it has shown since the war broke out, its Memorandum may do more harm than good.'[31]

A leading argument deployed by the ILP and its supporters at the Labour Party conference was that only by quitting the Government could the Labour Party hope to retain its authority with 'the men in the workshops' and thus avert 'the terrible danger of insurrection.'[32] W. C. Anderson – who had moved the Workers' and Soldiers' Council resolution at Leeds the previous June – pressed the point, warning:

> Side by side with the present food situation was the increasingly dangerous industrial position. A terrific industrial upheaval at the present moment might be dangerous from the standpoint of a democratic People's Peace. There was need for restraint. . . .[33]

For all its political militancy, the ILP was no less fearful of 'insurrection' than was Arthur Henderson. A handful of revolutionaries put their faith in industrial action: 'A general strike in the big key industries of Europe will put an end to the war in less than a week', declared *Solidarity*, a shop steward paper, early in February. John Maclean, appointed Soviet Consul in Glasgow by the Bolshevik Government, believed:

> There is a spirit of revolution developing in the work-shops. . . . Our unified purpose should be to seize the chance when our enemy at home was weak, to sweep the capitalist class out of the way and bring about peace. We were in the rapids of revolution.[34]

For the pacifist mainstream, however, the threatened industrial explosion fed nightmares of social collapse rather than dreams of international peace.

In the event the industrial upheaval was averted. By holding firm on the divisive issue of the 'comb-out', while making substantial concessions on the food question, the Cabinet successfully outfaced the shop stewards' movement. By early February it was clear that the skilled engineers had retreated from demands for peace negotiations into a narrowly sectional defence of their exemption from conscription.[35] With neither the political crisis that Labour's resignation from the Government would have caused, nor the industrial explosion, which – however much pacifists might fear it – would undoubtedly have created new possibilities for their politics, the momentum that had been building up since the Russian Revolution nearly a year earlier was sharply checked. When the Allied Socialists met later in February 1918 MacDonald's fears were fully realized – the keynote speeches insisted that the War Aims were not a basis for negotiation with German socialists: the latter would have to accept them wholesale before any 'Stockholm'-style conference of all belligerent socialist parties could be considered.[36] That put paid to 'democratic diplomacy' as anything other than 'the plaything of Governments'. On March 3rd, unable to hold out any longer in the hopes of a peace initiative from the West, Trotsky was forced to sign the Treaty of Brest-Litovsk. Germany now had its separate peace with Russia, and three weeks later it launched a new Western offensive. The opportunity for a negotiated peace had been lost – and with it the hope that anything good might come out of the Great War.

A banner headline in *The Herald*, an anti-war socialist paper, on 12th January 1918 had declared: 'A People's Peace – Now or Never.' This was correct. If the warring nations of Europe could be persuaded to abandon their dreams of victory, then there was some hope the peace they negotiated would be a just and lasting one. Pacifist hopes for a peace without victory, at first invested in American mediation, had been given a new lease of life by the Russian Revolution. Brest-Litovsk and the German offensive that followed finally shattered these hopes. From March 1918 it was clear that only a crushing military victory by one or other side would bring 'peace'. And a victor's peace, as pacifists had always understood, could be nothing but a temporary truce, setting the scene for new wars of revenge once the defeated powers had recovered their strength. The consequences of Lloyd George's containment of pacifism in the early months of 1918 were to be inscribed in the history of Europe over succeeding decades – down to 1945 if not beyond. It had indeed been 'now or never' for the peace movement.

For the Labour Party the outcome was more ambiguous. The fate of the War Aims Memorandum revealed clearly the tension between pacifist conceptions of democratic diplomacy from below, and Henderson's concern to use the 'political weapon' to supplement Allied military power. But the disappointment of pacifist hopes of winning the Labour Party to a genuine democratic diplomacy did not lead to a new rupture in the Party. The German offensive in March 1918 had swung public opinion so solidly behind the war that pacifists were reduced to morose inactivity and bitter post-mortems on the missed opportunities of the winter.[37] The dramatic military reversals and advances of following months left no space for a recovery of peace politics while the war continued.

Equally important to the maintenance of Labour's new-found unity in the closing stages of the war was that all leading figures now sensed the possibility of major political advances after the war. To many, Labour's independence had seemed finally lost when the Party agreed to join the Lloyd George Coalition in December 1916. Henderson's resignation eight months later, however, opened the way to a major overhaul of its structure and policy. The 1918 Reform Act, which greatly extended the franchise; the huge wartime growth of the trade unions; and the new popularity of collectivist ideas – all served to encourage the Labour Party to set its sights on power. And it did so, after the adoption of the Clause IV commitment to 'the public ownership of the means of production' in 1918, as an avowedly socialist party.

Labour's adoption of socialism evolved out of discussions among Labour leaders attempting to formulate a response, short of actual resistance, to the imposition of military conscription in 1916.[38] The key idea was to propose that in return for conceding the right of the state to conscript manpower, Labour should demand the 'Conscription of Riches'. At first there was some disagreement about what the slogan actually meant. Hyndman, now a keen supporter of the war, argued that Labour should be demanding general nationalization of industry in the name both of equality of sacrifice and of war-fighting efficiency. Other jingo socialists went so far as to attribute the same view to Winston Churchill, quoting him as saying:

> Our whole nation must be organised – must be organised and mobilised – MUST BE SOCIALISED. . . . There must be asserted, in some form or other by the Government, a reserve power to give the necessary control and organising authority, and to make sure that everyone, of every rank and condition, men and women, shall do their fair share. Democratic principles enjoin it; social justice requires it; national safety demands it.[39]

Whatever Churchill may have said, most of Labour's leaders were less ambitious, demanding only the addition of steeply progressive taxation to the existing apparatus of wartime control of industry. But however the 'Conscription of Riches' was interpreted, the secret of its success as a slogan was that it fused basic socialist ideas about state control and greater equality with patriotic support of the nation at war.

In popularizing this slogan Labour was enormously aided by widespread resentment against 'profiteers' – a word universally used during the war to describe the conduct of shipowners, food wholesalers, arms contractors, landlords and all the other 'Brit-Huns' who were said to be exploiting wartime scarcities to line their own pockets while workers and soldiers loyally gave their all for the war effort. 'The detestation of "the profiteer" by Labour', comments one historian, 'arose as much from an affront to its patriotism, as it did from latent class consciousness, and the victim of capital was seen as the patriotic community no less than the working class. . . .'[40] One did not have to oppose the war to oppose its consequences; and there was nothing in the least unpatriotic about the demands for 'equality of sacrifice'. A placard carried by the child of a Clydeside rent striker in 1915 declared: 'My father is fighting in France; we are fighting the Huns at home.'[41] There were moments during the war when popular hostility to 'profiteering' came close to providing a mass basis for pacifist politics. This was true in January 1918. But it was not a reliable basis. Popular anger against inequalities in the distribution of food could be swiftly transferred into a grim determination to defeat the Hun, as became clear when the military stalemate broke in March 1918.

Through its support for the war and its positive partici-pation in the construction of the war economy the Labour movement helped to create a fund of popular support for socialist objectives. Rent strikes secured state intervention to restrict the power of private landlords. Protests over food shortages forced the Government to implement rationing schemes first devised by the Labour and Co-operative movement. In these and other ways working people were able to translate their resentment of unpatriotic profiteers into a positive commitment to the use of state controls to impose democratic restraints on the unregulated operations of market forces. In late 1917, proclaiming Labour's new commitment to 'the democratic control of industry [through] the common ownership of the means of production', Arthur Henderson pledged the Party to 'strenuously resist every proposal to hand back to private capitalists the great industries and services that have come under Government control during the war . . . we do not mean to loosen the popular grip upon them, but on the contrary to strengthen it.'[42]

The rootedness of Labour's new-found socialism in war-time democratic nationalism posed serious problems to those who sought to use the Labour Party as a vehicle for pacifism.

Traditionally pacifists had looked to the evolution of a transnational civil society and the gradual withering away of the nation state as the key to human progress – a view elaborated most influentially by Richard Cobden. The implicit contradiction between such visions and the socialist emphasis on the state as the instrument of social justice had not prevented most pre-war socialists from accepting a broadly Cobdenite approach to the problem of peace. The collapse of liberal capitalism and the construction of the war economy made the contradictions between socialism's domestic and international politics harder to evade. Under war conditions, pacifist socialists were forced to rethink their attitude to the state, if only because many of them – not just conscientious objectors – suffered state repression.[43] Ramsay Macdonald, who before 1914 had treated the expansion of the power of the state as entirely unproblematic, now showed a quite new awareness of the danger that socialist ideas could be used to legitimate the construction of a state capitalist tyranny. It was essential, he asserted, to think again about 'the limits which democratic Socialism imposes upon the state.'[44]

The most sophisticated rethinking was undertaken by members of the National Guilds League.[45] Guild Socialists like G. D. H. Cole sought to reconcile syndicalist ideas of workers control with Fabian commitments to the rights of consumers and of citizens. Leading pacifists were drawn to Guild Socialism, and the ILP itself moved far towards endorsing the idea of self-government in industry.[46] Despite the appeal of such ideas among both socialist intellectuals and trade union activists, the attempt to develop a non-statist socialism was ultimately subordinated to a Labour Party socialism which placed its emphasis on nationalization and the power of the state. Wartime popular mobilizations demanding state intervention to establish equality of sacrifice laid the basis, not for a libertarian revolt, but for a fusion of socialism with the most powerful force of all – the democratic self-assertion of the nation-in-arms.

The explicit conflict between Henderson and MacDonald over the meaning of 'democratic diplomacy' was ultimately less important than the implicit contradictions in Labour's politics between liberal internationalism and socialist nationalism. Tensions over the degree to which hopes for peace could be invested in the processes of inter-state relations were already familiar to pre-1914 pacifists, and they will continue to exercise peace activists so long as nation states exist. What was new was that socialism and internationalism, the two basic components of Labour's ideology, were beginning to pull in opposite directions. On the one side stood Henderson's commitment to maintaining popular control of economic life. On the other side, faithful to the spirit of the UDC's liberal internationalism, Labour insisted on an early return to unrestricted free trade.[47] In 1918 the contradiction went largely unobserved. During the 1920s, however, the clash between these two legacies of the Great War for socialists was to become a central issue in their attempts to grapple with the problem of unemployment.

8

'Figs Cannot be Gathered from Thistles': the 1920s

In the course of the 1920s pacifist ideas moved towards the centre ground of British politics. There was a growing recognition that the war had solved nothing. Versailles was a victor's peace and it created a minefield of unresolved national problems in central Europe. Since the settlement rested on the simultaneous destruction of *both* the great powers dominating central Europe – Germany and Russia – it was extremely unlikely to last once those nations rebuilt their military and economic strength. Moreover the reparations clauses of the Treaty, far from helping to restore the economic life of Europe, merely complicated the enormous problems of putting the world economy back together again. Even the least sophisticated found it easy to blame the chronic unemployment which afflicted Britain on the war. The tenth anniversary of the armistice, in 1928, was marked by a cascade of anti-war literature, which set the seal on a broad pacifistic consensus that was to dominate the centre ground of British politics well into the 1930s.

At the heart of the new pacifist establishment was the League of Nations Union (LNU). Formed in October 1918, the LNU brought together advocates of the League who had supported a negotiated peace, with prominent patriots who wanted the Allies to consecrate their victory with the establishment of a League of Nations.[1] From small beginnings the LNU recruited 60,000 members in its first two years, and 600,000 – including half the MPs in the House of Commons – by 1926. The LNU was dominated by Lord Robert Cecil who, as a minister under Lloyd George, had been instrumental in persuading the wartime Government to take the idea of the League seriously. Product of an ancient and powerful Tory family (his father, Lord Salisbury, had been Prime Minister), Cecil combined leadership of a non-party mass organization with an insider role both at Westminster and Geneva, the headquarters of the League of Nations. During the 1920s the LNU steered a careful non-partisan path, involving leading members of all three political parties – though Liberals outnumbered the others: the League had become the favourite cause of Liberalism in decline.[2] Stanley Baldwin, the Conservative leader from 1923, included Cecil in his Government partly, no doubt, to help secure pro-League opinion in what increasingly appeared to be the key question of electoral politics: how to compete with Labour for the ex-Liberal vote.[3] Although Cecil, unable to cope any longer with the contradictions involved in his two roles, abandoned his ministerial career in 1927, the LNU continued to combine educational work, designed to foster a broad current of sentiment in favour of League ideals, with its role as a semi-official adviser to the Foreign Office. It was only in the 1930s that the attitude of the Government towards the growing international crisis forced the LNU to choose between its two roles. It finally cashed in its accumulated non-partisan capital in a campaign of truly massive proportions – the Peace Ballot of 1934–35.

For the LNU the lesson of the Great War was clear. So long as international affairs were left to the uncontrolled interplay of nation states, mutual suspicion would generate arms races which, in turn, would generate wars. In 1925, Viscount Grey, the first President of the LNU, who, as Liberal Foreign Secretary, had taken Britain into the war, endorsed the view that 'great armaments lead inevitably to war'.[4] The object of the League was to create the conditions of international security that would make general disarmament possible. Under the Covenant of the League, disputes between nations could be settled by discussion and arbitration. Since any delinquent state would face the combined power, economic and military, of member states, national armaments could be kept to a minimum. Even Conservative Governments could be persuaded of the wisdom of this approach since, so long as no powerful state threatened the status quo, support for the League was the cheapest way of maintaining the Empire. As Cecil explained in 1925:

> We have a small army and a vast Empire. . . . It is immensely important to us to preserve the status quo by the peaceful methods of arbitration and international co-operation, rather than by the maintenance of armies and navies which a return to the balance of power would force upon us.[5]

Although the League was a League of governments, not of peoples, it was officially committed to the view that public opinion was the ultimate guarantor of peace. Cecil told the first League Assembly:

> . . . by far the most powerful weapon at the command of the League of Nations is not the economic or the military weapon or any other weapons of material force. By far the strongest weapon we have is the weapon of public opinion.[6]

Despite this, the LNU invested its hopes less in the efficacy of a *transnational* effort to sustain a people's peace – no other country had an organized public opinion remotely comparable to Britain's – than in its capacity to influence *British* Governments. For all Cecil's faith in the power of public opinion, it was, in the end, the power of the British state that mattered:

> At the heart of the LNU, [writes its historian, was] . . . a faith in British public opinion as a force capable of moulding a new world order. A large and influential Union could sway the Government which in turn could lead the League and the world.[7]

Within the Labour Party there was considerable suspicion of the League, expressed, above all, by the UDC intellectuals on whose expertise in foreign affairs the Party was heavily dependent in the 1920s.[8] Since it was rooted in the 'victor's peace', little good could be expected from the League. Versailles, said Ramsay MacDonald in 1919, was 'a peace to end peace', and 'figs cannot be gathered from thistles.'[9] Far from opening the conduct of foreign affairs to democratic control, the League lacked any democratic assembly of the peoples and would merely provide a cover for all the bad old habits of secret diplomacy. 'The structure and composition of the league are thoroughly bad', wrote Hobson: 'The breath of democracy is nowhere to be found. Nations do not meet at all, only States. . . .'[10] Unless Versailles was radically revised, argued Morel, the League would become 'the most powerful engine of oppression the world has ever seen.'[11] The oppressors he had in mind were the French. Using all the propagandist flair he had deployed against slavery in the Congo, Morel ran a frankly racist campaign against what he called 'The Black Horror on the Rhine' – the (mythical) sexual marauding of African troops stationed with the French occupying forces.[12] In January 1923, France invaded the coalfields of the Ruhr in an attempt to enforce delivery of reparation coal, thereby triggering the hyper-inflation which helped to undermine the Weimar Republic and open the way for Hitler. Morel tried to organize an agitation to press the Government to take a strong line with France, but the UDC's local groups had long since disbanded,[13] and the LNU, which favoured a conciliatory approach to the French, warned its own local groups against agitation.[14]

Morel's objective was to win the Labour Party for a policy of radically revising the Versailles Treaty. But when MacDonald formed the first Labour Government in 1924, he brushed aside Morel's claim to the Foreign Office and took the job himself, combining it with the Premiership. In line with his overall political goal of proving that Labour was 'fit to govern', Macdonald abandoned the visions of democratic diplomacy which had so excited him in 1917 and proceeded to adjust to the reality of a balance of power mediated through the League, helping to resolve the Ruhr crisis by lending his support to the rescheduling, rather than the abolition, of German reparations payments.[15] Morel died soon after, but not before he had the bitter pleasure of seeing the Labour Government brought down with the aid of a 'red scare' engineered, it appeared at the time, by Foreign Office officials.[16]

In the 1924 election manifesto, the Labour Party explained

that it was by the *international* record of the Government, rather than by any direct schemes of job creation, that the electorate should judge its efforts to solve the problem of unemployment.[17] The appeasement of political tensions in Europe provided the key to the recovery of British exports and the reduction of unemployment. As Brailsford had noted some years earlier: 'The decline of our trade with Germany, Russia and Austria would alone account for the whole volume of our present unemployment.'[18] Two years later he told mutinous Clydesiders that a concentration on foreign affairs, far from indicating a neglect of the problem of unemployment, would lay the basis for its resolution.[19]

A more critical account of such thinking was given in 1922 by Elie Halevy, the French historian, and it deserves extensive quotation. Halevy, who had an acute eye for the ideological delusions of the British, observed that when Labour leaders looked for solutions to the problem of unemployment they turned, not to socialism, but to the traditions of liberal internationalism:

> So ideas already a century and a half old have returned to favour . . . (the ideas of Adam Smith & Ricardo). Their teachings were popularized by Richard Cobden three-quarters of a century ago, and by Norman Angell, the author of *The Great Illusion*, on the eve of the war; today John Maynard Keynes is their successor. The Labour Party has adopted these ideas. But are they the Labour Party's? Far from being socialists, Adam Smith and Ricardo, Richard Cobden, Norman Angell and Maynard Keynes are doctrinaire liberals, conscious opponents of socialism. . . . When (Labour) tries to define a programme capable of rallying the masses at the next general election, it falls back, not on a specifically socialist programme, but on the old programme that half a century ago had been that of bourgeois liberalism in England. Peace and Plenty. Plenty through Peace. . . . Peace everywhere, forever, and at any price.[20]

At the core of Labour's programme was an objective shared by all British Governments in the 1920s – the restoration of the gold standard as the basis of a new liberal internationalism run, as before 1914, from the City of London. In retrospect it is quite evident that this was a doomed endeavour.[21] The British economy was no longer sufficiently dominant in the world to sustain the balancing role it had performed before 1914. The obvious alternative was for New York to take over from London, but in financial matters, as in military ones, America was not yet prepared to undertake the role of world leadership which Britain could no longer fulfil. The determination with which, against the odds, British Governments attempted to restore economic liberalism in the 1920s partly reflected the influence wielded by the City of London. Just as important, however, was the power of ideas. After the Wall Street crash of 1929, with the slump forcing up tariff barriers around the world, Ramsay Macdonald's Second Labour Government clung dogmatically to Treasury orthodoxy and the defence of free trade.[22] The Conservatives returned to their panacea of imperial protectionism and even the Liberals, the historic party of free trade, began to question the dogma, influenced by Lloyd George's experience in running the war economy and Keynes's argument that deficit budgeting behind temporary import restrictions was the key to triggering a domestic economic revival. Philip Snowden, who had been a harder-line pacifist during the war than the more pragmatic Macdonald, was now Labour's Chancellor, and he stood like a rock against all attempts to introduce new economic thinking. Shoulder to shoulder with the bankers of the City of London, Snowden fought off the attack on economic internationalism, while, with the Cabinet refusing to follow through the full deflationary logic of the Treasury approach to the slump, Britain drifted into financial crisis. In August 1931 the Labour Government collapsed, and Macdonald emerged to lead a Conservative-dominated National Government which, within months, took Britain off the Gold Standard and introduced protective tariffs. Liberal internationalism was dead.

Between them, the success of the LNU and the Labour Party's revival of liberal internationalism, left little space for more radical pacifist or socialist currents. Early in 1921 the ex-absolutists of the NCF established the No More War

Movement, which had 3000 members in 1927 and continued to play a role on the pacifist left until it merged into the Peace Pledge Union ten years later. The No More War Movement denounced the League, with its reliance on force, as an affront to genuine pacifism, and looked to the more revolutionary currents within the labour movement to provide the basis for a politics of war resistance.[23] It was not easy to steer a course between absolute pacifism and revolutionary violence. For some leading feminists, pacifism ruled out revolution. In 1915, for example, Catherine Marshall condemned socialist ideas of class struggle as 'pure militarism'[24] and, responding to events in Russia in 1917, Helena Swanwick confided her belief that 'no real *building* can come out of revolutions which make a dust and a mess and bitterness and reaction.'[25] After the war, Philip Snowden, arguing against flirtations with the Communist International, appealed to the pacifist conscience of the ILP:

> The ruthless and bloody ways of Capitalism are not our ways. Better to continue to suffer under its domination and its oppression than gain economic power through blood and slaughter. For what shall it profit us if we gain the material world and lose our own souls?[26]

The founders of the No More War Movement were made of sterner stuff, and preferred to follow Clifford Allen's wartime advice that socialist pacifists should embrace the revolution and 'use our intelligence to restrain violence in the new revolutionary movement'.[27] In February 1919, Will Chamberlain, a leading absolutist, argued:

> . . . it will be the duty of those who have resisted militarism during the war to do all we can to stem the tide of militarism in the Labour movement. The time may yet come when we shall have to face the bullets of our fellow workers in warning them that armed force is no remedy, whether in the hands of the capitalist or the worker.[28]

During the period of extreme social instability immediately

following the war, when there was some possibility of revolutionary developments in Britain, these concerns appeared relevant. Trade unions were debating their right to use the strike weapon to achieve political demands (including the release of conscientious objectors still languishing in jail), while Cabinet Ministers suffered periodic bouts of panic that the revolution was about to break out.[29] When, in August 1920, the threat of British military intervention against Soviet troops advancing into Poland, triggered a massive upsurge of anti-war sentiment, it seemed that a new wave of revolutionary pacifism might erupt, taking up where the crisis of January 1918 had left off. In the event, however, the crisis served mainly to demonstrate the dominance of older pacifist traditions over revolutionary ideas.

Since early 1919, agitation against Britain's support for the various anti-Soviet armies in Russia had been co-ordinated by a Hands Off Russia Committee run by the far left, but supported by UDC intellectuals, Quakers and many Liberals.[30] The labour movement was generally unresponsive to this agitation until May 1920, when – with Polish forces invading the Soviet Union – there was an enthusiastic response to the action of London dockers in refusing to load munitions onto the *Jolly George*, a ship bound for Poland. Even so, calls for a general strike to force the Government to end all support for intervention were heavily defeated at the Labour Party Conference in June. What changed this situation was the defeat of the Poles in July, and the Red Army's counter-thrust into Poland. Intervention in Russia threatened the 'First Workers Government', but it didn't threaten world peace. A successful Soviet attack on Poland, on the other hand, would place the whole Versailles settlement in jeopardy. For a few days at the beginning of August 1920, it was widely believed that the Government was preparing to send a new British Expeditionary Force to relieve the Polish Army. This was August 1914, all over again.

The response of the Labour movement was immediate and impressive. On August 9th the TUC and the Labour Party issued a joint statement:

. . . war is being engineered between the Allied Powers

and Soviet Russia on the issue of Poland. . . . Such a war
would be an intolerable crime against humanity. . . .
[Therefore, the statement continued,] the whole industrial power of the organized workers will be used to defeat
this war.[31]

Constituting themselves as a Council of Action, the leaders
called a Special Conference of labour movement organizations
for August 13th, at which decisions would be taken to
'instruct their members to "down tools". . .'. When Lenin
heard about this, he believed that the revolution in the West
was going to succeed after all. The action of the labour leaders,
he wrote, had 'the same significance for England as the
revolution of February 1917 had for us . . . it is the transition
to the dictatorship [of the proletariat] and there is no other way
out of the situation.'[32] He was, of course, entirely mistaken.

  Ever since 1920 the belief that the threat of strike action
prevented war against the Soviet Union has inspired successive generations of socialist and peace activists.[33] Despite the
best endeavours of every serious historian who has written
about the subject, this myth is still widely believed. It is true
that some powerful people, notably Winston Churchill,
favoured military intervention. But Lloyd George never had
any such intention.[34] When the putative revolutionaries of the
TUC and Labour Party met Lloyd George the day after their
threat of direct action, it became clear that there was no real
disagreement. They all wanted to maintain peace, and they
were all committed to defending Polish independence, a point
which Bevin, on Lloyd George's behalf, impressed on Soviet
diplomats in London – 'his first experience of diplomacy', A.
J. P. Taylor remarks, with characteristic acerbity, 'but unfortunately not his last.'[35] When the delegates assembled for
the Special Conference on August 15th they heard a lot of
revolutionary-sounding rhetoric from leaders who knew that
they were kicking at an open door. The strike call was
endorsed and Local Councils of Action were set up throughout the country, to await events.

  As it became clear that the Bolsheviks were prepared to
make peace on terms which fully restored Polish territorial
integrity, the wave of anti-war feeling subsided as quickly as it
had appeared. On August 22nd only 6000 people turned up to

the London demonstration called by the Special Conference. In a bid to 'sweep away secret bargaining and diplomacy' Labour appointed two delegates to attend the Riga peace conference. But with the danger of a Soviet advance now over, Lloyd George no longer needed Labour's help and refused to allow them passports. The excitement of August did little to change attitudes to continuing *indirect* intervention. As before the Polish crisis, there was little protest except from the far left who kept the local Councils of Action going for some months as centres of mobilization and revolutionary propaganda.

On August 19th, Palme Dutt – revealing a capacity to assess political realities independently of the Moscow line which, in all his long years as Britain's foremost guardian of Communist orthodoxy, he was seldom to repeat – insisted the issue was 'not essentially a revolutionary class issue, but simply an expression of war-weariness and horror at the prospect of being dragged into another war.'[36] The Home Office agreed, attributing the upsurge to the 'general fear of war that exists in the lower middle and working classes, and not to any tenderness for Russia.'[37] If the Red Army had continued its advance into Poland things might have turned out differently. Had Lloyd George felt compelled to send British troops there would undoubtedly have been a massive outcry, including, quite possibly, strike action. However, the fact that Labour was committed to Polish independence, as well as non-intervention in the Soviet Union, suggests its opposition to a war to defend Poland, would have been rather less unanimous than the bold statements of early August seemed to promise.

There was, of course, no love lost between the leaders of the British labour movement and the Bolsheviks. In 1924 the First Labour Government devoted much effort to restoring normal relations with the Soviet Union. One motive was a desire to kill communism with kindness. As Philip Snowden told the House of Commons, increased trade would help to 'approximate the Russian system to that of other countries with whom they were having commercial relations.' Welcoming Lenin's New Economic Policy, he expressed the hope that the development of Anglo–Soviet trade would persuade Russia to 'throw away the last shreds of Bolshevism and Communism

by which it is at present fettered.'[38] Even more important was
the anticipated effect of increased trade on the British
economy. Without diplomatic relations, Morel explained,
'the whole machinery of commerce is semi-paralysed.'[39] In
the words of a Council of Action handbill issued in October
1920: 'Peace with Russia would mean for British workers
Cheaper Food, Cheaper Clothes, Cheaper Fuel, Cheaper
Building, and More Employment.'[40] It was the abiding
appeals of bourgeois pacifism, not any new-fangled ideas
about proletarian revolution, which informed popular
support for the readmission of Soviet Russia to the international community.

The most interesting controversy about the problem of
combining socialism and internationalism occurred within the
ILP. After the experience of the 1924 Labour Government,
Clifford Allen, now Chairman of the ILP, set up a small
commission to plan a coherent economic strategy for a future
Labour government.[41] Brailsford, who was editing the ILP's
newspaper, was a member, as was Hobson. The outcome was
a programme for 'The Living Wage' which called for an
incoming Labour Government to undertake a massive redistribution of income through family allowances, better
social services and increased social security benefits, all paid
for by taxing the rich. There was some ambiguity about
whether the object of the policy was to precipitate a capitalist
crisis and open the way for large-scale nationalization and
socialist planning, or whether – as Hobson preferred to think –
the result of such redistribution would be to increase demand
and put capitalism back on its feet. While this ambiguity
worried socialist doctrinaires, there was something to be said
for leaving the question open, since nobody actually knew
how capitalism would respond in practice to a determined
reforming government, and meanwhile the ambiguity would
tend to maximize the breadth of support for the programme.
  More problematic was a second tension. Despite the
predominance of liberal internationalists in the development
of the ILP's programme, those who followed through its full
logic could not escape profoundly nationalist conclusions. At
first, the most important of these was John Wheatley, a

socialist businessman from a Glasgow Catholic background who, as a highly successful Minister of Housing in the 1924 Labour Government, carried some political weight. Already in 1922, Wheatley was attacking the conventional view that internationalism held the key to ending unemployment:

> In their search for a market for great stores of goods, the capitalists screamed about the necessity of putting Germany on its feet, Austria on its feet, Russia on its feet, and talked about granting credits which would enable those countries to purchase from us, so clearing our markets and setting our industries going. But why not set Glasgow on its feet, Dundee on its feet, Lanarkshire on its feet? Couldn't the people in these places use more goods if they had the power to purchase them?[42]

Brushing aside Allen's pleas not to 'take as selfish view of Socialism, a national view', Wheatley argued that the 'Living Wage' strategy would only work if import duties were introduced to prevent foreign capitalists, employing sweated labour, from reaping the benefit of the increased demand in the British economy. Labour, he insisted, must abandon its commitment to free trade: 'If socialism is to be established piecemeal, it must be protected from capitalism as it is erected.'[43] Accepting that such an economic strategy would be difficult for Britain to sustain in isolation, he looked to the consolidation of the British Empire as a 'bloc against capitalism', working, perhaps, in co-operation with the Soviet Union.[44]

Wheatley died, in some political isolation, in 1930. But what Fenner Brockway called 'the Wheatley school of national socialists', did not die with him.[45] In 1925, Oswald Moseley and John Strachey were both members of the Birmingham ILP, and they collaborated to produce their own strategy for a socialist solution to unemployment.[46] Moseley, whose economic thinking owed more to Keynes than to Hobson, was more concerned with the expansion of credit than with the redistribution of income as the key to economic recovery. Nevertheless he was at one with Wheatley on the need to abandon free trade and develop a protected imperial bloc. More clearly than Wheatley, he identified the gold standard policies of the Treasury and the City of London as the major obstacle to national economic recovery. In 1929, Moseley became a minister in the Second Labour Government, with a brief to assist in the development of schemes to reduce unemployment. Exasperated by the resistance of the Cabinet to new ideas he resigned from the Government and took his case to the Labour Party Conference in October 1930, where he very nearly won it. Within six months, however, he had left the Party and set out on the road that led to the formation of the British Union of Fascists in 1932.

Moseley's political trajectory was an extreme reaction to the dilemma in which British socialists found themselves. John Strachey finally broke with Moseley in 1931 and became a Communist. This was not a solution either. Communism involved, as Orwell wrote, 'a kind of transferred patriotism and power worship'.[47] Since the Russian Revolution did not spread to the West, Communists became prisoners of a state with pretentions to a universal mission, and their identification with the foreign policy needs of the Soviet Union represented little advance over the subordination of an older generation of radicals to the interests of the City of London. In the 1940s, Communists (though not Strachey who, by then, was switching his allegiance to the other superpower), looked to the Red Army to enforce the peace with the same uncritical admiration as nineteenth-century 'imperialist pacifists' had looked to the power of the British Navy.

Another socialist who agreed with Moseley in 1930 was Nye Bevan. Twenty five years later, Bevan expressed his hostility to the EEC in terms redolent with the memory of 1930: 'Are we now expected to go back almost a century, reject socialism, and clasp free trade to our bosom as though it were the only solution of our social evils?'[48] In the 1950s, as in the inter-war years, it seemed that you had to choose between socialism and economic internationalism. No effective combination of the two was available within Britain's political culture. In between, during the Second World War, Bevan made an important contribution to finding a means of reconciling British socialism with a wider international vision. Unlike Strachey, he discovered a way of doing this which did not involve the subordination of British socialism to the ideological hegemony of either of the emerging superpowers. Before discussing this, however, we must face the 1930s.

9

'The Necessary Murder'? – Facing Fascism

The Wall Street crash, and the collapse of efforts to reconstruct the nineteenth-century liberal international order, set the world on the path to a second global war. As the descent into anarchy accelerated in the later 1930s, the British peace movement split apart as never before or since. This disunity, however, was not a symptom of declining activity – far from it. Militant anti-war protest has (with the possible exception of the early 1980s) never been so widespread in Britain as it was in the years immediately before the Second World War. In the Peace Ballot of 1934–5 the LNU conducted the largest exercise in doorstep campaigning ever undertaken by any pressure group. Thereafter peace groups proliferated. In 1936 there were 40 different peace societies in Birmingham alone.[1] Some co-ordination was supplied by local Peace Councils, many of them affiliated to the National Peace Council,[2] organizing a rich ferment of local Peace Weeks, Peace Exhibitions, Peace Pageants, Peace Demonstrations. There was, however, little coherence. 'Half of those who participate in these activities', remarked one frustrated local LNU branch in a letter to Gilbert Murray in 1936, '. . . want our Government to do one thing and the other half the exactly contrary thing. . . .'[3]

By the end of 1937, Gilbert Murray himself, now committed to rearmament, was confiding privately: 'We are no longer a peace Party opposing a Jingo Party. We are a "League of Collective Security" party opposing Pacifists, Isolationists and pro-Germans. We are actually for a "spirited foreign policy!" Hence a successful Peace Week with all the Peace forces well represented injures our cause, or at least muddles our supporters' minds.'[4] This was a minority position. Most peace activists remained united by their continuing opposition to rearmament, if by little else. As faith in the League declined, some called for a new alliance system – and a new Government – to stand up to fascist aggression. Others pinned their hopes on the appeasement of German grievances, supporting the Chamberlain Government's efforts in this direction. Through all this confusion, few individuals remained entirely consistent. Storm Jameson, a woman novelist active in the peace movement, later recalled: 'For some years after 1933 I lived in equivocal amity with pacifists and combative supporters of the League of Nations, adjusting my feelings, in good and bad faith, to the person I happened to be with. I swayed between the two like a tightrope walker.'[5] Similarly, Vera Brittain was finally converted to absolute pacifism – and rendered temporarily speechless – while listening to Christian pacifist speeches at a rally to which she had been invited to put the case for collective security.[6]

These confusions should not surprise us. The peace movement in the 1930s was faced with quite insoluble problems. Ever since the spring of 1918, when pacifist hopes that a 'peace between equals' could indeed turn the First World War into a 'war to end war' had been finally dashed, there had been no convincing reason to believe that a second global bloodletting could be avoided. With the exception of some Christian pacifists and a handful of far-left revolutionaries, no part of the peace movement, before 1939, came to accept that another war was unavoidable. This refusal of the activists to reconcile themselves to war testifies to their sincerity, not their naivety. They knew the odds were against them. But they also knew there was a remote chance that their efforts might help to prevent catastrophe. One historian has called this 'a mood of despairing hope'.[7] The probability of war informed everything they did. But without the hope that war could be averted there would have been no movement. Indeed when the hope finally collapsed, in the first six months of 1939, the peace movement collapsed with it.

It is important to grasp what it was that peace activists thought they were trying to prevent. Technology had advanced since the appalling slaughter of the Great War. Above all the aeroplane – in its infancy in 1914–18 – threatened to transform the nature of warfare, eliminating once and for all the distinction between soldiers and civilians. In 1932 Stanley Baldwin had revealed that, in the opinion of the experts, there was no defence against aerial bombardment. The bomber – like the ICBM which haunts a later generation – would always get through. 'The only defence,' Baldwin explained, 'is offence'. And he added, with a simplicity that subsequent proponents of deterrence have learned to avoid: '[this] means that you have to kill women and children more quickly than the enemy if you want to save yourselves.'[8] Those who contemplated a new war thought about it in much the same way as a later generation thought about nuclear war: most of Peter Watkin's film *The War Game* could have been made in the 1930s. Bombs and poison gas would rain down on undefended cities. Hunger, disease and civil disorder would destroy what was left of civilization. Only military dictatorship would be capable of sustaining an ordered society in the aftermath of such a conflict. Eventually perhaps – this was Bertrand Russell's speculation – the Americans would recolonize Europe and rescue it from barbarism.[9]

For some people – Russians and Germans among them – the Second World War *was* like that. But not for the Americans, nor the British who were not bombed heavily enough to prevent them from turning the experience into a basis for a cosy national myth. The prevalence of the idea of the Second World War as a 'good war' in Anglo–American culture[10] makes it very hard to appreciate that those who tried to prevent it had good reasons for doing so. It was only with enormous reluctance and great misgivings that even those most acutely aware of the evils of Nazism came to persuade themselves of what we, as beneficiaries of the Second World War, too often take for granted – that the catastrophe of another war was the lesser of two evils.[11] In 1936, Bertrand Russell, after rehearsing the expected consequences of a new war, posed the question: 'Can we imagine any great modern war which would do more good than harm?'[12] He was only slightly ahead of his time. Who, today, believes that a nuclear war would do more good than harm? Who would think it sane to use nuclear weapons against a new Hitler?

The efforts of pacifists to prevent the Second World War have won them few friends. The record of the peace movement in the 1930s has been a favoured weapon in the arsenal of its opponents ever since, and an astonishing amount of nonsense has been talked on the subject. The idea that the peace movement was *responsible* for the National Government's policy of appeasement will not withstand examination. There is now an extensive historical literature dealing with British appeasement.[13] Many diverse factors have been shown to have influenced the decision makers, amongst which public pacifism was of minor importance. This is not surprising. Throughout the 1930s a Conservative-dominated National Government was in power. It had an invulnerable Parliamentary majority. Its defence and foreign policies reflected the views and perceived interests of Whitehall, the Conservative leadership and those rich and powerful individuals who were in day-to-day contact with the process of government. Popular movements made little impact on this Establishment. On the one occasion when they did, in the run-up to the 1935 Election, it was – as we shall see – the peace movement that was agitating for a policy of resistance to aggression, and the Government that was forced by public opinion to suspend its deeply unpopular policy of appeasement – until the Election was safely out of the way. There is little point, however, in conducting this discussion as a polemic against ill-informed and malicious misrepresentations of peace movement history.[14] The point is not to seek to vindicate, but to understand the differing responses of pacifists to the most difficult situation they have faced in this century.

Within weeks of the 1931 Election, the Japanese invasion of Manchuria alerted public opinion to new threats of war which, within five years, were to destroy the League's credibility as an instrument for the maintenance of peace. The bombing of Shanghai, widely shown on newsreels early in 1932, helped to trigger the fears of civilian bombing which played such a large part in popular thinking about war and peace during the 1930s. In 1933, reacting to international condemnation of their aggression, the Japanese left the League. At the same time, Hitler's access to power dimmed prospects for the Disarmament Conference in Geneva. Germany finally quit the Conference – and the League – in

October. Meanwhile Anglo–Soviet relations had deteriorated to a point where many on the left feared that a renewed war of intervention was being prepared. A sudden wave of fear that a new world war was in the making found expression not through the LNU – whose recruitment declined sharply during 1933 – but in some rather less disciplined eruptions of protest.

Two weeks after Hitler became German Chancellor, the Oxford Union declared: 'This House will in no circumstances fight for its King and Country.' Amidst a blaze of publicity, the resolution was quickly taken up by student bodies all over the country. The final phrase carried a suggestion that they might be willing to fight for the League, but it seems unlikely that this thought had crossed the minds of many of the young gentlemen who voted for it.[15] In July Beverley Nicolls' *Cry Havoc* was published, an incoherent and emotional anti-war tract which predicted that a second world war would break out within a year. 'Not so much a book as a scream', commented a reviewer in *The Spectator*, fairly.[16] The book rapidly became a best-seller. At the Labour Party Conference in Hastings that autumn, a resolution committing the party to a policy of war resistance – including the general strike – went through unopposed. Charles Trevelyan, founder of the UDC, spoke for a substantial body of opinion when he moved the resolution in a spirit of revolutionary pacifism: '. . . the rulers must know that if war comes they will fight with a divided nation. They can make their bourgeois war themselves, but they will make it without the workers.'[17] More conventional thinkers in the Labour leadership saw discretion as the better part of valour and held their fire. When, a few weeks later, Labour overturned a large Tory majority in a by-election at East Fulham, this was widely seen as evidence of the popularity of pacifism – despite the fact that Labour's candidate, John Wilmot, had been more concerned to appeal to Liberal supporters of the League than to whatever sentiment may have existed in Fulham in favour of war resistance.[18]

Despite the Hastings resolution, John Wilmot was, in fact, more in tune with majority sentiment in the Labour Party than Charles Trevelyan. The destruction of the labour movement in Italy, Germany and, in 1934, in Austria boded ill for a strategy of international proletarian war resistance. By the summer of 1934 the Labour leadership had repudiated the Hastings resolution with a joint TUC/Labour Party statement reaffirming their commitment to 'preventing War by organising Peace'. The statement explained that war resistance was appropriate only if the Government engaged in military action unsanctioned by the League – a qualification that is nowhere to be found in Trevelyan's resolution.[19] These developments in the Labour Party reflected a more thoughtful mood among pacifists after the panic of 1933, a mood which opened the way for the LNU leadership to regain the political initiative.

Despite its enormous membership, the LNU in the 1920s had not been a popular *movement* – it did not see its function primarily as campaigning to change Government policy. After Cecil abandoned his ministerial career in 1927 there were moves towards a more campaigning stance, but these were held in check by the overriding need to retain the Union's Conservative supporters and, with them, its non-partisan character. The balancing act became increasingly difficult to sustain. Alarmed by falling recruitment, and by the growing isolationism apparent in Government circles, Cecil hit on the idea of the Peace Ballot – a nationwide house-to-house canvass of opinion.[20]

It was not until the 1940s that public opinion polling became an established part of the political process. Meanwhile the opinions of newspaper proprietors played a disproportionate role in determining politicians' views of what the public wanted. Cecil's immediate motive in proposing the Peace Ballot was to outflank Lord Rothermere's claims of growing public support for his isolationist and anti-League position. Most of the LNU leadership was sceptical. Could they reach enough households to make an impact? But Cecil, putting his prestige on the line, and buoyed up by favourable results in a number of local newspaper polls, persuaded them to go ahead.

The Peace Ballot was the largest and most sustained mobilization ever undertaken by a British peace movement – 'an attempt to mobilise Public Opinion on the scale of a General Election, but on a single issue.'[21] Between the autumn of 1934 and May 1935 more than 11.6 million individuals were polled in their own homes – thirty-eight per cent of the total electorate. A National Declaration Committee was set up to run the campaign, involving not only peace organizations, but also the Labour and Liberal Parties, the TUC and the Co-operative Movement, and churches of many denominations. Across the country local committees were formed to co-ordinate activity. Cecil's initiative brought together a huge army of 500,000 canvassers – 35,000 in London, 6500 in Birmingham, 3000 in Edinburgh, 500 in Gloucester. Men and (especially) women, pacifists and Communists, Liberal, Labour and (some) Tory activists, Co-operators and Christians trudged through the streets distributing and collecting Ballot forms and – despite the organizers' pretentions to scientific objectivity – persuading people to declare their support for the League of Nations. There was even a journal for the activists, *The Ballot Worker*.

One reason why the Peace Ballot was able to attract such enormous support was that it brought the LNU off the political fence. Against a background of bitter hostility from the right-wing press, alarmed Conservative politicians attacked the Ballot, complaining that the questions were politically biased and that the whole enterprise was becoming a front for anti-Government activity. This was a self-fulfilling prophecy. Increasingly the Ballot became exactly what its Tory critics most feared, a mobilization of protest against the half-hearted attitude of the Government towards the League. With a General Election in the offing the Ballot provided a perfect framework for opposition parties to co-operate in setting the foreign policy agenda, without in any way compromising their own independence. Moreover, because it retained the support of many establishment figures, the Ballot even isolated the Tory Party from some of its natural supporters.

The Ballot itself was carefully constructed to maximize support for the League, and minimize areas of disagreement. Three questions – on British membership of the League, multilateral disarmament, and the world-wide prohibition of the private manufacture and sale of armaments – received over ninety per cent support. More than eighty per cent of those polled also endorsed the 'all-round abolition of national military and naval aircraft', a formulation designed to evade pacifist opposition by implying, but not explicitly stating, support for an *international* airforce under League control.[22] The final question, on how to deal with aggressor states, was split into two parts:

  (a) by economic and non-military measures?
  (b) if necessary, military measures?

Nearly ninety per cent supported economic sanctions, but less than sixty per cent were prepared to endorse military sanctions, while twenty per cent opposed them and a further twenty per cent evaded the issue altogether by declining to answer the question. By offering voters the option of support-ing economic sanctions without military sanctions, the authors of the Peace Ballot were fudging the real issues.

This fudge was deliberate. Without it, it is doubtful whether the more extreme pacifists could have been persuaded to take part in the canvassing.[23] More important, support for the League would be maximized if people were given the opportunity to support it without supporting war. What the economic option appeared to offer was the possibility of coercion without bloodshed, of defeating an enemy without having to fight. As an official leaflet explained: 'All the organisations which ask you to fill up this Ballot paper believe that a boycott on trade and credit would in practice always be enough to stop any nation from starting a war.'[24] Thus, as Bertrand Russell was to point out, the nation could 'satisfy [its] love of power . . . without firing a shot.'[25] It was the prevalence of this illusion that held the key to the over-whelming popularity of the League and of collective security in Britain in the mid-1930s. It is hardly surprising that the LNU leaders did not go out of their way to point out that, without the final threat of military sanctions, an economic blockade against an aggressor power was most unlikely to succeed.

This belief in the efficacy of economic sanctions reflected the continuing hold of 'imperialist pacifism' in the popular imagination. Economic sanctions, as E. H. Carr, a leading critic of the League's supporters, was later to point out, are the weapon of the strong.[26] During the final months of the Peace Ballot campaign it was becoming clear that Mussolini was preparing to invade Abyssinia, and it was in relation to this danger that the issue of sanctions was generally debated. Even those who thought military sanctions might be necessary believed that this would be limited to using the Royal Navy to close the Suez Canal to the Italians. 'There is no doubt', wrote an LNU MP of his constituents during the 1935 Election campaign, that 'they're quite prepared *for the Navy* to have to fight.'[27] The use of the British Navy to enforce the will of the international community hardly counted as war. In Whitehall there was a deep awareness of the fragility of British power: one false move and the whole house of cards could come tumbling down. During the emerging Abyssinian crisis, Cabinet caution reflected a realistic assessment of the dangers to the British Empire of becoming entangled in a naval conflict with Italy in the Mediterranean, especially since Mussolini's colonial adventure posed no immediate threat to British interests.[28] Considerations like this played a major part in determining Government policy in the crises of the 1930s. But liberal public opinion, as expressed through the Peace Ballot, had no time for such cautious realism. In 1935 the League was genuinely popular with the British public because it allowed them to believe, not for the first time, that there was no limit to Britain's power to do good in the world. More or less deliberately, what Lord Robert Cecil had pulled off in the Peace Ballot was an irresistible fusion of pacifism and patriotism. For a few months this carried all before it.

By the time the Ballot result was declared in June, Mussolini's Abyssinian ambitions dominated the international agenda. There was also a British General Election in the offing. Paradoxically, the very success of the Ballot undermined its efficacy as an anti-Government front. Whatever their private reservations, Ministers were fully persuaded by the Ballot that their appearance of half-heartedness towards the League and sanctions had become a most serious electoral liability. This was all the more so since the most fervent supporters of the League were precisely those traditional Liberal voters whose vacillations between the parties tended to determine the outcome of inter-war elections. So the Prime Minister, Stanley Baldwin, assured Cecil that the League remained 'the sheet anchor of British policy'[29] and a policy of economic sanctions was adopted. Samuel Hoare, the Foreign

Secretary, used a meeting of the League Assembly in Geneva to declare British readiness to participate fully in 'collective resistance to all acts of unprovoked aggression'. The LNU leadership congratulated themselves: public opinion had forced the Government into a firm stance. Mussolini, however, was less impressed and he launched his invasion on October 3rd. An all-party rally under LNU auspices called on the League to close the Suez Canal to Italian forces. While negotiations continued in Geneva, the Tories went to the polls declaring that 'collective security by collective action can alone save us from a return to the old system which resulted in the Great War.'[30] Their Liberal and Labour opponents, whose foreign policy clothes had been so comprehensively stolen, were reduced to assertions – unconvincing to most voters – that the Government was lying through its teeth.

In fact, of course, it was. Within weeks of its return to power the duplicity of the National Government's support for sanctions became embarrassingly obvious. An agreement between Hoare and his French counterpart, Pierre Laval, was leaked to the press. They intended to offer Mussolini control of two thirds of Abyssinia provided he would save their faces by allowing Haile Selassie to continue to rule over the remainder. The outcry was spontaneous and virtually universal. Even *The Times* protested.[31] On December 18th Hoare resigned, to be replaced by Anthony Eden, widely seen as a champion of the League.[32] The overthrow of a Foreign Secretary was a considerable achievement for a popular agitation, but this was to be the limit of the Peace Ballot's success. During the months that followed, as Mussolini bombed and gassed the Abyssinians into subjection, no serious attempts were made by the British Government to implement effective sanctions. This put paid to Baldwin's attempt to pose as a champion of collective security. More importantly, it put paid to public faith in the League. Within a year of the triumphant conclusion of the Peace Ballot, the consensus that it registered had entirely disintegrated. Denied the comfortable illusion that the League could restrain aggression without killing people, pacifists now had to face a harsh choice. Should they reach an accommodation with traditional balance-of-power thinking by seeking to build an anti-fascist alliance? Or should they abandon all illusions in the capacity of military preparations to prevent, rather than precipitate, war and opt for a policy of peace at any price, of absolute pacifism?

10

Against Fascism *and* War

The Abyssinian war of 1935–36 hardened the emerging division between those who looked to collective security to prevent a repeat of the Great War, and those who totally refused the use of force in international relations. It was at this time that the modern meaning of the word 'pacifist' became established: the semantic change registered a deep and abiding split within the peace movement.[1] Not until the growth of the nuclear disarmament movement in the 1950s were significant bridges rebuilt between the two wings of what, in the 1920s, could be described as a single pacifist movement.

Normal Angell and Clifford Allen were among those who fought a rearguard action in defence of the older, more general, meaning of the word 'pacifism'.[2] They argued that since the concentration of military forces in the hands of the League would be a step towards their total elimination, absolute pacifists should have no difficulty in supporting collective security as a step in the right direction. The fundamental issue at stake here was not the merits or otherwise of the League, but whether the peace movement should lend its support to any reconstruction of security arrangements short of the total renunciation of the use of force. To do so, said the 'true' pacifists, was to collaborate in war preparations. Not to do so, said their opponents, was to cut pacifism off from any possibility of influencing practical politics. Clifford Allen said in 1933:

> I submit to you that Pacifism is not and never can be a political method so long as it is chiefly concerned with abstaining from the use of force. . . . You can, of course, *define* Pacifism by a reference to force, but you cannot thereby save the world from the use of force. . . . You must cease taking part in practical affairs and go instead into the wilderness as an educator of opinion or as a

religious evangelist. . . . Either therefore insist upon believing in Pacifism as measured by the use of force and go out of politics, or define Pacifism as something emphasising the power of reason and stay in politics.[3]

In the mid-1930s, however, most absolute pacifists were not yet ready to accept the apolitical logic of their beliefs. For the time being they could evade Allen's choice by challenging the assumption that the League represented anything more than the collective security of a group of satisfied imperial powers. This was the line taken by the No More War Movement, and most of the socialist left agreed with it in the early 1930s. During the Abyssinian crisis the Socialist League (the main left-wing grouping in the Labour Party) opposed the call for sanctions against Italy, fearing that Britain was being 'led under the banner of the League into another imperialist war.'[4] The ILP was so worried by this possibility that it eventually disassociated itself from calls for dockers to boycott coal and oil shipments to Italy for fear that '"working-class sanctions" could not be distinguished publicly from League sanctions and would help to create a psychology for war against Italy.'[5] The Communist Party, on the other hand, abandoned its earlier hostility to the League after the Soviet Union joined in 1934, and argued, with some subtlelty, that socialists should 'take full advantage of all existing institutions, peace pacts and covenants, and imperialist contradictions, that can place stumbling blocks in the path of the warmongers.'[6]

The Communist change of heart was part of a broader reorientation on the left. The Nazi threat to socialism and the working-class movement – whether in Germany, the Soviet Union, or the Western democracies – made it increasingly difficult to maintain an attitude of equal hostility to all imperialist powers. The ILP did so only at the price of appearing to abstain altogether from the politics of what almost everyone else took to be the real world. In the later 1930s, according to Fenner Brockway, the ILP:

recognized that so long as Capitalism continued the alternatives were either a patched-up imperialist peace or an imperialist war. A patched-up peace would mean an

extension of Hitler's tyranny over more peoples: a war
would be fought by Britain and France for their own
imperialist interests. We held it was the duty of revolutionary Socialists to denounce both imperialist peace and
imperialist war as the inevitable consequences of Capitalism and, whichever came, to carry on the independent
class struggle of the workers, directing it towards the
conquest of Worker's Power. . . .[7]

But mass movements cannot be built on denunciation alone,
and few people believed that 'worker's power' was on the
immediate agenda. The majority of socialists agreed with the
Communist Party in turning away from the abstentionist
logic embraced by the ILP. They *could* see a difference between
imperialist war and imperialist peace, and they fervently
believed that, even short of the revolution, their own actions
might be capable of preventing another Great War.

It was not primarily from the left that the groundswell of
absolute pacifism emerged in the later 1930s. In October 1934
a letter appeared in the press appealing for men to send
postcards to its author, the Revd Dick Sheppard, affirming the
statement: 'we renounce war and never again, directly or
indirectly, will we support or sanction another.' 50,000 people
responded. Sheppard, already famous as 'the radio parson' –
he had been the first person to broadcast a church service – was
Canon of St Pauls. Like his counterpart in the LNU, Lord
Robert Cecil, he was an eccentric member of the Establishment. The passionate sentimentality of his rhetoric reached
out to ordinary unpolitical people, while his personal charisma
provided a necessary substitute for political or ideological
coherence in the new movement.

While the Peace Ballot held the field among peace activists,
Sheppard made no attempt to establish an organization, but in
July 1935 the 'Sheppard Peace Movement' was founded, and
in May 1936 this became the Peace Pledge Union. The PPU
was the largest absolute pacifist organization in history. Its
governing body included church leaders, Christian Socialists
(notably the ex-leader of the Labour Party, George Lansbury),
and writers and intellectuals including Siegfried Sassoon, Vera
Brittain, Aldous Huxley and Bertrand Russell. By September
1939, 130,000 people had signed the pledge. Since membership

required nothing more than a signature, it is difficult to assess
the real weight of the movement. The pledge was perfectly
designed to register the horrified rejection of war with which
very large numbers of otherwise unpolitical people responded
to the various war scares of the later 1930s. Many must have
signed and left it at that. Nevertheless, with 30 full time staff
and more than 1000 local groups, the PPU was nearly as big as
CND fifty years later. Sheppard died in 1937 without having
developed any clear idea about what could be done to prevent
war, apart from renouncing it. Those who became active in
PPU groups, however, could not long avoid Clifford Allen's
question – did pacifism, as such, provide an adequate basis for
political action?[8]

One answer was provided by Gandhian philosophy, as
interpreted by an American pacifist, Richard B. Gregg. Non-
violent resistance was seen as the answer to international
aggression, and the job of the PPU was to train an élite core of
resisters. The process of training – small affinity groups,
personal regeneration, spiritual exercises – became the major
activity of many PPU groups. Aldous Huxley envisaged 'a
kind of religious order, membership of which involves the
acceptance of a certain way of life, and entails devoted and
unremitting personal service for the cause.'[9] Not everyone
was happy with the approach. 'Can't you tell them,' Sheppard
whispered to Kingsley Martin during a meeting with Gregg,
'that we haven't time for all this intensive cultivation and that
our job is to stop the next bloody war.'[10]

One alternative to 'Greggism' was for the pure pacifist
minority to seek allies elsewhere in politics. Having rejected
collective security and, with it, the great majority of left and
liberal opinion, the only potential allies available were Tory
isolationists and right-wing appeasers. Much stress was laid
on the demand for a World Conference at which a British
sacrifice of imperial advantages would create the space for
appeasing the grievances of the 'have-not' powers – Germany,
Italy, Japan – through a general scheme of 'territorial,
economic and monetary readjustments. . . .'[11] (Lenin would
have called it, with some justification, redividing the imperial
spoils.) While the PPU pointed out that their proposed World
Conference was quite different to Chamberlain's policy of

pragmatic concession to Hitler's demands, *Peace News* – the organ of the PPU – nevertheless backed the Munich settlement in 1938 and supported German demands against Poland a year later.

Pacifist denunciations of what some saw as the 'hate-mongering propaganda' of the left's anti-fascist stance became increasingly strident.[12] Communists responded with allegations that the Peace Pledge Union had become 'the pro-fascist tendency in the peace movement.'[13] Such allegations were not entirely without foundation. Pacifists needed no persuading that fascism threatened civilization. But, given the destructive power of modern weapons, they did not believe that civilization could be protected by war. In an increasingly desperate search for peace some pacifists were even prepared to make overtures to Fascist organizations.[14]

As war approached, growing numbers of PPU supporters came to accept the necessity of abandoning these unhappy attempts at political engagement. Instead they turned to the Christian quietism of the Fellowship of Reconciliation – the fastest growing absolute pacifist organization in the late 1930s. Pacifism could not be justified by its ability to prevent war. What mattered was its affirmation of human values in a world where war was inescapable. In a dark age the pacifist's role was to bear witness against barbarism, or, as Auden was to put it 'to show an affirming flame':

> No pacifist method has yet been perfected in this country to counter Hitler. If we do not oppose him by force then we must be willing to see all that we love and value go under for at least a generation. Can we face this?
>
> I know what Christ would have done. In his time the Jews must often have felt their culture and civilization was in danger of being swallowed up by Roman domination. But there can be no doubt as to the Christian method in face of that challenge.
>
> It is a frightfully difficult answer. We do not want more reason but more steadfastness. Can we rise to such a dispassionate judgement?[15]

Not many could.

As hopes for the League disintegrated and the Peace Ballot consensus broke apart, those who followed the logic of collective security found themselves forced to unlearn many of the lessons of the First World War. In the absence of a viable League, they turned back towards alliances. One left-wing enthusiast for the League, Konni Zilliacus, claimed that an alliance of anti-fascist states would constitute the embryo of a future World Government.[16] But he did not explain how a government excluding some of the world's most powerful states could establish its authority – short of a new world war. And nobody advocated that. The point of an anti-fascist alliance was to prevent war, not to prepare for it.

Collective security, which had been understood as an alternative to the diplomacy discredited by the catastrophe of 1914, became increasingly difficult to distinguish from the traditional pursuit of a balance of power in Europe. The extent of the retreat was masked, however, by the existence of the Soviet Union. Alarmed by Hitler's rise to power, Stalin was actively pursuing an alliance with the Western democracies. In September 1934 the USSR had joined the League of Nations, and six months later they signed a pact with France. In the late 1930s, the demand that Britain make an alliance with the Soviet Union became the key alternative to Chamberlain's foreign policy – the only combination that had the power to resist Hitler and thus prevent war. 'I see no hope of avoiding war,' wrote Brailsford in the summer of 1936, 'unless we can soon create a firm defensive alliance of England, France and Russia plus some smaller "Left" States. But', he added, 'only a Left Government in this country would enter such an alliance with Russia. . . .'[17] This assumption – that nothing would persuade the Chamberlain Government to make an alliance with the Soviet Union – was axiomatic on the left. It was generally assumed that Chamberlain would prefer to sacrifice imperial interests in a compromise with Hitler, than to join the USSR in an anti-fascist alliance.[18]

A 'pact with the Soviet Union to defend democracy against fascism' sounded like a very different proposition from an 'alliance with Russia to sustain the British Empire against German imperialism' – however difficult it might be to distinguish the two things in practice. The ideological loading of the new language of international relations served to obscure the degree to which the left had capitulated to traditional balance-of-power diplomacy. If the pursuit of a Soviet alliance lent strategic and ideological coherence to the alternative foreign policy, it was – for most of those involved –the civil war in Spain which provided the emotional core. For nearly three years, from July 1936 to March 1939, the elected Spanish Government held out against Franco's fascist rebellion. While Hitler and Mussolini, on the one side, and Stalin on the other sent military assistance, Britain and France refused aid to the beleaguered Government in the name of 'non-intervention', knowing that this policy favoured the rebels. Socialists often presented the Spanish issue in balance-of-power terms, accusing the National Government of standing idly by while fascism gained control of Britain's vital Mediterranean sea routes.[19] But the real issues had nothing to do with the balance of power, which merely dictated that Britain should be on terms of benevolent neutrality with whoever won in Spain. Support for the Republic provided an escape from the complexities of international relations and the frustrations of confronting an apparently immovable reactionary government in Britain. Here the individual could act directly – raising cash, medical supplies, taking in Basque refugee children, or – for more than two thousand young men – volunteering for the International Brigade.[20] Solidarity with the Spanish Republic undermined the pacifism of many on the left,[21] and Russell knew that he was swimming against the tide when he urged the friends of peace to 'avoid the crusading spirit . . . in relation to Spain, on the grounds that even the best cause is not worth a great war.'[22] Those who campaigned against 'non-intervention', however, clung to the belief that if Britain could be persuaded to join the Soviet Union in active resistance to fascism, then a general war could still be avoided. The small war in Spain had to be fought, they argued, precisely in order to check the fascist advance before Hitler felt strong enough to launch the big war.[23]

The more difficult issue, however, remained. If the National Government as presently constituted could not be persuaded to ally with the Soviet Union it would have to be replaced. But how? The obvious vehicle was the Labour

Party. But no Election was due until 1940 – and that might well be too late. Even if there was still a peace to be saved in 1940, it seemed most unlikely that Labour would win the election. The continuing electoral hegemony of the Conservatives rested not only on the division of the anti-Tory vote between Labour and Liberals, but also on the fact that large numbers of manual and white-collar workers, benefitting from the rapid growth of new industries, services and housing in the Midlands and the South of England, felt that they had good reason to be grateful to the Government. As in the 1950s and 1980s, and for many of the same reasons, Labour's 'forward march' seemed far from guaranteed.[24] Where was the breakthrough to come from? The Government could only be brought down if sufficient Conservatives were prepared to vote with Labour and Liberal MPs to defeat it in the House of Commons, forcing a new election or opening the way to a reconstituted anti-fascist National Government. Such a split in the Tory ranks had no precedent, and would only become imaginable when public outrage at Government policy was aroused to such a pitch of fury that large numbers of Conservative backbenchers felt obliged to break ranks. Moreover the Labour Party would also have to be prepared to co-operate with Liberals and dissident Conservatives in the formation of a new Government. Most Labour stalwarts, patient people who had set their sights on achieving unencumbered Labour rule however long it took, were distinctly unenthusiastic about such a prospect. Soured by the extreme sectarianism of Communist attacks on the Labour Party in the early 1930s, many Labour activists agreed with their leaders that all the talk of an anti-Government alliance merely disguised a Communist ploy to subvert the Labour Party. Far from lending their weight to agitation for political realignment, Labour's leaders organized to resist and ultimately expel those who persisted in advocating it.[25] In the face of such obstacles, what is surprising is not that the movement for an alternative Government failed. Rather, the fact that it made any headway at all bears witness to the degree to which wide sections of the British public became alarmed by the apparent drift of Chamberlain's foreign policy.

From the mid-1930s, in the places where members of

different political parties met, there was much talk about possible realignments in the political middle ground.[26] After the 1935 election, the LNU, aware of its potential as the biggest non-party organization in Britain, edged towards a more direct political challenge to the Government. Convinced of the need for a more rapid rearmament programme, the LNU leaders joined with Winston Churchill, leading Liberals and Walter Citrine of the TUC, to sponsor a new campaign for 'Arms and the Covenant'. There was talk of the emergence of a new centre party. But most LNU members remained hostile to rearmament, while Churchill was distrusted in all parts of the political spectrum. The new campaign put down few roots.[27]

Left-wing engagement with this process of realignment was delayed by a concerted attempt by the 'United Front' campaign of the three main left organizations – the ILP, the Communists and the Socialist League – to gain a secure foothold within the Labour Party. When this was defeated, early in 1937, the way was open for the 'People's Front' – a broad anti-fascist alliance intended to involve Liberals and dissident Tories as well as socialists and the Labour movement. Advocates of the popular front made little attempt to build a single co-ordinated organization. Such an organization would have been an easy target for Labour's disciplinarians. In any case, they had no wish to construct a new political party. The point was to persuade existing ones to work together. The case for the people's front was argued out in existing organizations – local Peace Councils or Aid for Spain Committees, trade unions, the Co-operative Party, the LNU. The resignation of the Foreign Secretary, Anthony Eden, early in 1938 provided an opportunity for the popular forces to intervene. Around the country LNU branches held meetings demanding Chamberlain's resignation, but the leadership pulled back from direct involvement in party politics. And Eden, who wanted the leadership of the Tory Party, offered no support to the movement triggered by his resignation. In the spring the left launched a new popular front campaign – the United Peace Alliance – with support from the Co-operative Party. After a promising start, the campaign fizzled out in the summer when the full Co-operative Congress refused to back it.[28]

The nearest thing to a sustained campaign for a People's Government was the Left Book Club. Established, in close co-operation with the Communist Party, by the publisher Victor Gollancz in March 1936, the Club rapidly became rather more than a purveyor of books – though, with 50,000 members by the beginning of 1938, it did that effectively and in vast numbers. G. D. H. Cole's *The People's Front*, the Club choice for July 1937, looked to local readers' groups as the main basis for developing the agitation. By the end of 1937 there were 730 such groups, and 1200 by the spring of 1939. In many places the Left Book Club made the Labour Party look like a stagnant backwater, while demanding a less disciplined or full-time commitment than membership of the Communist Party.[29] The success of the Left Book Club leant some credence to popular front politics. New alignments among MPs and electoral pacts amongst the parties would be necessary to the overthrow of the National Government. But these were seen as consequences, not causes. The central concern was less with lobbying amongst the powerful, than with creating an irresistible tide of popular opinion that would force the politicians into appropriate action. The very fact of unity between diverse political forces, popular frontists believed, together with an agreed programme of resistance to fascism and domestic social reforms, would transform the political situation in the country. Left-wing and progressive opinion, disorientated by Baldwin's election victory and the seeming immovability of the National Government, would be reinvigorated. Precisely how these new popular energies would influence the world of high politics could not be anticipated: perhaps the movement would have to wait for one of Cobden's 'accidents'. But it was reasonable to believe that, as the international crisis mounted, the politicians would react differently if surrounded by a mass of mobilized and informed opinion than if left to their own devices.[30]

Until the autumn of 1938 Hitler's direct expansionism caused less passion among the British public than events in Spain or, before that, Abyssinia. Neither the reoccupation of the

Rhineland in March 1936, nor the annexation of Austria two years later caused any great stir. But the Czech crisis of September 1938, which took Europe to the brink of war, did produce the kind of public response which popular frontists were looking for to transform the political situation.

In a series of dramatic and highly publicized meetings with Hitler, culminating at Munich on September 29th, Neville Chamberlain ensured that the effective destruction of Czech independence did not immediately precipitate a general European war. In the House of Commons, Labour called for a firm stand in alliance with France and the Soviet Union. But when war seemed most imminent they faltered, hoping against hope that Chamberlain would be able to find an acceptable way out.[31] Even the Communist Party was momentarily shaken by the apparent imminence of war – was it possible that Chamberlain was going to fight Hitler after all? – but the errant comrades were quickly pulled back into line.[32] The general public were frightened, relieved and (many of them) finally outraged by Chamberlain's diplomacy.

Munich fully exposed the divisions and confusions within the peace movement. The Peace Pledge Union, which had praised Chamberlain's efforts, subsequently issued a leaflet describing Munich as a pacifist victory:

> A War Has Been Stopped
> War Can Be Abolished
> By The People
> Disarmament can be achieved, because if you can stop a war, you can abolish armaments. The statesmen of Europe heard your voice and dared not disobey. Complete the job you began so well in September. . . .[33]

This was absurd. As Gandhi pointed out at the time, Munich was a victory for Hitler's violence, not for pacifist protest.[34] But many more thoughtful pacifists still clung to the hope that the appeasement of Germany's Versailles grievances would serve to moderate, or even undermine, the Nazi regime. Clifford Allen, who since 1934 had built up an all-Party group of experts committed to collective security and domestic reform, resisted pressures to take up the cause of the People's Front, and, instead, devoted the last year of his life to actively assisting Chamberlain's diplomacy. While he did not glamourize the Munich settlement, he insisted that 'the Prime Minister was right to choose the catastrophe of yielding to improper procedure rather than to choose the terrible catastrophe of war.'[35] Another leading pacifist, Cyril Joad, put the same point more succinctly:'Ce n'est pas magnifique, mais ce n'est pas la guerre.'[36]

During the crisis itself, the most effective intervention came from Victor Gollancz. In the last week of September, using the Left Book Club groups, he organized the distribution of two million copies of a leaflet explaining clearly and simply why peace could not be preserved by giving way to Hitler's demands. A quarter of these were on the streets the day they were delivered from the printers.[37] In sixty-seven different towns the Left Book Club organized public meetings to discuss the crisis. Within days of the settlement Mass Observation reported widespread shame 'that we had let down the whole tradition of England's pledges for honesty, fair play and resistance to threats.'[38] Buoyed up by a wave of patriotic outrage rooted in the well-established propensity of liberal England to display shame at the actions of its Governments, the left was quick to seize the opportunities presented by Munich.

Outside Parliament attention focused on two by-elections. Even before the crisis there had been talk of fielding a Popular Front candidate in Oxford. Eventually both Labour and Liberal parties agreed to withdraw their candidates in favour of A. D. Lindsay, Master of Balliol (and a long-standing member of the Labour Party), who fought the election exclusively on the issue of Munich. He was opposed by Quintin Hogg (the future Lord Hailsham). Lindsay's supporters included not only Communists, Liberals and a quarter of the Parliamentary Labour Party, but also four future Tory Prime Ministers – Churchill, Eden, MacMillan and the young Edward Heath. The by-election provided a timely opportunity for even the least politically-minded people to express their disgust at the Munich settlement.

Louis MacNeice, who went to Oxford to help, later spoke for:

> Those who by their habit hate
> Politics . . .
> The nicest people in England have always been the least
>   Apt to solidarity or alignment
> But all of them must now align against the beast . . .
> That prowls at every door and barks in every headline.[39]

When the votes were cast on October 27th, Hogg won, but with a greatly reduced majority.

Three weeks later, in a by-election at Bridgewater, the People's Front triumphed. Here the combined efforts of Richard Acland, Liberal MP for a neighbouring constituency, and the local Left Book Club helped to persuade the local Liberal and Labour parties to stand down in favour of Vernon Bartlett, a journalist, broadcaster and former employee of the LNU. Bartlett's surprise victory overturned a large Tory majority. For a moment it looked as though the desperate urgency of the international situation might enable peace activists to shift the dead weight of the party system.[40]

Within the Palace of Westminster things were also moving. Previously Labour's leaders had qualified their rejection of a Popular Front by hinting that they might consider if there was evidence of a serious backbench Tory revolt. After Munich this seemed possible. Dalton was excited: 'to split the Tory Party would be real big politics.'[41] For several weeks he scurried back and forth in the corridors of power, trying to patch together an arrangement for co-operation with the Tory dissidents. Dalton seems to have been worried that the Party rank and file would be bewildered by the turn around. Events in Oxford and Bridgewater should have told him otherwise – as should the call, by representatives of 120 local Labour Parties meeting to discuss Spain, for Labour to take the initiative in forming an alliance of progressive forces to bring down Chamberlain.[42] John Strachey, a leading Left Book Club and Communist intellectual, wrote to his schoolfriend Robert Boothby – now a left-wing Tory MP – reassuring him that the left would support a pact with the Tory dissidents, even if the Communist Party was excluded (which it was bound to be). The Communists, he pledged, would keep a low profile in the interests of overthrowing Chamberlain.[43] But all the excitement was premature. By December it was clear that nothing would happen. For the time being Chamberlain survived – largely because Eden, the big fish among the Tory dissidents, would not jump.[44]

Stafford Cripps, erstwhile leader of the Socialist League in the Labour Party, had been keen on a deal with Tory rebels in October. Now he gave up on them. Following Bartlett's victory at Bridgewater, he launched a grass roots campaign for an electoral pact with Liberals and Communists. On January 25th, 1939, the day Barcelona fell to Franco, he was expelled from the Labour Party. A few other Labour MPs lent support, and met the same fate – notably Charles Trevelyan, last of the surviving ex-UDC Liberals in the Parliamentary Party. Despite an outcry from local Labour Parties, the leadership easily won the day at the Labour Party conference at Southport in June. The movement for a People's Front was dead.[45]

One reason the movement collapsed was the imminence of a General Election. In 1935 the fact that an Election was anticipated had probably increased support for the Peace Ballot: but that was because the LNU had steered clear of party politics. The popular front movement was, however, openly aiming not just to popularize alternative policies, but also to produce a realignment of the parties. While the General Election remained remote, loyal party members were prepared to flirt with realignment and even to admit that Labour stood no chance of victory if it fought alone. But, as the Election approached, Labour activists were more likely to place wishful thinking before any realistic assessment of the electoral facts. With new confidence, speaking as though the secret post-Munich negotiations had never occurred, Attlee condemned talk of alliance as a defeatist betrayal of the Party's socialist purpose.[46]

Advocates of the popular front remained fundamentally anti-war. They never campaigned for military preparedness. Despite their *de facto* acceptance of balance-of-power politics, few were prepared to accept its corrollary – the arms race. Thus they laid themselves open to the jibe that, while demanding 'Arms for Spain', they were indifferent to the defence of Britain. It is true that some opponents of the Government saw rearmament as the main issue – notably

Churchill. But there was no popular basis for this view, as the LNU leaders discovered when they tried to mobilize support for Churchill in 1936. In the Labour Party the supporters of rearmament – Dalton and Bevin – were forced to work behind the scenes. In 1937 they persuaded the Parliamentary Party to abstain, rather than vote against, the arms estimates, and during 1938 the Labour Front bench started to attack the Government for not rearming faster.[47] But there was no groundswell of support for this position – not until 1940.

Most popular frontists remained content with the reassuring doctrine that collective security was a substitute for rearmament. If Britain had more allies, they argued, it would need fewer armaments. Underlying this refusal to face up to the logic of resistance was not merely a residual pacifism, but, more importantly, an inability to accept that armaments in the hands of the Chamberlain government would make the world a safer place. Many feared that the object of rearmament was not collective security, but merely a desire to deter Hitler from moving West. Chamberlain, they expected, would stand idly by – or even join in – when Hitler attacked the Soviet Union. Opponents of rearmament in the Labour Party (and until 1938 this included the leader Attlee) argued that, however desirable under a Labour Government, the Party could not support Chamberlain's rearmament without appearing to endorse the foreign policy that went with it. This was not merely a question of parliamentary tactics. 'Acceptance of rearmament', Attlee wrote in 1936, 'will lead to demand after demand being made on your liberties. It will in effect lead to a demand that you shall accept Fascism practically, in order to conquer Fascism. We shall not be a party to that.'[48] If Fascism was, as the Communists insisted, simply capitalism with its back to the wall, then it was realistic to see in Chamberlain's rearmament programme not the promise of defence against German Fascism, but stage one in the construction of British Fascism.[49] Bevan put the point forcefully at the 1937 Labour Party Conference:

> If a strongly armed British Government is necessary, a united nation behind the Government is also necessary. If the immediate international situation is used as an excuse

to get us to drop our opposition to the rearmament programme of the Government, the next phase must be that we must desist from any industrial or political action that may disturb national unity in face of fascist aggression. Along that road lies endless retreat, and the end of it is a voluntary totalitarian state with ourselves erecting the barbed wire around.[50]

After Munich the idea that the main danger came from Chamberlain rather than Hitler became difficult to sustain. Some leaders of the popular front movement – Victor Gollancz for one – began to call openly for an acceleration of rearmament: though here he parted company with the Communist Party.[51] It had occurred to some popular frontists that rearmament as an instrument of social control could cut both ways.[52] Rearmament created bottlenecks in the supply of skilled labour, placing trade unions in a position to press for changes in foreign policy as a condition of their support for the 'dilution' of labour. The fear of precisely such pressure had played a part in persuading the Government not to push ahead too fast with the construction of a war economy.[53] But no-one on the left formulated a clear strategy of supporting military preparedness as a way of enabling the labour movement to increase its economic and political muscle – and thereby its ability to influence British foreign policy.

In April 1939, under pressure from Tory backbenchers, the Government announced the introduction of military conscription. Brailsford was one of the few popular frontists prepared to go the whole hog and accept this.[54] The CP, after some initial confusion, made it clear that, while it did not oppose conscription in principle, it was unacceptable under Chamberlain.[55] Labour, with a more tender concern for civil liberties, was less prepared to endorse the principle, and equally opposed to the practice. Conscription, they protested, had less to do with military preparedness than with providing the Government with the power to coerce the labour movement. Attacking British liberties, said Bevin, was no way to persuade Hitler that Britain was ready to fight. If Chamberlain really wanted to do that he should resign and make way for a government of genuine anti-appeasers.[56] The fact was that distrust of Chamberlain ran so deep that even the most

unequivocal supporter of rearmament in the labour movement could not give unreserved support to his Government's
military preparations.

Munich had inspired a last-ditch attempt to bring down
Chamberlain and save the peace. When that failed many
activists became demoralized. The point of the alternative
foreign policy had always been to prevent war, not to prepare
for it. Despairing hope gave way to hopeless despair. Moreover many lost faith in Britain's ability, under any government, to prevent the slide into war. After Munich the initiative
lay with Hitler. People as diverse as the Communist Palme
Dutt and the Tory Hugh Cecil concluded that Britain no
longer held the key to the world situation.[57] The belief in
Britain's power to do good in the world, which had for so long
underpinned popular internationalism, no longer seemed
tenable.

Paradoxically they may all have been wrong. There *was*
something Britain could still have done. When Hitler took
over the rump of Czechoslovakia in March 1939, Chamberlain was finally persuaded to adopt a stance of resistance to
further German expansion, and to open negotiations for a
Russian alliance. That in itself was a minor triumph for the
Popular Front agitation; Chamberlain moved partly because
he feared the domestic consequences of not doing so. But the
change was only cosmetic. Over the summer, Anglo-Soviet
negotiations were allowed to drag on until, in August, Stalin
despaired of a Western alliance and signed the Nazi-Soviet
pact.[58] We cannot know whether a British Government that
genuinely wanted a Russian alliance could have produced a
different result – but it would have stood a chance. At the time,
however, the opportunity for an alliance failed to trigger a
new mass movement. Few believed that war could now be
prevented, and hardly anyone understood that the real issue in
Moscow was not whether Britain and Russia could prevent
war by agreeing on a joint policy of resistance, but whether
Stalin could be persuaded not to make a separate peace with
Hitler. The tragedy is that, at the moment when a massive
explosion of agitation in Britain for a Soviet alliance might
have substantially shortened the coming war, the popular
movement was inert. The activists had given up on a people's

peace – and they were not yet ready to explore the possibilities of a people's war.

11

Socialist Patriotism and People's War

Despite Labour's election victory in 1945, there can be little doubt that it was the Right who – in the long term – picked up the winnings from the Second World War. Not only did the post-war Labour Government make no decisive encroachments on the economic basis of capitalism, it also accepted without question the underlying foreign policy assumptions of the Establishment. It is often assumed that the Second World War had a more radicalizing impact on British politics than the First. In the field of foreign policy this is quite untrue. The First World War produced not only a mass peace movement while it lasted, but also a post-war current of public pacifism which, for a time, threatened to overwhelm the traditional operations of the Foreign Office and the Ministry of War. The second great European blood-letting produced no such peace movement, and the lessons it taught were those of militarism, not of pacifism. In 1944 the Labour Party, in sharp contrast to its statements at the end of the First World War, declared: 'It is better to have too much armed force than too little.' Labour insisted on the war guilt of the German nation as a whole, and issued an explicit refutation of the Angellite thesis that wars could produce no economic gain for the victor:

> The Germans have clearly demonstrated by their heavy exactions and by their systematic exploitation of the occupied territories that very large contributions, in labour and in goods, as well as in money, can be collected from one country for the benefit of another.[1]

It is the brutalizing effects of warfare, not any pacifist

revulsion against them, that rings through the language in which international politics were discussed in Britain throughout the 1940s.

In the First World War radicals had looked to the emerging superpowers to enable democratic movements to set Europe to rights – whether by the enforcement of a Pax Americana, or by the boost given by the Russian Revolution to the campaign for a negotiated peace. By 1939 the radicals were older, and sadder. Everything had been tried: and everything had failed. H. N. Brailsford, whose 1916 book had done much to popularize the idea of the League, spoke for a generation whose hopes had been shattered by the events of the inter-war years when, at the end of 1939 he confided to his ex-wife:

> I have hideous moments in which I go shivering, cold and physically sick before writing a war-like article. . . . I see all the horror, and yet my reason can find no way out. So when the shivering fit is over I write my bellicose article and no one would guess that I ever hesitated.

Three years later he wrote:

> I'm beseiged by pleas . . . to write something to help my day and generation. But what? I'm so pessimistic about the coming settlement that I'm paralysed. Am I just once again to write, as I did in 1916, a book of amiable daydreams, which everyone will ignore?[2]

After the war, of course, the superpowers did move in to set Europe to rights. But the establishment of the bloc system in the late 1940s was to be a sad end to visions of the New World – Western or Eastern – restoring the balance of the Old.

The Second World War brought to full maturity the deep-rooted affinity between nationalism and socialism. Writing in 1942, Franz Borkenau argued that 'internationalism is essentially a bourgeois-democratic affair', and he added:

> If there is any social force which, pre-eminently, has worked towards making the nation-state important again after its partial abeyance in the age of liberalism, that force is socialism.[3]

Before 1914, when European socialist parties had little prospect of power, the contradiction between their ambition to establish democratic control over economic life, and their sympathy for a liberal internationalism rooted in the principles of the free market, remained largely unacknowledged. But as labour movements gained influence in their respective nation states, the nationalism implicit in their socialist goals came to the fore. Labour movements embraced nationalist economics 'because they coincided with their most urgent interests.'[4] Workers looked to the national state, over which democracy gave them some influence, to protect them against the ravages of an unregulated world economy. As E. H. Carr put it in 1945:

> The socialisation of the nation has as its natural corollary the nationalisation of socialism. . . . [Hence] the loyalty of the masses to a nation which had become the instrument of their collective interests and ambitions. . . . "Planned economy" is a Janus with a nationalist as well as a socialist face.[5]

Against this powerful combination of socialism and nationalism, liberal economics stood little chance.

In Britain, as we have seen, the 'nationalization of socialism' was delayed by the continuing power of liberal internationalism in the political culture. Although the popularity of the war economy lay at the root of the growth of socialism during the First World War, liberal internationalism was quick to reassert itself once the war was over. The collapse of post-war attempts to reconstruct the world economy in 1929–31 opened the way for a new wave of economic nationalism in Britain. During the 1930s, however, it was the Conservatives who capitalized most effectively on the larger consequences of the Wall Street Crash, using them not only to bring down a Labour Government and introduce tariffs aimed at imperial consolidation, but also to promote among the masses the spirit of patriotic self-congratulation so eloquently projected by Stanley Baldwin:

> I think that we must all be full of the sense of profound thankfulness that we are living in this country, under a

> system of National Government. . . . True to our
> traditions, we have avoided all extremes. We have
> steered clear of fascism, communism, dictatorship, and
> we have shown the world that democratic government,
> constitutional methods and ordered liberty are not
> inconsistent with progress and prosperity.[6]

The collapse of appeasement put paid to Baldwin's isolationist
patriotism, and opened the way for the Left. In the prosecution of the war, the Left discovered far greater opportunities
for political advance than any that had arisen from the anti-war
struggles of the 1930s. As in the First World War, the
imperative need for active working-class collaboration in the
war effort greatly enhanced the importance of the labour
movement in the industrial and political life of the country.
The Labour Party's part in bringing down the Chamberlain
Government in May 1940 was recognized by the central roles
allotted to Labour Ministers in Churchill's Coalition Government. The transference of Ernest Bevin direct from the
leadership of Britain's largest trade union to the Ministry of
Labour, symbolized Labour's role in the new order – not least
because Bevin's control over the allocation of manpower came
to displace the traditional operations of the Treasury, as the
lynch-pin of Government economic management.[7]

The infusion of Labour's socialist ambitions with nationalist
sentiment was one consequence of gaining power on the back
of the war economy. In 1945, when the Labour Party asked
and received retrospective electoral approval for the transformation of 1940, it did so in the language of nationalism.
Nation-alization – like the *National* Service that had won the
war and the *National* Health Service – placed working-class
demands for justice and equality firmly within the context of a
nation taking control of its destiny:

> Each industry must have applied to it the test of national
> service. If it serves the nation, well and good; if it is
> inefficient and falls down on its job, the nation must see
> that things are put right.[8]

Only in this way could Britain, competing in a world of
emerging economic giants, 'keep her place as a Great Power'.[8]

The power of Labour in the War Cabinet helped to channel the energies of radical activists into support for the People's War. Equally important, however, was the surge of popular nationalism unleashed by the catastrophic military events of 1940 – Dunkirk, the fall of France, the threat of imminent Nazi invasion, the Battle of Britain, and, finally, the Blitz. It is worth pausing for a moment to examine the nature of this sentiment since, more than any other factor, it explains why all attempts to build a mass peace movement, both during and after the war, were to fail.

Despite the affinities between socialism and nationalism, not many British socialists before the 1940s had framed their message in unashamedly patriotic language. This was a consequence not only of the continuing pull of liberal internationalism, but also of the deeply undemocratic character of the generally available language of patriotism. In the 1930s Popular Frontists had sought to 'follow the French example . . . win from the enemies of peace and the working class those symbols and that "heritage" that are the British equivalents of Liberty, Equality, Fraternity and the *Marseillaise*.'[9] Unfortunately, as one British Communist explained to the French comrades: 'Il y a une toute petite différence entre *La Marseillaise* et *God Save the King*.'[10] There is no need to discuss here the critical role of the monarchy in structuring the 'Ukanian' identity: this has recently been dissected with great brilliance by Tom Nairn.[11] As I revise this chapter, celebrations of the anniversary of the so-called Glorious Revolution of 1688 once again bring home the fact that while other nations trace the origins of their freedom and identity to popular uprisings, the British happily attach the word 'revolution' to a mere *coup d'état*. The essential point was made by R. H. Tawney:

> In the transition to political democracy, this country underwent . . . no inner conversion. She accepted it as a convenience, like an improved system of telephones; she did not dedicate herself to it as the expression of a moral idea of comradeship and equality, the avowal of which could leave nothing the same. She changed her political garments but not her heart. She carried into the democratic era, not only the institutions, but the social

habits and mentality of the oldest and toughest plutocracy in the world. She went to the ballot box touching her hat.[12]

In 1940, for a brief moment, the democracy stopped touching its hat. Confronted by the imminent threat of Nazi invasion, and convinced that only by straining every nerve could Britain avoid the fate of France, millions of people came, perhaps for the first time, to perceive the nation not as something to which they were admitted by the grace of kings, but as their own authentic community. J. B. Priestley's celebration of the 'little holiday steamers' which 'snatched glory out of defeat' at Dunkirk gained him an enormous radio audience. He used it to attack paternalistic officialdom and to articulate demands for social progress: 'I'd tell people to forget their old ordinary life because ultimately, anyhow, we'll either have a better life than that, or bust.'[13] The Establishment didn't like this kind of thing and Priestley's broadcasts were, eventually, stopped. When the bombs fell in the autumn the intellectuals were quick to celebrate the initiative and self-generated activity of the common people, and to discover within it a basis for a new reconciliation between patriotism and democracy.[14]

It was George Orwell who gave the most memorable expression to the socialist patriotism of 1940. Britain's existing rulers could not, he argued, organize effective resistance to Hitler. It would need a revolution to eradicate 'inefficiency, class privilege and the rule of the old' and thus liberate 'the native genius of the English people. . . . We cannot win the war without introducing Socialism, nor establish Socialism without winning the war.'[15] Orwell's socialism would reflect the democratic virtues characteristic of the English working class – 'the genuinely popular culture . . . that goes on beneath the surface, unofficially and more or less frowned on by the authorities.'[16] Against the Nazi war machine, English socialism would deploy, not merely an efficiently planned economy, but a popular will to victory rooted in 'the English genius' – gentleness and anti-militarism; defence of the autonomy of local communities against centralizing power; respect for liberty and the rule of law. At the root of Orwell's socialism was a belief in the decency of ordinary working people and their capacity to prevent the necessary centralization of a socialist economy from degenerating into totalitarianism.[17] They were, he acknowledged, deeply zenophobic:

> In all countries the poor are more national than the rich, but the English working class are outstanding in their abhorrence of foreign habits. . . . During the war of 1914–18 the English working class were in contact with foreigners to an extent that is rarely possible. The sole result was that they brought back a hatred of all Europeans, except the Germans, whose courage they admired. In four years on French soil they did not even acquire a liking for wine.[18]

For the time being, however, the political implications of English insularity were overshadowed, for Orwell, by his belief that 'patriotism, against which the socialists fought for so long, has become a tremendous lever in their hands.'[19]

It is, of course, difficult to disentangle the reality of popular attitudes from the myth-making of the intellectuals. Nevertheless the evidence of opinion polls and by-elections suggests that the new democratic nationalism was not merely imagined by the intellectuals who sought to articulate it.[20] It is sometimes suggested that the inconvenience, misery and personal tragedy caused by the war outweighed the appeals of patriotism.[21] This probably misconstrues the function of patriotic sentiment. Patriotism did not exist *in spite* of the inconveniences caused by the war, but *because* of them. At the simplest level, patriotism lent meaning and purpose to personal catastrophies that would otherwise appear intolerable. A more complex linkage might be found between the disruptions of individual lives and local communities, the extraordinary geographical mobility of individuals, and the sense of 'the nation at war' as a concrete lived reality.[22] Be that as it may, what is clear is that the events of 1940 precipitated a popular nationalism which – unlike Tawney's deferential democracy and Baldwin's conservative nation – the Left could work with. Just at the moment when France's Jacobin revolutionary tradition reached its lowest ebb, the British Left discovered the radical possibilities of patriotism.

The Labour leadership, fully committed to the Churchill coalition, tended to see pressure from below more as a threat to the orderly regimentation of the people, than as a source of constructive initiative. The Labour Party ceased to contest by-elections and ruled out extra-Parliamentary agitation of any kind as incompatible with its membership of the Government. As a result, membership slumped and in many parts of the country the Party ceased to exist as a mass organization. Large numbers of Labour Party activists rejected the ban on political agitation, believing that pressure for a more socialist approach to the war effort was a precondition of victory. Some argued that the Party should threaten to withdraw from the coalition unless the Tories accepted demands to extend war controls to the nationalization of major industries. Although most Labour activists drew back from a direct challenge to the Coalition Government, the victory of two independent left candidates in by-elections in the spring of 1942 increased pressures on the Party to abandon its adherence to the electoral truce. By fighting by-elections, it was argued, while remaining in the Government, Labour could demonstrate the public demand for more radical measures and increase its muscle at the Cabinet table.[23]

At the Labour Party Conference in May 1942 the dissidents were narrowly defeated. This left the way open for the consolidation of the independents around a new organization: Common Wealth.[24] Founded in June 1942, Common Wealth was a cross between a political party and a non-party campaign. Its main activity was contesting by-elections. For most of the membership the purpose of doing so, however, was not to build a new political party, but to bring pressure to bear on the Government to conduct the war in a more radical spirit. It provided a channel for protest while the war continued. About 15,000 people joined, and three MPs were returned in wartime by-elections. When the Labour Party returned to the electoral politics in 1945, Common Wealth rapidly disappeared from the political scene. It belongs to a tradition of tactical independent electoralism alongside the post-Munich Popular Front candidacies of 1938 and the attempts to put up independent anti-nuclear candidates in the 1950s and 1960s. Indeed some of the same individuals were involved in all three episodes.

Common Wealth was formed by the merger of two organizations – J. B. Priestley's '1941 Committee' and Richard Acland's 'Forward March'. In the winter of 1940–41 a number of public figures contacted by the left-of-centre owner of *Picture Post*, Edward Hulton, agreed to work together for greater efficiency, vigour and democracy in the prosecution of the war. Priestley was the best known member of the '1941 Committee'. As in the 1950s, when he played a similar role in the emergence of CND, he was primarily interested in a committee of notables lobbying the powerful, and had no intention of starting a mass movement. When Common Wealth was formed – 'a vague sort of national movement, with provincial branches etc', as he recalled with distaste in 1968 – he quickly withdrew.[25]

The dominating figure in the new organization was Richard Acland – MP, an ex-Liberal converted to socialism in 1936, and a vigorous supporter of the pre-war Popular Front movement. In May 1940 he told Lloyd George:

> In my view this country is filled with immense new moral forces which have been dammed back for ten years by the great dead bulk of the Labour Party Machine lying like a fallen tree across the road to progress.[26]

Acland placed himself at the head of the 'moral renaissance',[27] consolidating a personal following built around his best-selling books and endless public meetings into a loose organization called 'Forward March'. Acland brought moral-ity to the forefront of politics. More than any other wartime figure he addressed himself to the conscience of middle-class radicalism, arguing that the only worthwhile victory possible was one based on the common ownership of the means of production and a moral revolution in which selfishness and the profit motive would give way to an ethic of service to the community. In a curious way, and despite its commitment to vigorous prosecution of the war, Common Wealth provided a refuge for pacifist-minded individuals who could not bring themselves to oppose the anti-fascist war. By investing the war with a transcendent moral purpose, Acland may have helped his followers to silence the promptings of their pacifist consciences. Equally important in this respect was Common Wealth's approach to foreign policy, acutely summarized by one historian: 'The LNU and the Popular Front might have failed, but the People's War fostered a vision of a progressive Utopia arising phoenix-like from the ashes of Europe.'[28] This vision, by no means confined to members of Common Wealth, represented the main achievement of peace politics during the Second World War. It is discussed fully in the next Chapter. First, however, it is important to examine some rather less visionary – but certainly more influential – exponents of People's War.

The major focus of popular agitation during the war years was provided not by Common Wealth but by the Communist Party. When, in the autumn of 1939, Chamberlain chose, after all, to go to war with Hitler, and Stalin chose not to, the Communists were, understandably, thrown into some confusion. After a brief flirtation with a policy of 'War on Two Fronts' – supporting the war while opposing the Chamberlain Government – the Party settled for the Moscow line, calling for an immediate 'People's Peace' to end the 'Imperialist War'. As Hitler extended his European empire, and the threat to the British Isles came closer, this policy lost all credibility. By the spring of 1940, the Communists had tacitly accepted that agitation for an immediate peace with Hitler was out of the question. During the autumn and winter of that dramatic year they put themselves at the forefront of agitation for more effective air raid precautions, and used their influence in the war factories to defend workers' living standards while criticizing the inefficiency of management. The Nazi-Soviet Pact and the 'Imperialist War' line certainly lost the Party members, and, more importantly, disrupted its close working relationship with the non-communist left in Popular Front organizations like the Left Book Club. Nevertheless the constructive work of Communists in the Blitz and the war factories kept the Party alive and put it in a good position to exploit the opportunities for expansion that followed Hitler's invasion of the Soviet Union in June 1941.[29] From this point until the end of the war the Communist Party proclaimed its enthusiastic support both for the war effort and for the maintenance of Churchill's Coalition Government. As – to many people's surprise – Russian resistance first held up and then began to turn back the Nazi forces, the Communists' identification with the Soviet Union became their major attraction to tens of thousands of new recruits. By the autumn of 1942, claiming 64,000 members, the Communist Party was a quarter of the size of the much depleted Labour Party. Common Wealth was a marginal protest movement: but the Communists seemed set to become a major force in British politics.

It was not only solidarity with the Soviet resistance that brought members flooding into the Party. Equally important was its decision to combine support for the war effort and for the Government with the most vigorous campaigning politics. In the factories the major focus of Communist activity was the campaign to increase production, waged in such a way as to increase the power of shop steward organizations, often in alliance with Government officials, at the expense of traditional managerial prerogative. It was the Communist Party which seized most fully the opportunities for extending working-class power on the shop floor created by wartime full employment and the intervention of the state in the economy. Alongside Ernest Bevin's conduct of the Ministry of Labour, they were at the forefront of the process by which workers came to see their interests as identified with the extension of state power in economic life. Thus they contributed greatly to the popularity of national economic planning which underpinned Labour's election victory in 1945.[30]

But the Communists' most dramatic political intervention was the Second Front Campaign. For three years, from the autumn of 1941, the Party mounted successive agitations for the immediate opening of a Second Front against Hitler in North Western Europe. The Government's refusal until June 1944 to cross the Channel left the bulk of the fighting to the Russians. Brushing aside military and logistical arguments, the Communists claimed that this reflected the continuing influence of the 'Men of Munich' within the Government, men who wanted Britain to stand on the sidelines while Russia and Germany fought one another to a standstill. They were

supported by the press lord, Beaverbrook, and the combination of the *Daily Worker* and *Daily Express* created a unique
political movement which still awaits its historian. The
Second Front Campaign produced the biggest demonstrations
of the war period and, most of the time, opinion polls showed
that the demonstrators spoke for the majority of a public
moved by both feelings of solidarity with the hard-pressed
Russians and by a desire to get the war over with.[31]

These were difficult times for the voices of pacifism to make
themselves heard. The only substantial oppositional movements in Britain were demanding, not peace, but the more
vigorous prosecution of the war. Most sections of the left were
interested, not in stopping the war, but in using it to swing the
balance of social power away from Britain's traditional rulers.
Whatever else divided them, the Labour leadership, the
Communists (after June 1941) and much of the independent
left had embarked on a parallel course – promoting popular
power through People's War. Not since the Crimean War
nearly a century earlier, when middle-class radicalism latched
on to the opportunities for attacking the aristocratic Establishment in the name of efficient prosecution of the war, had
pacifist opinion found itself so isolated in Britain.[32] And it had
been the experience of that war that convinced Richard
Cobden of 'the utter uselessness of raising one's voice in
opposition to war when it has once begun.'[33]
    During the 'phoney war' – the eerie nine months between
Chamberlain's declaration of war and Hitler's attack in the
West – there was a substantial current of support for a
negotiated peace. R. R. Stokes, a Catholic Labour MP who
feared that the price of resistance to Hitler would be the
establishment of Communism throughout Europe, led a small
group of MPs in calling for peace negotiations – a position
which accepted the partition of Poland as a *fait accompli*.[34]
There was, at first, significant support for this position among
Labour activists, as well as in the PPU. Many PPU leaders
shared Stokes's fear that Communism might prove an even
greater evil than Nazism. In October 1939 Vera Brittain
wrote:

> Even supposing that we do destroy Hitler . . . [this will]
> probably lead . . . to a revolutionary situation in
> Germany, controlled by puppets who owe allegiance to
> another Power. We, the democracies, will still be faced
> by totalitarianism, in a form less clumsy but no less
> aggressive, and even more sinister in its ruthless un-
> exhausted might.[35]

Given such an approach it is hardly surprising that relations
between pacifist and Communist opponents of the war during
1939–40 proved difficult. The PPU launched its own
Women's Peace Campaign in direct competition to the Stop
the War agitation promoted by the Communist-led Women
Against War and Fascism.[36]

Hitler's assault in the summer of 1940 put paid to the
agitation for peace negotiations. Several leading supporters of
the PPU resigned, and, even among the Quakers, 'a silent
majority' seemed ready to condone the war.[37] After Dunkirk,
pacifists concentrated, not on stopping the war, but on trying
to ameliorate the barbarism with which it was being conducted. They protested against the saturation bombing of
German cities, and campaigned to allow famine relief supplies
into German–occupied Europe.[38] Although there were nearly
four times as many conscientious objectors as during the First
World War, there was no organization remotely like the NCF.
Anxious to avoid confrontation with pacifists, the authorities
made life relatively easy for the objectors. Fenner Brockway
paid tribute to the understanding and respect for individual
conscience shown by the state.[39] Some of the more militant
resisters complained that they were being 'diddled' by the
'ingenious' tolerance of a state which deprived them of the
opportunity, welcomed by Clifford Allen twenty-five years
earlier, 'for the young men of our generation . . . [to bear]
witness to the faith that [was] in them.'[40] Only three per cent
of COs went to jail, compared with thirty per cent in the First
World War. The great majority of pacifists quietly performed
various kinds of alternative service. Some set up agricultural
communities where they could take refuge from public
contempt for 'conchies' and convince themselves that their
experiments in communal living would, once 'the grim period

of war is over . . . be remembered as the forerunner of the new society.'[41]

So long as Hitler threatened Europe the prospects for a revival of peace politics were minimal. It is true that, while outright military victory remained improbable, Labour leaders (hoping for a German revolution) resisted calls for the post-war de-industrialization of Germany and toyed with the idea of placing Britain at the head of a revolutionary European resistance to Hitler. Hugh Dalton wrote in June 1940:

> We have got to organise movements in enemy-occupied territory comparable to the Sinn Fein movement in Ireland. . . . The 'democratic international' must use many different methods, including industrial and military sabotage, labour agitation and strikes, continuous propaganda, terrorist acts against traitors and German leaders, boycotts and riots. It is [he added, engagingly] quite clear to me that an organisation . . . of this character is not something that can be handled by the ordinary . . . machinery of either the British Civil Service or the British military machine.[42]

A few weeks later Churchill put him in charge of organizing the Special Operations Executive (SOE), charged with 'setting Europe ablaze'. The romance, however, did not survive. In the course of 1941, Attlee accepted that neither he, nor, more importantly, Winston Churchill, were really interested in fomenting revolution. When it came to subversion, one historian has remarked, 'the Coalition was more politically vulnerable than the Nazi Government.'[43]

With the entry of Russia and America into the war, victory became conceivable and Labour's German policy hardened accordingly. Labour's war was against the German nation, not just the Nazis. Attlee, however, was no more anxious than Churchill to actually fight the Germans. The Labour Ministers fully supported Churchill's resistance to the opening of a Second Front. In June 1942 the Cabinet formally agreed that there would be no attempt to invade Northern Europe until the Russians had broken the back of the Nazi offensive in the East. The Russians could win the war, while Britain conserved her young men and concentrated on the defence of her Empire. It was realized that such a policy risked leaving Soviet Russia as the dominant force in a post-Nazi Europe. But there would be time enough to intervene on the Continent if and when the Russian advance began. Meanwhile Attlee was just as keen as Churchill to maintain Britain's extra-European Empire. In July 1943 Attlee pointed to the need to draw the Americans into sharing the burden of maintaining order in post-war Europe, in order to liberate British resources for the maintenance of the Commonwealth. The alternative, as he saw it, was that the Americans would take over the Empire, while Britain exhausted herself trying to set the continent to rights. Attlee's arguments pointed clearly to the foreign policy eventually pursued by the post-war Labour Government – attempting to manipulate the emerging US superpower in a way that was compatible both with the maintenance of Britain's overseas Empire and with her traditionally limited commitment to entanglement in European affairs.[44]

12

A 'Third Force': Vision versus Cold War

While the major forces of the left were fully commited to co-operation with Churchill in imposing unconditional surrender on Germany, more radical ideas about foreign policy retained a small foothold in the margins of British political life. Throughout the war, members of the Labour Party, Common Wealth and a variety of unattached intellectuals continued to debate alternative approaches to the problems of war and peace in Europe. Most of the non-communist left put up a stubborn defence of internationalism in their objection to blaming the German people, rather than the Nazis, for the war. No stable peace, they insisted, could be built on the destruction of the German nation.[1] The terror bombing of German cities was condemned by some on moral grounds. Others continued to believe that the German working class held the key to the eventual democratic overthrow of fascism. In bombing Hamburg, wrote Tom Wintringham in 1943, 'we . . . bomb the revolution'.

Wintringham, an ex-Communist who had fought in Spain and was now one of the leaders of Common Wealth, advocated a revolutionary war strategy in which invading conventional armies would co-operate with the resistance movements in occupied Europe to facilitate the emergence of genuine popular power across the continent.[2] It was widely believed on the left that the capitulation of the old ruling classes in the face of the Nazi onslaught had opened the way for socialist revolution. Many looked forward to a Labour Britain co-operating with the heirs of the resistance movements in the construction of a new democratic and socialist Europe. Speaking at the Labour Party Conference in May 1945, the young Major Denis Healey called on British socialists not to be too squeamish about the inevitable excesses of popular movements engaged in the revolutionary over-throw of collaborationist regimes. 'The crucial principle of our own foreign policy should be to protect, assist, encourage, and aid in every way the Socialist revolution wherever it appears.' And he warned:

> The upper classes in every country look to the British Army and the British people to protect them against the just wrath of the people who have been fighting under-ground against them for the past four years. We must see that does not happen. There is a very great danger, unless we are very careful, that we shall find ourselves running with the Red Flag in front of the armoured cars of Tory imperialism and counter-revolution.[3]

Visions of an alliance between British Labour and a European revolution were reinforced by some radical new thinking about the limits of national sovereignty and the nation state. The error of 1919, wrote E. H. Carr, had been to seek to found a new world order on the anachronistic principle of national self-determination. National sovereignty was increasingly a myth. The scale of modern industry needed a transnational sphere of operation. Military technology – the aeroplane and the submarine – made all but the very largest states indefensible except in alliance with others.[4] In such circumstances it was absurd to attempt to establish an international society by 'the piecing together of national units':

> Instead of basing our settlements on a recognition of the unrestricted right of national self-determination, and then seeking to build up an international system out of independent national units, we must begin by creating the framework of an international order and then, as a necessary corollary, encourage national independence to develop and maintain itself within the limits of that framework.[5]

In the late 1930s an American critic of the League, Carl Streit, had called for political union between the British

Empire and the United States as the embryo of world government. As the European situation worsened Streit's idea of 'Federal Union' was taken up in Britain, but predominantly in the context of a merging of European, rather than Atlantic, nations. In the summer of 1940 even the Cabinet was prepared to contemplate the merging of French and British citizenship, if this would help to prevent French capitulation to the Nazis.[6] Throughout the 1940s, Federal Unionists kept up an organized propaganda for a federal European state, attracting support from a wide range of individuals in the Labour and Liberal Parties, and in Common Wealth.[7]

The problem with Federal Union was that it offered no mechanism for the transcendence of nationalism. National sentiments could not just be wished away by the drafting of Federal constitutions. Some believed that Hitler's New Order had put paid to the nation state in Europe. But, despite occasional declarations of Europeanism by some Resistance leaders, there was no guarantee that the movements would fight for a United States of Europe rather than the restoration of the unrestricted sovereignty of their respective nations.[8] And in Britain itself the war had enormously reinforced popular nationalism – not only because of the direct threat of invasion, but equally because the construction of a war economy encouraged ordinary people to look to the national state as the main protector of their material well-being. The answer to what E. H. Carr called 'the nationalisation of socialism' lay not in anachronistic attempts to restore *laisser-faire*, but in the promotion of transnational controls over economic life. In such improvisations as the Middle East Supply centre and the United Nations Relief and Rehabilitation Agency, Carr perceived:

> a striking parallel with the financial and economic system of the nineteenth century, operated all over the world by the organs of an anonymous authority having no precisely defined status, but enjoying in virtue of its non-political services and its prestige the toleration and approval of national governments.[9]

Underlying the Era of World Wars, Carr argued, was the breakdown of the Pax Britannica and the liberal world economy that it had sustained. In place of the invisible operations of Victorian bankers, Carr – echoing Hobson at the turn of the century – looked to the proliferation of trans-national economic agencies to make 'a modest clearing in the jungle of international relations.'[10] The road to world government would be paved, he believed, not with federal constitutions but with functional agencies created to carry out particular transnational economic tasks. To the extent that the common people came to look to such agencies to guarantee their material interests, argued Carr, nationalism would tend to wither away. It would be the experience of international agencies fulfilling particular economic functions, not any vision of federal political union, that would lay the soundest basis for a stable post-war order. 'Internationalism, like nationalism, must become social.'[11]

A few socialists used this same principle of function to question the sovereignty of the nation state from within as well as from without. While Labour leaders were content to see the national state – over which they at last had the prospect of control – as an adequate instrument for the democratizing currents unleashed by the People's War, radicals looked for a more thoroughgoing process of political change. G. D. H. Cole, who defined himself in 1942 as 'a West European liberal (with a small "l") with an intense belief in democratic socialism', found, in popular responses to the emergencies of war – bomb shelter committees in London, resistance movements in occupied Europe – echoes of that grass-roots democratic spirit which had inspired his Guild Socialist writings in the First World War. For every new supra-national agency, he insisted, there should be a proliferation of self-managing co-operatives, trade unions, neighbourhood groups – the small-scale voluntary associations which had always provided the best environment for active democracy.[12] This approach harked back to the Guild Socialist idea of 'functional representation' – the division of sovereignty between democratic bodies separately elected to carry out different social functions. Membership of a wide range of distinct functional democracies, both smaller and larger than the nation state, would enable ordinary people to retain their national identities without reducing all political life to the dangerous discourses of nationalism.[13] The nation state was both too big and too small to provide a focus for effective popular self-government.

There was no easy way of accommodating such visions to the military and political realities of the late war years. From 1943 the war was being won – but not by revolutionary means. For every self-managing partisan band, there were thousands of conscript soldiers obeying orders. For every successful guerilla engagement, scores of bombs fell from the sky on undefended civilians. And there was only one Tito. As the Allied armies occupied liberated Europe, it became clear that neither in the East nor in the West would they act as midwives for a democratic socialist future.

Those who pinned their hopes on the British Labour Party to resist the use of Allied military power to prevent socialist revolution in liberated Europe were to be sadly disappointed. The British intervention in Greece in December 1944 revealed how very far the Labour leadership was from endorsing the principles of a socialist foreign policy. On 3rd December 1944 Greek police, defending a right-wing regime installed by the British against the broad-based communist-led resistance movement, ELAS, machine-gunned an unarmed crowd in Athens' Constitution Square. Within a week fierce fighting had broken out between ELAS and the British troops who had been occupying Athens since the German withdrawal in October. Winston Churchill, determined to restore the Greek monarchy and to keep Communists out of the government, ordered that there should be no negotiation with ELAS until they had been driven out of Athens. 'In Athens as everywhere else our maxim is "no peace without victory".'[14]

Churchill's policy provoked a popular outcry in Britain. British troops had been conscripted to fight fascism, not to put down popular resistance movements. While the fighting in Athens was at its height, 20,000 people demonstrated in Trafalgar Square – a remarkable number for a demonstration called at less than two weeks notice – demanding negotiations and the inclusion of ELAS representatives in the Government. There were even some strikes – though the Communist Party did its best to prevent any disruption of war production.[15] Mass Observation reported 'a deep underlying apprehension'

that the trouble in Greece was only a foretaste of what was
going to happen in all the liberated countries.[16] Churchill's
refusal to negotiate was opposed not only by public opinion,
but also by most of his advisers in Greece, by the Foreign
Secretary (Anthony Eden), by the President – and the press –of
the United States, and even by *The Times*, which one of
Churchill's few supporters described during the crisis as 'a
more expensive edition of the *Daily Worker*.'[17] (The most
notable absentee from the ranks of Churchill's critics in
December 1944 was Stalin. Loyal to the sphere of influence
agreement he had struck with Churchill in Moscow two
months earlier, he remained silent throughout the crisis.) If
ever there was a moment when the alliance of Britain with
counter-revolution in Europe stood open to challenge, this
was it.

No one did more to sustain Churchill during this crisis than
the leadership of the Labour Party. Feelings ran high in the
Party and the trade unions, and – by chance – the Annual
Conference was scheduled to meet a few days after the
massacre in Constitution Square. It was clear that the great
majority of delegates supported an emergency resolution
condemning Government policy. Using a combination of
procedural manoeuvre and threats that the passage of such a
resolution would force Labour Ministers to withdraw from
the Government, the leadership stifled the protest.[18] Given
Churchill's isolation there can be little doubt that a sharp vote
of censure at the Labour Party Conference would have
produced, not the end of the Coalition, but a backdown by the
Prime Minister. The Labour Ministers, however, shared
Churchill's imperialist and anti-communist objections to
allowing the left to take control of Greece: 'The British
Empire cannot abandon its position in the Mediterranean',
Bevin told the Party Conference.[19] Subsequently the Trade
Union Congress lent its services to a campaign to discredit
ELAS with the British public by circulating allegations of
atrocities committed during the fighting.[20] The policy which
Healey was later to condemn – 'running with the Red Flag in
front of the armoured cars of Tory imperialism and counter-
revolution' – had been fully rehearsed by Labour's leadership
well before they came to power in July 1945.

It was widely understood that a critical factor in Europe's future would be the relationship between the emergent superpowers. No one, witnessing the critical role of Russia and America in making the defeat of Hitler possible, could believe that post-war Europe – however united – could be the master of its own destiny. 'The question . . . is not *whether* the great Powers will influence European developments,' remarked *Tribune* in December 1944, 'but *how* they will do it.'[21] Writing in 1942, G. D. H. Cole had acknowledged that unless America was prepared to pour capital into post-war Europe, the process of reconstruction would involve levels of austerity and repression comparable to Stalin's Russia between the wars. But he denied that this need for American aid ruled out the possibility of socialism in Europe. Cole remained convinced that the 'final crisis' of *European* capitalism had arrived. The revival of capitalism in post-war Europe as a dynamic and expansionist system was, he believed, inconceivable. But there was no reason why capitalist America should not work harmoniously together with Communism in the Soviet Union and a democratic socialist reconstruction process in Europe. Indeed, Cole believed, only under socialism would the European economies be capable of sustaining the expansionist momentum which, alone, would make them viable trading partners for the United States. It was the restrictive practices and autarchy, characteristic of capitalism in decay, that threatened the prospects for economic internationalism after the war. Socialism, in Europe, was in the best interests of capitalism in America. 'Expanding economies', wrote Cole, 'can work together.'[22] This was a position very widely held on the British Left in the closing stages of the war.

Just as Woodrow Wilson's rhetoric of democratic internationalism in 1917–18 had appealed to the imagination of British radicals, so did the liberal internationalism projected by the United States during the Second World War. Roosevelt resisted Churchill's balance of power diplomacy in the name of a universalistic doctrine of free trade and economic internationalism.[23] It was the autarchy and trade wars which followed the slump of 1929–32 which had made war inevitable. Post-war peace and prosperity could best be guaranteed by the integration of all the major powers – the British Empire no less than the Soviet Union – into a single world economy sustained by the free flow of American capital. No matter that American capitalism was pursuing its own interests under the cloak of universalism; Roosevelt's hostility to Churchill's schemes for carving up Europe into spheres of influence coincided nicely with the concern of radicals to prevent a polarization between East and West. Once again, as in 1913, British socialists found themselves drawn towards Angellite notions of international capitalism as the guarantor of peace; and, as in 1917, it was to the New World rather than to European capitalism that they looked for salvation. The capitulation of much of the left to Cold War Atlanticism in the later 1940s owes much to their continuing commitment to what one historian has referred to as 'the search for a "possible America" . . . through which failure could be redeemed, weakness remedied, and ideals re-habilitated.'[24] The affection felt on the British Left in the 1930s and 1940s for 'classless' American democracy is too easily forgotten.[25]

By a similar chain of reasoning, the Communist Party came to the conclusion that the best hope for social progress in Europe lay in the maintenance of the wartime alliance. If this was allowed to break down, wrote the leader of American Communism, Earl Browder, the prospects for humanity were grim: 'the spread of civil war over vast areas, cul-minating finally and inevitably in a new world war.' Only by promoting free trade and international economic co-operation could the catastrophe of a return to the trade wars and imperialist rivalries of the 1930s be avoided.[26] It was clear, argued Harry Pollitt in October 1944, that capitalism and socialism could co-operate through the United Nations to serve the interests of the people.[27] The dynamism of American capitalism, argued the Party's chief economic spokesman in January 1945, 'holds out hope not only for America, but for the world.'[28] The British CP was as keen to prevent an American return to isolationism after the war as it was to support American pressure against British attempts to sustain the Empire as a closed economic bloc.[29] In such ways did European Communists, anxious to avoid a new world war, join forces with the ideology of American imperialism.

The Communists were far more sensitive than other sections of the left, to the danger that socialist revolutions in post-war Europe might frighten the Americans back into isolation, thereby crippling the prospects for a new world order based on co-operation between the victorious allies. Such considerations underlay the Communist strategy of working for the establishment of left-of-centre progressive Governments in Britain and Europe, rather than for any immediate socialist transformations.[30] If both the Communists and the independent left could convince themselves in 1945 that large-scale American investment was a necessary condition of social progress in Europe, then it is hardly surprising that the incoming Labour Government perceived a link, not a contradiction, between its domestic programme and the cultivation of a special relationship with the United States.

But relationships with the Soviet Union, whose armies were liberating Eastern Europe, would be no less important to Europe's future. The Communists were confident that the expansion of Soviet power in the East was perfectly compatible with the strengthening of socialist forces in the West. Others were not so sure. Commenting, at the time of the Greek crisis in December 1944, on the apparent understanding between Churchill and Stalin over post-war spheres of influence, *Tribune* pointed to the dire consequences of the breakdown in Allied unity that such an agreement forshadowed:

> Once relations between Britain and Russia are founded on strategic distrust, the same must become true, inevitably, of the relations of each of them to all independent democratic forces on the Continent. Mr Churchill already sees in every democratic movement a potential ally of the Communists. Hence, he concludes, he cannot trust any democratic movement within the British sphere of security. Similarly, Stalin is beginning to see in every democratic workers' or peasants' party which is not under Communist control a potential ally of the West. Hence, he concludes, he cannot trust any of them within *his* sphere of security.[31]

The only hope for democracy in Europe, therefore, was the construction of 'a joint system of security for the whole continent'. If the defeat of Hitler was to be followed by a new military confrontation between East and West in Europe, the political space within which radical visions of democratic socialism could be promoted would vanish: 'unless the forces of democracy kill the zoning agreement, the zoning agreement will kill the forces of democracy all over Europe.'

Such fears were eventually to find their most powerful expression in *Nineteen Eighty Four*. Though not published until 1949, the novel was first conceived by Orwell in the winter of 1943–44 as a way of exploring 'the implications of dividing the world up into "Zones of Influence".'[32] The emergence of 'a continuous phoney war' between rival blocs created the conditions for the world-wide diffusion of totalitarian regimes impervious to internal revolt:

> The war is waged by each ruling group against its own subjects, and the object of war is not to make or prevent conquests of territory but to keep the structure of society intact.[33]

If Orwell gave way to pessimism, others, sharing the same starting point, believed that Britain had a key role to play in preventing such a future.

After the Nazi invasion of the USSR, many British socialists had looked to Anglo-Soviet unity to provide the framework for post-war peace and prosperity in Europe. While many clung to this belief, others came to recognize, not only that US economic aid would be essential to any European reconstruction but also that the Soviet Union was unlikely to welcome European unity. Understandable fear of renewed Western attack would, argued Nye Bevan, inevitably lead Stalin both to emphasize the need for a *cordon sanitaire* under Soviet control in Eastern Europe, and to oppose Western European unity as a threat to Soviet security. 'That is the price we have to pay for the bitter recent past, and only time and normal intercourse can assuage its evils.' In the meantime, Bevan continued, British Labour should work with socialist forces on the continent to build 'an organic federation of

Western European nations.' Although such initiatives might face initial opposition from the Russians, they would, he argued, in the long term lay the basis for the reunification of Europe as a whole and of *détente* with the Soviet Union. As the only surviving European state with the power to negotiate an independent role for Western Europe between the two superpowers, Britain had a critical part to play in preventing complete polarization between East and West.[34]

If the incoming Labour Government had assigned to Britain a pioneering role in the maximization of European unity and independence in the new world of the superpowers, it might have been able to ameliorate the emerging Cold War. It might also have laid the basis for a successful transition for Britain from the global role it could no longer sustain towards full partnership in a reconstructed Europe. Nothing, however, was further from the thoughts of Labour ministers. Like the great majority of their contemporaries, they were quite unable to comprehend what the war had done to Britain's status as a great power. Neville Chamberlain and the appeasers had warned that the British Empire could not survive a second world war. While the war was being fought, Treasury officials never ceased calculating its appalling economic conse-quences.[35] Post-war Britain, they demonstrated, would be bankrupt: incapable of funding the revolution in social security expected by the voters or – though they were less forthcoming on this point – of paying for the overseas military presence necessary to maintaining Britain as one of the Big Three. In 1945 such pessimism was out of fashion. Hadn't Britain stood alone in 1940? Hadn't Hitler been defeated? Hadn't the British people earned their welfare state? The new Labour Government was going to set the example to the world in social reform while ensuring that Britain kept her rightful place as a Great Power. Both socialist nationalism and a commitment to maintaining Britain's global role were strongly represented in the Cabinet. Neither commitment left much room either for realistic adjustments to straitened circumstances or for the European vision advocated by sections of the left.

Economic reality was quick to make itself felt. Britain was

bankrupt. For five years, industry had been geared almost exclusively to war production. Exports were down to a mere third of pre-war levels. While war lasted, the balance-of-payments gap was filled partly by selling off foreign assets and partly by the inflow of American Lease-Lend. The abrupt and unexpected ending of US aid in August 1945 left the incoming Labour Government facing what Keynes described to the Cabinet as a 'financial Dunkirk':

> This would take shape abroad in a sudden and humili-
> ating withdrawal from all our onerous responsibilities,
> with great loss of prestige (and of beneficial and pacifying
> influence), and our acceptance in the world of the
> position of a second-class power, like that of France on
> the morrow of the German surrender. . . . At home
> more severe austerity would be necessary than at any
> time during the war, and an indefinite postponement of
> the best hopes, and the social and economic pro-
> grammes, of the new Government.[36]

There was, Keynes advised, no alternative but to go to the US for a loan. Few disagreed.

During the war, radical thinkers had argued that acceptance of American aid was not incompatible with the construction of democratic socialism in Britain. Their premise, however, was some kind of alliance between Labour Britain and progressive forces on the continent – both socialist and Communist. A united Western Europe, reconstructing on democratic and socialist lines, while cultivating as friendly a relationship with the USSR as Stalin's paranoid behaviour in Eastern Europe would permit, might have been well placed to invite American investment without sacrificing either its independence or its socialism. Labour's unrelenting hostility to communism, and even left social democracy, on the continent, together with its failure to project a co-ordinated European strategy for socialist reconstruction, left the field free for the consolidation of right-wing free market regimes on the continent with which even the most European-minded of British socialists found it difficult to envisage an economic partnership.[37] Whatever interest Labour showed in enhancing Western European co-operation – and at times this was real enough – it always gave priority to the maintenance of national sovereignty.[38] Hugh Dalton, in his contemptuous dismissal of the foundation stone of the EEC – the 1950 Schumann plan to integrate the European iron and steel industries – expressed Labour's nationalistic arrogance with characteristic verve:

> No doubt . . . the experiences of war, including the experience of being occupied by the enemy, has broken the back of nationalist pride in many of these countries and this helps to popularise the federalist myth.[39]

No such fate had befallen Britain, and the arrival of the first majority Labour Government was hardly the moment for socialists to lose faith in the nation state.

> In its approach to European co-operation the Labour party must above all else have regard for the preservation of democratic socialism in Britain. . . . There can be no surrender of the Government's power to control the economic policy of the nation and thereby to carry through its programme; this requires retention by the Government of final control over the economic power of the State. . . .[40]

While the rhetoric of socialist nationalism could be deployed against the European vision, no such stubborn defence of national sovereignty was apparent in Labour's relations with the United States. The untrammelled economic sovereignty of bankrupt Britain was not sustainable – but Labour preferred to cultivate a special relationship with the United States than to throw its lot in with Europe. At the root of that preference was the overriding concern of Labour's foreign policy with containing the Soviet threat and sustaining Britain's global role.

Bevin, who became Foreign Secretary in 1945, fully shared Churchill's obsession with the containment of Soviet power. Like Churchill he made no distinction between the Red Army and the European Communist Parties, seeing both as mere agents of Russian expansion. By thus ruling out the possibility of co-operation between democratic socialists and communists at any level, Bevin turned his back on the possibilities of a socialist reconstruction in post-war Europe. Obsessed by the Soviet threat, his primary goal was to secure from the Americans not only the economic aid – which, given the overwhelming predominance of their economy in the post-war world, everyone agreed was essential – but also a permanent commitment of American military power as the keystone of a Western European bloc, capable of withstanding any conceivable threat from the East.

As the Truman administration came to terms with the fact that even the post-war muscle of the US dollar would be insufficient to draw the Soviet Union into the world capitalist economy, Bevin devoted his energies to steering America towards a full-scale military commitment to the defence of Western Europe. His greatest fear was that an American withdrawal could open the way for a reunified Germany building up its war-making potential in some kind of *rapprochement* with the Soviet Union – as had indeed occurred in the 1920s. To prevent this, he was determined to ensure the continued partition of Germany between East and West: a priority which ruled out positive responses to Soviet proposals for a neutral Germany. His announcement in February 1947, made under pressure from the Treasury, that Britain could no longer afford to underwrite right-wing regimes in Greece and Turkey, persuaded the Americans to take over the burden of policing the Eastern Mediterranean against Communism. It also provided the occasion for Truman to mobilize the American public against the temptations of isolationism by proclaiming his vision of a world-wide mission to 'help free peoples to maintain their institutions and their national integrity against aggressive movements that sought to impose on them totalitarian regimes'[41] – whether the aggression came from without or from an 'armed minority' within. This set the scene for the use of Marshall Aid to strike a sharp line between East and West in Europe, and for Stalin's over-reactions in the Czech coup of 1948, the persecution of 'Titoism', and the Berlin blockade. Through these troubled waters, Bevin steered a consistent course towards the eventual consolidation of Western European and American military policy, culminating in the NATO treaty and the siting of American nuclear bombers in Britain.[42]

While the Labour Government led the way in establishing the Atlantic Alliance, it never saw this as an alternative to the maintenance of Britain's role as a global power. Withdrawal from India was inescapable, but Labour had no intention of closing down the British Empire, and it was prepared to undertake a major colonial war to retain control of the dollar-earning resources of Malaya. Arthur Creech-Jones, who had been a conscientious objector in the First World War, now tackled his job as Colonial Secretary in a spirit of constructive imperialism worthy of Joseph Chamberlain.[43] The Government looked to the development of empire trade and the sterling area as an alternative to continuing dependence on US aid, and dollars earned by colonial exports were used to support the UK economy. In 1946 and 1947 Attlee floated the idea that Britain should cut its losses in the Middle East, abandon the defence of Greece, Turkey, Iraq and Persia against the Soviet Union, withdraw from Egypt, and fall back on its east African colonies. The Chiefs of Staff were horrified, and Bevin vetoed the idea: it 'would be Munich over again, only on a world scale.'[44] The Government's commitment to maintaining Britain's great power status underlay the secret decision to manufacture the atom bomb: 'we've got to have this thing over here whatever it costs. . . .' said Bevin. 'We've got to have the bloody Union Jack flying on top of it.'[45]

The failure of the post-war Labour Governments to take the measure of Britain's wartime decline produced bizarre contradictions in its stance. During the war, US officials had made no secret of their desire to break up the British Empire as part of their drive to make the world safe for the global penetration of US capital. Yet in 1945 the Labour cabinet went cap in hand to Washington begging for dollars, even at the cost of agreeing to terms designed to make it impossible for Britain to maintain its own economic sphere of influence – the sterling area – against dollar imperialism. The irony was that they only needed the loan to sustain a global role that its acceptance, in practice, was bound to undermine. Though Keynes had played up the threat to the social programme in order to persuade Labour ministers to accept the American terms, he later recognized that it was overseas military spending which made the loan unavoidable.[46] In fact, between 1946 and 1951, British Government spending overseas (most of it military) was more than double the amount borrowed from the US in 1945.[47] Cutting back on such spending would have done more to conserve Britain's real influence in world affairs than sustaining it at the price of subordination to America. 'Britain', wrote George Orwell in 1947, 'can only get free of America by dropping the attempt to be an extra-European power.'[48]

Perhaps the ultimate absurdity of Labour's policy was the belief that British world power could be promoted by opening up East Anglia to the American airforce. For several years after US forces returned to Britain in 1948, there was no legal basis whatsoever for their exercise of extra-territorial rights. This was put right by the Visiting Forces Act of 1952, under which Parliament ceded greater liberties to the American forces than did any other country in Europe except West Germany – which had lost the war.[49] The paradox of a global power permitting the establishment of foreign military bases in its homeland symbolized the true place of Britain in the post-war order, in a way that no amount of talk about Atlantic partnership and special relationships could ever quite obscure.

The long term results of Labour's foreign policy were disastrous both for the peace of the world and for Britain's place within it. By turning their backs on the possibility of socialist reconstruction in Western Europe, Labour's leaders gave hegemony to the Right in the emerging economic community. By their obsessive anti-communism, they did much to intensify the pressures leading to the Cold War and the division of Europe. By their double-think about Britain's global role – a show of great power status paid for with borrowed dollars – they went a long way towards turning Britain into a satellite of the United States. Cut off from the emerging economic miracle of Western Europe, and saddled with military commitments quite disproportionate to the strength of its rather old-fashioned economy, Britain was ill-prepared to face the demands of the post-war world. The precipitous relative decline which set in from the late 1950s, as foreign competition revived, revealed the full consequences of the failure of the post-war Labour Governments to think radically about the future of Britain.

The Government's foreign policy did not go unopposed. In November 1946 Richard Crossman moved an amendment to the King's Speech calling for a socialist 'middle way' between Soviet Communism and American capitalism. He attacked the Government's failure to seek common ground with continental socialist parties, a failure which, he argued, was forcing Labour's natural allies in Europe to choose between the more dynamic superpower alternatives, thus making the division of the continent into two hostile blocs inevitable.[50] The amendment was not pressed to a vote, but seventy Labour MPs abstained and the whips decided to avoid upheaval in the ranks by taking no disciplinary action.[51] A few months later the leading rebels published *Keep Left*, a pamphlet setting out an alternative agenda for the Labour Government. Alongside arguments for the development of a more effective machinery of economic planning, *Keep Left* called for closer co-operation with France:

> Working together, we are still strong enough to hold the balance of world power, to halt the division into a Western and Eastern bloc, and so to make the United Nations a reality. ·But if we permit ourselves to be separated from France, and so from the rest of Europe, and if we take cover under the mantle of America, we shall not only destroy our own and Europe's chances of recovery, but also make a third world war inevitable. . . .[52]

This marked, however, only a brief revival of the socialist Europeanism that had been embraced by many sections of the left during the war. As the consolidation of right-wing regimes in the major Western European states put paid to earlier visions of a new Europe of the resistance movements, the continent no longer offered an inviting basis for left-wing advocates of a democratic socialist 'third force'.[53] Instead some looked towards the other plank of the *Keep Left* foreign policy – the development of the British Commonwealth – as an alternative pole of attraction in world affairs to Russia or

America. If democratic socialism had little future on the Continent, perhaps the Indian Congress Party and the Australasian Labour Parties could provide a firmer base.[54]

Though clothed in different language from that normally employed by Bevin, this did not differ in substance from his own policy of looking to empire development to strengthen Britain in its dealings with the US. The significance of the fact that Britain's world role could only be sustained with the aid of the Americans seems to have been lost on the Labour left no less than on the Labour leadership. As one historian puts it:

> The third-force idea failed because it did not confront in any systematic way the . . . fundamental issue, namely . . . whether Britain in its reduced economic condition could afford to continue its world commitments. Ironically, the Left too accepted that Britain was a world power – they just wanted it to act differently – and therefore they lacked a viable alternative to Bevin's policies.[55]

This fantasy of a post-imperial global role was to haunt the left's discussion of foreign policy for several decades, and it formed a major obstacle to the revival of wartime socialist thinking about a European future for Britain.[56]

By the late 1940s most of the Left, shocked and saddened by events in eastern Europe, had lost faith in the capacity of 'third force' politics to prevent the Cold War and, with more or less reluctance, accepted the need for a military alliance with the United States. Well over 100 Labour MPs abstained when the establishment of NATO was put to the House of Commons in 1949, but, apart from a frankly pro-Soviet minority, the major figures on the left of the Labour Party had no alternative to offer. In 1951, Bevan resigned from the Government because the Chancellor of the Exchequer, Hugh Gaitskell, insisted on introducing Health Service Charges to help finance a hugely expanded arms budget, but he did not question either NATO membership or British participation in the Korean War.[57]

Keep Left was a narrowly Parliamentarian grouping. Despite substantial support among Labour activists, particularly those in Southern middle-class constituencies which had little chance of returning a Labour MP,[58] there was no significant extra-Parliamentary agitation against the Government's foreign policy – unless one can count a series of scintillating radio talks by A. J. P. Taylor which were ended by discreet Foreign Office pressure on the BBC.[59] There was little basis in popular sentiment for any agitation about foreign affairs. Apart from some nagging doubts over the mass bombing of civilians, and a moment of moral outrage over the December 1944 shootings in Constitution Square, the war had knocked the stuffing out of popular internationalism. According to Mass Observation, among the public at large, initial hopes for the United Nations were in danger of giving way to 'a narrow *faute de mieux* nationalism.'[60] The 1940s saw the apex of socialist nationalism in Britain, and this temporarily overwhelmed peace movement traditions.

Two exceptions to the collapse of peace politics may be worth noting. The first reveals the residual strength of an old pacifist belief; the second points forwards to the new agenda of the peace movement. In March 1947 seventy-two Labour MPs voted against the Government on conscription. This was easily the biggest challenge from the backbenches to the post-war Labour Government: they acted in defence of the liberal principle that peacetime conscription was unacceptable. The vote forced a temporary compromise, reducing the length of National Service from eighteen months to twelve.[61] But National Service, which was abolished in 1958, never became a mass campaigning issue.[62]

The second exception to the absence of peace politics in this period was the success of the Stockholm Appeal launched in Britain by the British Peace Committee at the height of the Cold War in 1950. A million people signed the Appeal which called for a world-wide ban on nuclear weapons.[63] The bombing of Hiroshima and Nagasaki in 1945 had planted a seed of terror which would, when conditions were ripe, germinate into a rebirth of pacifist politics. In the early 1950s conditions were not ripe, and the Stockholm Appeal was in any case too closely identified with the uncritically pro-Soviet politics of the Communist Party to have any significant impact on British political life. But one million signatures meant something. Less than a year after Hiroshima a Mass Observer wrote in her diary:

Our daily [cleaning] woman told us this morning that she had been very upset by a dream she had last night. Atomic bombs had been falling and the Thames was rising. . . . She saw buildings being carried away by the floods. Her one idea was to get to higher ground and she said to a man near her: 'I know, I'll go to Swindon' – because she had relatives there. And he said: 'It's no good your trying to go to Swindon. It isn't there.'[64]

Ten years later CND tapped into millions of private nightmares to build a new, and very resilient, politics of peace.

13

'Damned Fools in Utopia': CND's First Wave

> We try to avert the unimaginable by pursuing the unthinkable. . . . I must admit that I feel deeply pessimistic about the outcome. I think our utopia will never come, will always be nowhere, until the awful consummation of the world. I think the 'damned fools' will be right, as they usually are, and the real damned fools will go and drop their damned bombs on each other's damned utopias. I think this is the way the world will end, with a bang and a whimper of *I told you so*. And my only brief consolation will be that I joined the right damned fools in utopia. (Nicholas Walter, 1962)[1]

Nuclear weapons rehabilitated the pacifist consensus that Hitler had undermined. After Hiroshima there was no disputing the claim that, given the destructive power of modern technology, no political cause could be worth another great war.[2] Even the leaders of superpowers came to understand that all-out warfare would result in the total destruction of their societies, and could no longer be conceived as a realistic means of achieving political goals. To that extent, the pacifist case became the conventional wisdom, and it is probable that nuclear weapons have done something to restrain superpower leaders from embarking on military adventures which they know would be perceived by 'the enemy' as a threat to its vital interests.

As a long-term solution to the problem of international anarchy, however, nuclear weapons have some potentially fatal flaws. The system of deterrence, as pacifists have frequently pointed out, only has to fail once. The balance of terror has been, not a stable state of Mutually Assured Destruction, but an arms race driven at every stage by the technological search for overwhelming predominance. More-over, the devotion of massive resources to nuclear weapons research, development, production and deployment has created major social and political obstacles to any attempt to wind down the military confrontation between the super-powers. The vested interests of the military-industrial complex penetrate every artery of our nuclearized societies, and they mesh with a Cold War politics which has served to legitimate the continuing diversion of resources to feed the insatiable appetite of the arms race.

Against this formidable array of forces, pacifism has one major advantage – the human instinct of survival. Hiroshima and Nagasaki demonstrated that humanity was acquiring the power to destroy utterly both itself and its environment. The new peace movement rested on a despairing hope – Nicholas Walter articulates the downbeat phase of that in the quotation at the head of this chapter – that there might still be time to pull humanity back from the brink of self-destruction. This mentality was not dissimilar to that which underpinned the pacifist consensus of the early 1930s. In the nuclear age, however, even a new Hitler would be unlikely to divide pacifists in the way they were divided in the face of fascism. It is safe to assume that, whatever may happen in international politics, peace movements will continue to find an indestruct-ible base in the simple imperative of human survival. That does not, of course, mean that they will necessarily succeed. Nor does it exempt them from the normal pressures of political life – a fact well illustrated by the sharply fluctuating fortunes of the Campaign for Nuclear Disarmament (CND) since its emergence in the late 1950s.

For all its novelty – its heady sense that it was inventing a new politics of survival appropriate to a post-nuclear world – the first wave of CND (1957–1962/3) was clearly a product of the traditions of radical protest which we have been discuss-ing. It belonged to a moment in domestic politics when the Labour Party, dismayed by election defeats in 1951, 1955 and again in 1959, was engaged in a sharp struggle over its future direction. CND was partly a product of that struggle, and its fortunes were intimately linked to those of the left within the Labour Party. At the same time many peace activists believed that Labour's chances of returning to power were so remote – and the nuclear threat so imminent – that more direct and unorthodox methods of banning the bomb would have to be employed. Negotiating the frontiers with electoral politics was a major issue for the new peace movement, as it had been for its predecessors.

The first wave of CND occurred during a period of great uncertainty about Britain's role in world affairs. In the Suez crisis of 1956, the projection of British power in the Middle East was brought to an abrupt and humiliating halt by American threats of economic sanctions.[3] The crisis called into question the post-war political consensus on foreign policy, and triggered a burst of protest activity celebrated by the left as 'democracy militant, democracy on the attack and asserting its power by a thousand hurriedly organised initiatives.'[4] The Labour Party's anodyne slogan for its 1956 Trafalgar Square rally – 'Law not War' – was less revealing than the obvious anger of the demonstrators. The wag who coined the quip 'Britain Waives the Rules'[5] touched a nerve of national humiliation which demanded something more than polite appeals to the United Nations to take over the white man's burden. To many, in the months that followed, the unilateral renunciation of nuclear weapons came to seem an appropriate way for the people of a once great empire to regain their self-esteem.[6]

In the short term, Suez precipitated a reassessment of Britain's defence policy, which placed greater emphasis on the role of nuclear as against conventional forces. The Soviet announcement of the ICBM in August 1957, and their demonstration of its capacities with the launching of Sputnik in October, increased uncertainties about Britain's nuclear role and helped to open up the whole issue for the first time to extensive public debate.[7] It was the American cancellation, in April 1960, of Blue Streak, the missile Britain intended to buy, which gave CND its major political success of the period, opening the way for the passage of a unilateralist resolution at the Labour Party's Scarborough Conference that autumn.

In the longer term Suez contributed to a dawning realization among Britain's élites that the goal of maximizing their freedom of action in world affairs could no longer be served by turning their backs on the successful consolidation of the Western European economy. MacMillan's first, unsuccessful, application for membership of the EEC was made in 1962. The response of CND and the left to this initiative reveals, in retrospect, the extent of the failure of this first wave of anti-nuclear activity to escape from traditions of 'imperialist pacifism' which, even at the time, had begun to look distinctly old-fashioned to the more thoughtful members of Britain's governing classes.

Since the first of Britain's atomic tests in 1952 there had been sporadic attempts from various quarters to launch a campaign against British nuclear weapons. But the most effective anti-nuclear initiative of the early 1950s did not address itself specifically to the British bomb. The H-bomb National Campaign of 1954 sponsored by a group of Labour MPs working with Canon Collins, Fenner Brockway and others, collected a large number of signatures called – like the Stockholm Appeal before it – for all-round nuclear disarmament. A report, by the local vicar, of the activity of the Barnet Hydrogen-Bomb Committee in 1954 reveals a combination of the prosaic and the apocalyptic which remains characteristic of anti-nuclear campaigning:

> At a meeting held last evening it was decided to [hold] a second public gathering in my Church Hall – so as to let people know about the crisis facing civilisation.[8]

But for most left-wing activists, the campaign against German rearmament had much higher priority. It was the announcement, a few months after Suez, that Britain was to test its first H-bomb that triggered the proliferation of anti-nuclear activity and laid the basis for the foundation of CND a year later. A small group of pacifists conceived the idea of a Greenpeace-style disruption of the tests, due to take place on Christmas Island in the Pacific. In March they established a Direct Action Committee to raise money for this enterprise. A number of well-known figures, including Bertrand Russell, agreed to lend their names to the appeal.[9] Though the attempted disruption never occurred, the Direct Action Committee was to play an important part in the new peace movement.

In February 1957 a National Campaign Against Nuclear Weapons Tests was set up on the initiative of a group of North London radicals who had been campaigning on the issue for the previous two years. The initiative had been taken by members of the Golders Green Co-operative Women's Guild, led by an ex-suffragette, Gertrude Fishwick. In May, 2000 women wearing black sashes and carrying black flags walked in pouring rain from Hyde Park to Trafalgar Square.[10] Though Peggy Duff, Pat Arrowsmith and April Carter were all involved in this march, none of them subsequently gave priority to developing a *women's* peace movement. These were difficult years for feminism, and the few women's actions organized during the first wave of CND focused on women's role as mothers: 'the lovers of life' rather than the 'great creators'.[11] The new Campaign called on the Government to halt or postpone the planned tests in order 'to give a moral lead to Russia and America to reach agreement on the banning of all further tests.' The idea of Britain taking a unilateral initiative to break the deadlock between the superpowers proved popular, and local groups sprang up rapidly across the country. The new organization emphasized public education work – petitions, poster-parades, street stalls. It sought above all to change public attitudes and was suspicious of short cuts –whether by winning the Labour Party, or by the less orthodox tactics of the Direct Actionists. The adhesion of the United Nations Association, which occupied a position in the political spectrum equivalent to the pre-war League of Nations Union, represented a major success for the founders of the National Campaign. The decision of the British Council of Churches, by a narrow majority and against the advice of the Archbishop of Canterbury, to oppose the H-bomb tests gave further encouragement.[12]

Meanwhile pressure against nuclear testing was building up among Labour activists, many of whom went further, and called for the unilateral renunciation of nuclear weapons by Britain. A resolution on this topic was chosen for debate at the Labour Party Conference in October. Nye Bevan, bidding for the Foreign Office in the next Labour Government, opposed the motion on the curious grounds that without nuclear weapons Britain would lack the power to prevent the further polarization of the world between the two superpowers. He dismissed unilateralism as 'an emotional spasm' which would 'send a British Foreign Secretary, whoever he was, naked into the conference chamber.' He won the vote overwhelmingly, but the gratuitous offensiveness of his remarks destroyed his capacity to go on acting as the accepted guardian of the socialist conscience within Labour's establishment. This encouraged the Labour Left to look to extra-Parliamentary politics to rebuild their influence within the Party. [13]

Two bodies which might have been expected to play an active role in the new movement were curiously absent. The PPU took the view that a single-issue campaign against nuclear weapons would be a diversion from genuine pacifism. Happily most pacifists disagreed. More importantly, the Communist Party was uncomfortable about the unilateralism of the emerging movement, fearing that it would alienate public opinion and 'divide those who are today united in demanding that the tests should be stopped.' [14] Many Party members disagreed. Unlike the PPU, however, the Communists were capable of responding flexibly to the pressure of events, and the obvious momentum of CND in the late 1950s eventually pulled them into support for British unilateralism. Paradoxically, their initial hesitation probably helped CND to establish itself, by making it impossible to stigmatize the new organization as just another Communist front.

Following Bevan's apostasy it was clear the time had come for the establishment of a non-party campaign against British nuclear weapons as such – not just the tests. J. B. Priestley – who once before, in 1940, had found the words to express the patriotism of the left – now provided the final catalyst: an article in the *New Statesman* responding to Bevan's Conference speech. Priestley made no secret of his patriotism. He spoke highly of the Queen and advocated a citizens' army – 'taking their rifles to the ranges at the week-end'. But nuclear weapons were useless to Britain, whether as instruments of defence or of prestige. Far from giving Britain the power to mediate between Russia and America, as Bevan asserted, the attempt to keep up with the superpowers in this lunatic race for one

'ultimate' weapon after another merely made us look ridicu-
lous. In 1945 Britain, though stripped of its power, could
nevertheless have taken over the 'moral leadership' of the
world.

> There is nothing unreal [he continued] in the idea of a
> third nation, especially one like ours, old and ex-
> perienced in world affairs, possessing great political
> traditions, to which other and smaller nations could look
> while the two new giants mutter and glare at each other.

But it was Bevan's own party which had, after the war,
rejected the Third Force idea and presided over a decisive
moment in the polarization of the world when, in 1948,
'without a single protest from all the noisy guardians of our
national pride, parts of East Anglia ceased to be under our
control and became an American air base.' Unilateral nuclear
disarmament offered one final chance to restore British
prestige and, in doing so, to break the spell under which the
civilizations of the world were rushing towards self-
destruction. Britain's material power was now slight, but 'the
force of our example might be great. . . . There may be other
chain-reactions besides those leading to destruction; and we
might start one.' Only unilateralism now had the moral
power to 'lift this nation from its recent ignominy' – the
reference was presumably to Suez – and restore it 'to its former
grandeur.'[15] Priestley's peroration was redolent with
nostalgia for Britain's wartime glory:

> Alone, we defied Hitler, and alone we can defy this
> nuclear madness into which the spirit of Hitler seems to
> have passed, to poison the world. . . . The British of
> these times, so frequently hiding their decent, kind faces
> behind masks of sullen apathy or sour, cheap cynicism,
> often seem to be waiting for something better than party
> squabbles and appeals to their narrowest self interest,
> something great and noble in its intention that would
> make them feel good again.

Unilateralism was to the nuclear threat what the little boats of
Dunkirk had been to Nazism – the beginning of the end.[16] Or,

in the words sung by Aldermaston marchers a few months later: 'We're going to stop the loonies and preserve the human race, We're going to save our country for we like the dear old place. . . .'[17] Unilateralism provided a morally unimpeachable haven for lingering delusions of imperial grandeur.

This appeal produced a flood of correspondence which Kingsley Martin, the editor, sent on to Peggy Duff, secretary of the National Campaign Against Nuclear Weapons Tests. Peggy Duff was an old campaigner, with much experience of translating the rhetoric of left-wing notables into solid organizational achievement.[18] On this occasion she had more than her fair share of notables to cope with. When CND emerged in February 1958 most of its self-appointed Executive Committee were middle-aged men with established public reputations. Most of them knew each other already. It was, according to Jaquetta Hawkes, Priestley's wife and one of the few women on the Executive, 'a compact sort of little campaign [which] depended very substantially on friends'.[19] Cannon Collins, chairman of Christian Action and veteran of several previous single-issue campaigns, took the chair. Betrand Russell was made President. The Labour Left was represented by Michael Foot (chosen because he was *not* an MP, having lost his seat in 1955), and the United Nations Association by its Treasurer. The new movement took over the assets of the Campaign Against Tests, but admitted only two of its members onto the Executive – in addition to Peggy Duff who became Organizing Secretary.

At the outset there was some uncertainty about nailing the full unilateralist flag to the masthead. It was clear that the United Nations Association could not go that far. The initial agreed policy statement called on Britain to unilaterally suspend nuclear patrol flights, tests and the construction of new missile bases as a first step to a general disarmament conference. It was only after the inaugural meeting, on February 17th, 1958, that the policy was 'clarified' to include an unambiguous statement that CND's purpose was 'to persuade the British people that Britain must . . . renounce unconditionally the use or production of nuclear weapons and refuse to allow their use by others in her defence.' This made the position impossible for the United Nations Association, which promptly withdrew.[20]

The unilateralist commitment prevented CND from occupying the political centre ground which the Campaign Against Tests had so carefully cultivated. It is, however, difficult to imagine that a mass movement of such vigour could have been built around anything less. The key to unilateralism's success as a mobilizer lay in its fusion of morality with politics. As an absolute moral principle, it expressed the refusal to comply with preparations for genocide. Unless we resist, declared Ralph Schoenman in 1961, 'Eichmann stands for Everyman'[21] It was the moral need to *refuse* which impelled thousands of often not very politically-minded people to give time, effort and money to the campaign. But unilateralism was never simply a moral statement. CND's founders placed the unilateral gesture firmly in the context of its intended consequence: 'negotiations at all levels for agreement to end the armaments race'.[22] The point was not for Britain to opt out of world affairs, but, by her independent action, to break the log jam in international disarmament politics. CND's founders did not advocate unilateralism to the superpowers, and they disregarded resolutions to that effect passed by CND's annual conferences, where morality had a tendency to supersede, rather than complement, politics.[23] Unilateralism offered a political strategy, and one moreover which spoke directly to that nostalgia for a more glorious past which simmered below the surface of British political consciousness, on the left as much as on the right, in the aftermath of Suez. Unilateralism enabled pacifists to move towards political engagement, and it lent moral vision to the politics of the left.[24]

CND's founders wanted a mass movement, but they had no time for democracy. From the Campaign Against Tests they inherited a network of local groups and a practice of patient public education work. The Direct Action Committee – casting around for something to do after their abortive project of disrupting the Christmas Island tests – was organizing a march from London to Aldermaston at Easter. CND's leaders, after some hesitation, were happy to join in. More than anything else it was Aldermaston which established

CND's public presence. In subsequent years, CND reversed the direction of the march, in order to emphasize that its message was aimed primarily at politicians, not at workers in the nuclear industry. The colour and the noise, the discomfort and physical exhilaration, the informality and sense of purpose, the intense political discussions and the sentimental moralizing songs, all contributed to Aldermaston becoming the central unifying experience of the new peace movement. But the leadership resisted attempts to enfranchise the marchers or the groups. They had issued a call to action, not an invitation to debate policy or strategy. They thought they knew what needed to be done and how to do it. They were wrong.

For CND's founders the key task was to win the Labour Party:

> I know of no way of obtaining a non-nuclear Britain except by converting the Labour Party [wrote Kingsley Martin in the summer of 1960, when this conversion appeared imminent]. Unless they work through the Labour movement, nuclear disarmers are simply marching about to satisfy their own consciences and expressing their sense of sin and horror of nuclear war.'[25]

This did not mean that CND's leaders were unsympathetic to the campaign's character as a movement beyond party. Indeed they realized that only a broad non-party movement would be capable of addressing the floating voters, without whose support a unilateralist Labour Party could not hope to win an election.[26]

CND's agitation had a significant impact, both on public attitudes and on the Labour Party leadership. Opinion polls suggest that support for British unilateralism shifted significantly during the first two and a half years of the campaign – from a quarter to a third of the population.[27] In 1959 one large union went unilateralist, and this breakthrough turned into an irresistible tide when the cancellation of Britain's Blue Streak ballistic missile programme in April 1960 forced the Government to turn openly to the United States to supply the missiles. Meanwhile, the Communist Party, abandoning its earlier caution, added its not insignificant weight to unilateralism in the unions.[28] By the early summer of 1960 it was clear that the case for unilateralism could be won that autumn at the Labour Party Conference at Scarborough.

But major obstacles remained. The nuclear issue was inextricably bound up with power struggles inside the Labour Party.[29] After the 1959 election, Hugh Gaitskell, convinced that Labour would never become electable without major changes in its programme, set out to remove the Party's traditional commitment to socialism – Clause IV of the 1918 constitution. This put many activists in a fighting mood, ready to give free reign to their anti-nuclear consciences in order to keep up the pressure on the party leader to abandon his crusade against Clause IV. At Scarborough Gaitskell declared that he would 'fight, fight and fight again' to reverse the decision, making it quite clear that persistence in unilateralism would split the Party, and destroy its electoral prospects. There was never much doubt that Gaitskell would win his fight. Many constituency party delegates switched their positions during the 1960 conference itself, and voted with the platform. In 1961 most trade unions, satisfied that the row over defence had indeed turned aside a new assault on Clause IV, were happy to heal the civil war in the Party, deserting unilateralism as rapidly as they had adopted it the previous year.

CND's problem was intensified by a lack of clarity about what they were trying to achieve. 'Ban the Bomb' was an excellent slogan for demonstrations, but it afforded little guidance in the debates about the fundamental shifts in Britain's defence and foreign policy that unilateralism implied. CND's 1960 Annual Conference committed the campaign not only to banning the British bomb – although this had been the limit of the ambition of several of CND's founders – but also to removing US nuclear weapons and to leaving NATO. Labour Party leaders were prepared to compromise on the question of British nuclear weapons: though Gaitskell was reluctant to publicize his opposition widely because *British* nuclear weapons – unlike the US bases which he *did*, of course, support – were popular with most of the public.[30] More Atlanticist than the Conservative Party – many of whose members were still angry about American actions during the Suez crisis – Labour leaders were uneasy about the Gaullist implications of the Government's insistence on the 'independence' of British weapons. The Labour front bench was quite ready to expose the fact that, with the cancellation of Blue Streak, 'independence' was a technological impossibility for Britain. On NATO and the US bases, however, they were not prepared to move, and CND's most influential supporters in the Party showed minimal interest in developing the foreign policy alternatives which would have been essential to making the anti-NATO position into a serious political option. Picking up the threads from the 1940s 'Third Force' movement was, as we shall see, left to a new generation of socialists.

After Scarborough, while the Gaitskellites homed in on the NATO issue, Labour unilateralists cast around for a compromise formula which would limit the damage. At the 1961 Party Conference a pro-NATO and pro-nuclear policy was endorsed by a three-to-one majority. In the atmosphere of triumph – and despair – surrounding Gaitskell's reassertion of his authority, no-one placed much significance on the fact that delegates had faced both ways on US bases, voting to oppose the deployment of US Polaris submarines at Holy Loch. Potentially more important was the leadership's continuing skepticism about British nuclear weapons. When, in 1962, Macmillan persuaded the Americans to agree to supply missiles for British Polaris submarines, the Labour Party opposed the deal, and it fought the 1964 Election apparently committed to cancelling Polaris. These developments persuaded some CND supporters that more could be achieved by quiet lobbying and backstairs fixing than by noisy demonstrations in the streets. In 1963 Marghanita Laski, believing that the Campaign's utopianism had become a major obstacle to the adoption of 'a sensible nuclear policy' by 'responsible opinion', suggested, in effect, that the time had come to close CND down.[31] In a similar vein, the left-wing Labour MP Ian Mikado remarked:

> Another 10,000 or 20,000 or 50,000 non-political people don't compensate for the loss of those who can exert *political* pressure at the point of *action*.[32]

The fate of Labour's apparent intention to abandon British

nuclear weapons provides a classic illustration of the danger for peace movements of allowing inner-party manœuvre to displace mass mobilization. By 1964 CND as a mass movement was in rapid decline, and in the absence of tens of thousands of 'non-political people' prepared to take to the streets, there was nothing to prevent civil servants and military chiefs from quickly convincing Harold Wilson that his earlier opposition to Britain's 'independent' nuclear forces had been sadly mistaken.[33]

Even before the Scarborough Conference of 1960, the CND leadership's reliance on orthodox political campaigning had come under serious challenge from within the movement. Especially critical were the young people in whose energy, inventiveness and sense of urgency much of the freshness and novelty of the movement was rooted. Growing up in the depoliticized years of the Cold War, this generation flocked to the CND symbol and gave it meanings far beyond the nuclear issue itself. As a point of reference for a new rebellious youth culture – itself a product of the very affluence that seemed to be undermining traditional Labour politics – the Aldermaston marches came to embody a new kind of politics: a forerunner of 1968. Youthful impatience with the aging radicals who had founded CND helped to turn differences over direct action into an irreconcilable split. Most to blame for the split, however, was the incompetence of CND's founders in managing the democratic forms of organization forced on them by the mass movement. They provided, in the words of a devastating indictment written in 1963: 'a leadership which disassociates itself from every new departure and does nothing to create its own activity.'[34]

For the first two years, CND's leaders and the Direct Action Committee maintained an uneasy truce. After handing over control of the Aldermaston march, the direct actionists concentrated on organizing actions at the bases. In December 1958, actions at two East Anglian US rocket bases – Swaffam and North Pickenham – led to several arrests and gained substantial press coverage. The same tactics were used on many subsequent occasions: prior liaison with the police, small numbers of activists well briefed on the techniques of non-violence, systematic leafletting of local residents to explain what was going on. Actions of this kind were widely supported in CND groups and the leadership, though unenthusiastic, accepted a position of 'neutrality' on direct action while vigorously opposing any attempt to overturn CND's own refusal to engage in any but 'legal and democratic methods'.[35]

Labour's defeat in the Election of October 1959 did not bode well for CND's strategy of relying on a Labour Government to deliver disarmament. At the same time direct actionists were losing faith in the increasingly ritualized confrontations at the bases. Feeling that direct action had become stuck in a 'pacifist rut',[36] they began to consider more revolutionary ideas of mass civil disobedience. The mood of urgency was intensified in May 1960 when a planned meeting between Kruschev and Eisenhower – the first summit meeting since 1945 – was called off at the last minute amidst bitter diplomatic recriminations. Following the 1960 Aldermaston march – the largest so far with numbers doubling since the previous year – an intense debate had developed about the need for a new direction. The most extreme position was taken by a young American post-graduate student, Ralph Schoenman. As a member of the Youth CND Executive, Schoenman advocated 'this extraordinary proposition of surrounding the Houses of Parliament and not letting the legislators out until they gave way.'[37]

For Schoenman the existing democratic institutions were entirely fraudulent. CND's 'political' strategists were 'strutting in vain over cadavers, for our political institutions are empty.' The 'politics of the long haul' – waiting for a Labour Government – were an exercise in futility. Power was concentrated in the hands of a secretive nuclear state, bent on death. Britain, like all other modern industrial societies East or West, was 'essentially totalitarian',[38] its people alienated, isolated and de-politicized; its public life degraded by the mass media – 'a concentration camp for the mind':

> I have tried to argue that these mass societies have stripped us of democratic responses or rights. I wish to see understood that the mass media, statements in courts,

the entire reliance on the institutions of the closed
society, will never serve as the basis for reaching the
people; for these institutions legitimise and we must
expose the fraud. Our confrontation effects the tearing of
the veil.[39]

Mass civil disobedience, filling the jails, making Britain
ungovernable, forcing the Government of the day to acquiesce
or abdicate – this was Schoenman's message. Wiser heads in
the Direct Action Committee were hesitant, fearing that such
an approach would lead to violence and alienate more people
than it would convert.[40] Such doubts, however, were swept
aside by Schoenman's master-stroke – the recruitment of
Bertrand Russell to the politics of mass civil disobedience.

When Schoenman first contacted him, in July 1960, Russell
was cautious about plans for a mass sit-down in central
London. His response is worth quoting at length because it
puts very clearly arguments against indiscriminate calls for
mass civil disobedience that were often to be repeated during
the second wave of CND in the 1980s:

> I feel that the question as to what form civil disobedience
> should take is somewhat delicate and, moreover, one the
> answer to which must vary with circumstances. I have
> thought about it a good deal since our talk together and I
> am still convinced, perhaps even more firmly than when
> we talked, that we should begin by only obstructing
> activities which, in themselves, we find objectionable,
> i.e. launching sites, etc. I think this for various reasons.
> One is that it would be very much easier to get massive
> support for this form of civil disobedience. Another is
> that, although the authorities could not tolerate it, the
> general public would not be antagonised by it. A third is
> that our action would not appear to ordinary people to be
> subversive or anarchical or such as to cause serious
> inconvenience to average unpolitical people. I think that
> the other project which we discussed [presumably the
> central London sit-down] should for the present be kept
> in reserve.

Russell had sounded out Canon Collins who, he reported,
was 'quite willing to give his platonic blessing to such action as

obstructing work at nuclear and launching bases and sites . . . [and] to contemplate more general obstructive action . . . at some moment of crisis.' But it was quite clear that the CND leadership would not endorse a planned campaign of mass civil disobedience designed, not to express anger over some immediate outrage – Russell gave the example of the resumption of nuclear testing by the United States – but to provoke an all-out confrontation with the powers of the state. And he added: 'I think that a considerable proportion of the members of CND would agree with this point of view.'[41] Canon Collins, who had reluctantly tolerated direct action at the bases, condemned mass civil disobedience – at a time when there was no popular majority for nuclear disarmament – as a form of blackmail offensive both to democratic and to pacifist principles: 'It is the attempt of a small group to force its views upon the community . . . a kind of violence, provoking violent reactions.'[42]

Eventually, however, Russell allowed himself to be convinced. What appears to have moved him in the end was not Schoenman's theorizing, but a despairing sense that only the most dramatic of gestures could awaken the public to the danger of war before it was too late. For Russell civil disobedience was essentially a publicity stunt, a catalyst to awaken support for CND's campaign, not a revolutionary alternative to orthodox politics. The key was to persuade enough well-known public figures to put themselves at risk of arrest to force the 'average unpolitical people' to take notice. Hence the galaxy of writers, actors and artists assembled for the launch of the Committee of 100 in October 1960.

When Russell allowed himself to be convinced by Schoenman, a split with the CND leadership became inevitable. Despite an agreement to postpone any announcement of the new initiative until after the Labour Party Conference at Scarborough, news leaked out. Russell resigned as CND President and his relations with Canon Collins became poisonous. Meanwhile the leading spirits of the Direct Action Committee – Mike Randall and April Carter – put their doubts on one side, welcomed the inflow of new energy and new ideas, and moved into the Committee in an attempt to instil some discipline and restraint into its actions. Despite the unhappy circumstances of its birth, the Committee of 100 became, for the next twelve months, the cutting edge of the peace movement, offering a way forward as the hollowness of CND's Scarborough victory became clear.

In December 1960 plans were announced for the initial action – a sit-down in Whitehall in February – which would only go ahead if at least 2000 individuals had pledged themselves to participate. On the day more than enough people turned up and sat down. While a vigorous direct action campaign got under way in Scotland against the use of Holy Loch as a US Polaris base, a series of London sit-downs culminated in the arrest of more than 1300 people (of the 12,000 who attended the action) in Trafalgar Square on September 17th, 1961. Since the summer the apocalyptic sense of urgency that drove the Committee of 100 – 'Act or Perish' was the title of its founding manifesto – had been intensified by the diplomatic crisis that followed the building of the Berlin Wall in August, and the resumption of nuclear testing by both superpowers a few weeks later. But what ensured the success of the September action was the arrest and imprisonment of nearly a third of the Committee of 100, including the 89-year-old Russell, two weeks before the demonstration. The organizers were euphoric at the success of the demonstration; but puzzled about what to do next. In a misjudged attempt to maintain the momentum a call was issued for simultaneous actions in December at Wethersfield, a US air base in East Anglia, and six other locations. Again the authorities cracked down, but this time to much greater effect. The organizers, arrested on conspiracy charges, faced substantial sentences. 5000 people nevertheless took part in the actions and 850 were arrested. But 'filling the jails' seemed further away than ever, and the state was not beginning to crumble. Heavy jail sentences passed on the Wethersfield 'conspirators' in February 1962 had a deterrent effect. Never again was the Committee able to organize actions on the scale of 1961.

Even before the authorities got tough in the autumn of 1961, many members of the Committee of 100 had lost whatever faith they may temporarily have had in Schoenman's one-dimensional revolution. There was a growing realization among direct actionists that, as April Carter put it: 'to create a revolution with no political preparation or solution would be to invite disaster. . . .'[43] When, in the week after the Trafalgar Square sit-down, *Peace News* turned its thoughts to 'the problem of power', it recognized that direct action was not enough. Only in the context of a broader political movement could unilateralists hope to achieve their goals. With the alliance between Canon Collins and the traditional Labour Left in a state of impasse, *Peace News* suggested that perhaps the New Left had something to offer.[44]

14

The New Left and the Politics of Unilateralism

Suez triggered the patriotism of the established Labour Left and sent them in search of a new assertion of (pacifist) imperial greatness. But it was the events of 1956 in the Eastern bloc which opened the way for a younger generation of socialists to take up once again the abandoned search for a third way between Stalinist totalitarianism and American hegemony. Kruschev's denunciation of Stalin in 1956 threw the world communist movement into crisis. In the autumn, the Hungarian revolution lifted the spell of 'Nineteen Eighty-Four',[1] reviving the possibility of building a genuinely democratic socialism in Eastern Europe. Two days after the invasion of Suez, the Russians moved in to suppress the Hungarian uprising. As the conflict dragged on, the sight of workers and students confronting Soviet tanks in the streets of Budapest brought the crisis of international communism to a head. In Britain, a group of Communist dissidents led by the historians John Saville and Edward Thompson broke away to form one nucleus of a 'New Left', based mainly in the North of England. In 1960 they merged with a younger group of independent Marxists based in Oxford – Stuart Hall, Raphael Samuel and others – to launch the *New Left Review*.[2]

Unlike the Trotskyist splinters from earlier Communist splits, the New Left were frankly revisionist and uninterested in a return to Leninist purity. Harking back to the days of the Left Book Club – and, less explicitly, to the socialist revival of the 1880s and 1890s – Thompson urged the 'active minority of convinced socialists' not to lock themselves up in a new 'vanguard' party or in mere resolution-mongering within the Labour Party. Instead they should get together in local groups or clubs to discuss, educate and make propaganda – 'this,' he wrote, 'is of the essence of socialist action.'[3] In response to such appeals a modest movement of Left Clubs did emerge – perhaps thirty or forty of them, in various parts of the country.[4] Small though this 'active minority' was, Thompson had large hopes for its influence:

> . . . the Clubs and discussion-centres will be places beyond the reach of the interference of the bureaucracy, where the initiative remains in the hands of the rank-and-file. If the bureaucracy reacts by anathemas and prescriptions, the Clubs and publications will continue, staffed by socialists who are members of no party, but who intend to provide a service to the whole move-ment. . . . Their influence will pervade the Labour Movement . . . but because this influence derives from ideas it will elude administrative control. The bureauc-racy will hold the machine; but the New Left will hold the passes between it and the younger generation.[5]

In fact, the major political impact of the New Left was not in the Labour Movement, where it gained little influence, but in the peace movement.[6]

When, in the autumn of 1961, *Peace News* turned to the New Left for ideas on how to break the political impasse, Thompson rose to the occasion. Since he took seriously 'the positive values in the British democratic experience', he did not share hostility of *Peace News* to working through estab-lished institutions. But he was fully persuaded of the import-ance of sustaining 'a dynamic movement outside the Labour Party and free from its bureaucratic gags and tactical chloro-form'. The sit-downs, like the Aldermaston marches, took the issues beyond conference halls and committee rooms to 'the arena of the whole nation'.[7] This was the way to force the labour movement to take notice. To the question of what to do next, after Trafalgar Square and the setback in the Labour Party, Thompson had a clear answer. Building on the experience of a recent fight by the unilateralist miners' leader, Lawrence Daly, against a right-wing Labour candidate in West Fife, Thompson proposed that the Committee of 100, *Peace News* and the New Left should join with leading figures from CND and (if possible) the Labour Party, to launch a campaign of independent nuclear disarmament candidatures in appropriate by-elections.

Thompson argued that this did not mean abandoning the Labour Party and starting again. Evoking the example of the post-Munich by-elections and the Common Wealth Party during the war, Thompson asserted that it was 'bang in the central tradition of the left. Crucial issues have *always* been an occasion for independent by-election fights. . . .'[8] Merfyn Jones, who knew the Bevanite MPs well, argued that the Left's historical failure to get its way in the Labour Party arose from the fact that it could never 'envisage building a movement outside the party'. Now that CND existed as a mass movement free from party allegiance, the obvious next step was to run independent candidates – a much more effective way of making propaganda than demonstrations and sit-downs. So long as there had been a chance of a quick victory in the Labour Party it was, perhaps, sensible to hesitate. But Gaitskell's defeat of unilateralism cleared the way. If, he concluded – going rather further than Thompson – 'this ultimately means the formation of a new party, let that be the logic.'[9]

Peace News was interested, and so were leading members of the Committee of 100. Peggy Duff, always to the left of her Executive, also agreed with Thompson, but was not prepared to abandon her role as Organizing Secretary of CND to pursue the idea. But Michael Foot – representing the established Labour Left on the board of *New Left Review* – wouldn't hear of it, and he persuaded most other members of the board to reject the idea, effectively killing the threatened challenge to Labour's unity.[10] An attempt was eventually made, during 1962, to get independent election fights off the ground. But the group involved had little political weight, and it came to nothing.[11] The revival of Labour's electoral fortunes from 1962–63 put paid, for the time being, to further attempts at socialist renewal from without.

The convergence between the revolutionary pacifism of *Peace News* and the New Left had little staying power without the by-election project to sustain it. Their different attitudes to the labour movement was only one problem. More fundamentally, they disagreed about the implications of unilateralism. For Mike Randall, secretary of the Committee of 100, it was clear that unilateral nuclear disarmament was unattainable within the existing political system. Only a revolutionary upheaval could put it on the practical agenda.[12] Nicholas Walter, a leading anarchist, agreed, arguing that by embracing unilateralism the CND leadership had unwittingly opened the way for the transformation of their organization from a polite pressure group into an 'unwilling vanguard of utopia'.[13] But Walter had no illusions about the capacity of the Committee to create the revolution, dismissing its 'anarchopacifist' doctrine as 'a predominantly middle-class, purposely non-violent form of syndicalism developed by amateurs in an atmosphere of affluence'.[14] Not that he had anything better to offer: his own pessimistic position has been quoted at the head of the previous chapter.

The New Left, aware that 'the link between utopianism and despair is dangerously intimate',[15] adopted an entirely different approach to the politics of unilateralism. Their concern throughout was to examine the foreign policy implications of British nuclear disarmament. Unilateralism, they believed, only made sense as part of a larger shift to a position of 'positive neutralism'. But they did not confuse their advocacy of neutrality with planning the foreign policy of a *socialist* Britain. Positive neutralism was, they insisted, 'a policy which capitalist Britain *could* pursue': that was why it was possible to conceive of the popular movement imposing it on the Labour right and even on the Tories.[16] Such a breakthrough in foreign policy would certainly open new opportunities for the left: indeed, breaking the Cold War deadlock was a precondition for any serious socialist advance in the West. But British neutralism was not in itself a socialist measure, and its achievement did not require a revolution. The politics of survival took precedence over the politics of socialism. And this was fortunate since socialism was not, yet, on the agenda. Like their predecessors in the popular front politics of the 1930s, the New Left were concerned to engage, urgently and effectively, with the existing structures of power. In this they had more in common with the CND leadership – and, indeed, with traditions of pacifist politics stretching back, via the UDC, to pre-1914 radicalism – than they had with the Committee of 100. Despite the flirtation with *Peace News* and independent electoralism, the New Left's most important contribution was to the development of CND's thinking about foreign policy.

Elaborating the foreign policy implications of British unilateralism fell largely to the New Left. Canon Collins, who dominated CND's international work, rapidly came to the conclusion that the idea of Britain giving a moral lead – however popular with the marchers – cut little ice in Germany, Africa, or Moscow. His skepticism about the likely consequences of British unilateralism was reinforced by the French acquisition of the bomb in 1960. Unilateralism, he came to believe, was primarily for home consumption, and hardly compatible with an internationalist stance abroad. His leading concern was to open up discourse with the Soviet Union and he claimed a certain success when some leading Soviet intellectuals were persuaded to sign a statement 'deploring' the resumption of Soviet nuclear testing in the autumn of 1961. Collins's insistence on inviting World Peace Council representatives to international conferences caused bitter arguments within CND. The fiercest criticism came from direct actionists who applied their unilateralism equally to Britain and the superpowers. In 1962 these differences were played out at a conference in Moscow when the direct actionists handed out a leaflet condemning Soviet nuclear weapons in Red Square.[17] CND's condemnation of this action was echoed in *Pravda* by Yuri Zhukov who, only two weeks earlier, had been lauding the readiness of the Committee of 100 to break (bourgeois) laws.[18]

With Collins putting unilateralism on a back burner, and the direct actionists seeking to extend its application from Britain to the superpowers, it was the New Left, picking up the divided legacy of 1940s 'Third Force' thinking, who made the only serious attempt to elaborate the foreign policy implications of *British* unilateralism. One starting point was the socialist Europeanism of the war years, particularly as elaborated by Communist dissidents: Polish intellectuals struggling to define a humanist socialism in the immediate post-war years; the democratic alternative for Eastern Europe glimpsed in Germany in 1953 and Hungary in 1956; Claude Bourdet, an ex-leader of the French resistance, who had attempted to launch a movement for a democratic socialist third way as the Cold War closed in on Europe in the late 1940s, and who contributed many of the key ideas of New Left thought on neutralism.[19]

Canon Collins, who accepted the post-war division of Europe as immutable for all practical purposes, could play the honest broker between the deadlocked superpowers.[20] The New Left sought no such role, but aspired instead to a third force of democratic socialists reaching out to each other from within their respective blocs. As Edward Thompson put it, writing a script to which he was repeatedly to return during the next quarter century:

> . . . the assertion of democracy in the Communist area cannot take place without a hundred contests with the entrenched bureaucracy, its intentions and ideology. And, equally, the regeneration of the Western socialist movement cannot take place without a fundamental break with the policies and orthodoxies of the past decade. And this two-pronged offensive is (it becomes increasingly clear) carrying the left Socialist in the West, and the dissident Communist in the East, towards a common objective.[21]

For Thompson, the object of British unilateralism was to initiate, not merely a process of superpower *détente* and disarmament, but a more fundamental break-up and fragmentation of the bloc system itself.

> If we want the Polish compromise to broaden into democracy, if we want the embittered labour movements of Western Europe to find a new direction and unity, if we want to create the preconditions for further advance at home – then we must persuade Britain that it is time to 'do it herself'.[22]

Thompson's perspective of a disintegrating bloc system, which was to inform so much peace movement activity in the 1980s, had little purchase on the realities of European political life in the years after 1956. Hungary, it turned out, was more an end than a beginning, and the promise of de-Stalinization was not, for the time being, fulfilled. Nor did any major breakthrough occur in Western Europe. As in the 1940s, socialist advocates of a closer European co-operation were confronted by uniformly right-wing regimes in Western Europe, and the consequent probability that any purely Western moves towards 'European' unity would be likely simply to intensify the Cold War.[23] Moreover, apart from a brief period in the late 1950s, when the West German SPD lent its weight to the peace movement, European social democracy remained firmly Atlanticist. The withdrawal of SPD support in 1959, and the Berlin crisis of 1961 disrupted the West German peace movement – though it was later to revive in the less politically focused form of the 'Easter Marches', a German echo of Aldermaston. Outside Germany the only significant European peace movements were in Scandinavia and Holland. At no time, during the first wave of CND, was the consent enjoyed by NATO and its nuclear commitment among the peoples of Western Europe as a whole, seriously undermined.

In this situation Thompson's focus on the discourse of European dissidents was much less influential on the left, than the alternative vision of an alliance with progressive forces in the post-colonial Commonwealth. This was a long-standing concern of the Labour Left, and the foundation of the Movement for Colonial Freedom by Fenner Brockway in 1953 helped to strengthen such links. The development of the Non-Aligned Movement, following the Bandung conference of 1955, appeared to point to an alternative way for Britain to escape from the logic of the blocs, whatever happened on the European continent. The agenda of a positive neutralist foreign policy, it turned out, had less to do with initiating a chain reaction of bloc dissolution in Europe, than with adding Britain's weight to the non-aligned movement in the Third World. If Britain was in danger of becoming a marginal 'offshore island', this was not because it failed to cultivate its European connections, but because it was cut off from the 'huge expanding mainland of [post-colonial] Afro–Asia.'[24] By abandoning NATO in favour of associating with the non-aligned powers Britain could capitalize on its history as an extra-European power to attack the bloc system from without. 'What India has achieved would be as nothing compared to the immense pressure Britain could generate, in alliance with India, Ghana, Yugoslavia and backed by the uncommitted countries, for world peace and active neutrality.'[25] Ghana became particularly important to the British peace movement, both because of the involvement of members of the Direct Action Committee with a Ghanaian-based protest movement against French nuclear testing in the Sahara, and because Nkrumah agreed to host an international anti-nuclear conference in Accra in 1962. Peggy Duff's account of this conference suggests that it probably did more to expose the differences between the political style favoured by Non-Aligned governments and that of the peace movements, than it did to promote their ongoing collaboration. Eventually, the overthrow of Nkrumah in 1966 was to put paid to further explorations in this direction. Well before that, some peace activists had problems with the New Left's often uncritical enthusiasm for Nehru and Nasser, Castro and Nkrumah.[26]

Neither the New Left line on foreign policy, nor the proposed by-election initiative, provided the key to rescuing the anti-nuclear movement from the decline that set in after Gaitskell's triumph and the climax of direct action in the autumn of 1961. Various explanations have been offered for this decline. Simple exhaustion had something to do with it. As Merfyn Jones points out, CND 'owed its following and significance to the support of people who were drawn out of private life only by an exceptional tug of conviction.'[27] As he explained to groups meeting at the time: 'You're up against professional politicians. They're in this business for a lifetime. They don't intend to argue with you – they're waiting for you to get tired.'

More important than simple tiredness was frustration with an agitation that seemed to be getting nowhere. The frantic sense of urgency that impelled some – especially the young – activists was finally deflated by the confrontation between Kennedy and Kruschev over the presence of Soviet missiles in Cuba in October 1962. For a week, the world stood on the brink of the often imagined holocaust. During the crisis

activists went through the rituals of protest with little sense
that what they did could make any difference to the outcome.
When it was over, and the bomb hadn't dropped, nothing was
ever quite the same again.[28] Probably the Cuba crisis did no
more than lend focus to a change of mood that was already
well underway – ever since the Committee of 100's ineffective
confrontation with the state a year before. A similar point can
be made about the Partial Test Ban Treaty of 1963. Certainly
the Treaty lent force to the argument that the arms race was
now under control and that CND's warnings of imminent
catastrophe were no longer relevant. But in different circumstances it would have been perceived as a victory for the peace
movement and a spur to new activity.

Shortly after the Cuba crisis, CND issued a new policy
document. Written by the New Left intellectual Stuart Hall,
'Steps to Peace', reflected the belief that a more detailed
elaboration of transitional measures was necessary if unilateralism was to have any purchase in the political process.
This document caused much argument in the movement: the
complexity of its proposals fed grass roots suspicion that the
leadership – egged on by its unofficial New Left think-tank –
was abandoning unilateralism.[29] Again, however, we are
dealing in symptoms not causes. The level of rank and file
paranoia about leadership backsliding reflected, not any
change in the way CND was run, but a general sense of
political impasse affecting all parts of the movement.
Conventional campaigning had failed to capture the Labour
Party. But the mass sit-downs of the Committee of 100 had
not worked either: the weight of thousands of bums on
London's imperial pavements had proved quite insufficient to
bring down the nuclear state. Nigel Young has remarked:
'Most movements have a definite life cycle, during which a
certain range of possibilities are explored. . . .'[30] By 1961–62
the available possibilities had all been explored and there was
nowhere left for the movement to go. CND remained a
substantial organization for several more years, but as actual
killing in the Vietnam War replaced the potential nuclear
holocaust in the imagination of activists, a new range of
organizations and issues came to the forefront of peace
politics. What remains impressive about the early years of

CND, as Perry Anderson remarked in the mid–1960s, was its capacity to mount 'a passionate pressure for change' despite 'the most adverse historical circumstances'[31] – in particular an international situation deeply unfavourable to a movement attempting to break free from the structures of bloc politics in Europe.

If the Suez crisis set the scene for CND's first wave, the debate about British membership of the EEC in 1962 is an appropriate place to leave it. Three weeks before the Cuba crisis broke, Gaitskell had reunited the Labour Party Conference with a speech opposing British entry to the Common Market: 'the end of Britain as an independent nation state . . . the end of a thousand years of history . . . just a province of Europe. . . .'[32] 'All the wrong people are cheering', remarked his wife as Gaitskell sat down, and Frank Cousins, hero of the unilateralists, committed the Transport and General Workers Union to distributing a million free copies of the speech.[33] The tide of nationalist sentiment unleashed by MacMillan's application for membership of the EEC in 1961 not only transcended the disputes between left and right in the Labour Party, it also carried all before it in the peace movement. There were, of course, powerful arguments against British membership – the EEC was a rich man's club designed to exploit the Third World; it would harden the division of Europe, fusing economic with military confrontation and tending towards the emergence of a third European nuclear superpower; it would deprive a Labour Government of the sovereignty needed to pursue an independent foreign policy abroad, or a socialist one at home. But that was not all there was to be said. 'Socialism in One Country is a sad slogan for a Gaitskell to inherit from a Stalin', remarked Alasdair MacIntyre, one of the few voices on the left to support British entry into the EEC:

> I do not understand those socialists who are against Franco–German capitalism, but somehow prefer British capitalism. I detest the anti-German chauvinism of the anti-Common marketeers.[34] I can see nothing but good in an enforced dialogue with the exciting movements on the Italian Left. Labour leaders should be using the demand for equalisation upwards of welfare benefits in

the Treaty of Rome to dramatise the conservative
dreariness of our (false) national belief that Britain leads
in welfare. CNDers should be considering international-
ised non-violent action against nuclear crimes.[35]

Few socialists agreed with him, preferring to pose the issue
as 'a choice between Europe and the world.'[36] The CND old
guard were no less convinced that Britain's proper sphere of
influence remained global. In 1962 A. J. P. Taylor declared,
uncompromisingly: 'We set an example to the world, not to
Europe.'[37] Despite Suez, the old delusions of grandeur
remained. 'We were the last Imperialists', Taylor was to write
of CND's founders twenty years later.[38] And Tom Nairn,
discussing Labour attitudes in the early 1970s to the EEC, put
the issue clearly:

> After all, the rooted conviction that only the whole wide
> world will serve as a natural sphere of action for one's
> nation is, itself, the frankest expression of an immensely
> inflated national ego.[39]

At a time when the British Establishment was painfully
abandoning the globalist assumptions which were its birth-
right, and edging towards recognition that only by settling for
a narrower sphere of action in Europe could Britain regain the
freedom of manoeuvre which the cost of sustaining her
worldwide commitments denied her, the left rallied to the
good old causes: national sovereignty and – the phrase remains
apt – imperialist pacifism. The peace movement, in so far as it
considered the issue, agreed. As so often in the past, part of the
drive behind peace politics was an 'inflated national ego'. It
took a further twenty years, and drastic changes in the
relationships between British, West European, Soviet, East
European and American power, to open the way to a
genuinely European peace movement capable, perhaps, of
finally transcending the imperialist legacy carried for so long
by British radicals.

15

Protest and Survive: CND's Second Wave

Had the peace movement not already succumbed to anti-fascism, the Cold War of the late 1940s would certainly have destroyed it. The new intensification of superpower conflict at the end of the 1970s, however, had the opposite effect. This probably reflected the fact that, by the 1970s, the bi-polar division of the world was already becoming an anachronism. The new flare-up in the Cold War revealed, not the power, but the fragility of the superpower grip on world politics.

While the Soviet invasion of Afghanistan certainly played a major role, the chief cause of the new Cold War was to be found in the United States. Defeated in Vietnam; worried by an upsurge of Third World revolutions; anxious about the relative economic advance of Western Europe and Japan; alarmed by the Soviet Union's approach towards nuclear parity and its increasing projection of naval forces into oceans previously reserved for themselves – America's leaders in the late 1970s were attempting to re-assert the fading glory of the American Century.[1] One aspect of this global sabre-rattling was the decision to deploy new intermediate range nuclear missiles in Europe, announced in December 1979, two weeks after the Soviet invasion of Afghanistan. Intended to demonstrate the solidity of the NATO alliance, cruise and Pershing missiles had the opposite effect, placing an un-paralleled strain on popular consent to the US nuclear presence in Europe.

By announcing the planned deployment date as 1983, NATO gave the peace movement a timescale as well as a target, and the early 1980s saw a popular anti-nuclear move-ment of unprecedented proportions.[2] In 1984, at the peak of the new movement, CND claimed 90,000 national members and a quarter of a million in its local groups. The demonstration of October 22nd, 1983, was probably the largest in British history, with the possible exception of the women's suffrage rally of 1909. Its impact was multiplied many times by the fact that, as in 1981, it coincided with mass rallies throughout the capitals of Western Europe. Altogether some five million people took to the streets of Europe in the autumn of 1983 to demonstrate their opposition to nuclear weapons.[3] The other major mobilization of the early 1980s occurred independently of CND. Since its establishment in 1981 the Greenham Common peace camp had became a centre for international, as well as British, pilgrimage. The women of Greenham Common affected parts of the public psyche that more conventional campaigning could not reach. On December 12th 1982, 30,000 women linked hands to 'Embrace the Base'. With a characteristic sense of the power of symbolic gestures, they decorated the fence with pictures of their loved ones, messages, patchwork and flowers. This was probably as important in bringing cruise missiles to public attention as CND's very much larger, but less imaginative, demonstrations.

The new Cold War stimulated both fear and hope. As superpower relations worsened, the nuclear threat, forgotten during the years of *détente*, reasserted its hold over the popular imagination. And the threat appeared more menacing than ever before. Developments in missile technology and new strategic doctrines appeared to place a premium on striking first if war seemed imminent. During the early 1980s, the inbuilt fragility of the so-called balance of terror was at the forefront of protesters' minds. Fear that the bombs would go off more or less by accident was as important to mobilizing the movement as moral revulsion at the threat to use them deliberately. Moreover, public exposure of the 'limited nuclear war' scenarios, beloved of military planners, lent credence to the view that the real purpose of the new missiles was to enable NATO to fight a nuclear war in Europe without involving the destruction of the US homeland. Gene le Roque, a dissident American ex-Admiral much quoted by the new movement, put the issue forcefully: 'We fought World

War I in Europe. We fought World War Two in Europe. And, if you dummies let us, we'll fight World War Three in Europe.'

After Mrs Thatcher came to power in 1979 her Government was quick to nail its flag firmly to the nuclear mast, not only over cruise missiles, but also with the decision to vastly expand Britain's nuclear capacity by purchasing missiles for Trident submarines from the Americans. At the same time it induced both fear and ridicule among the population by issuing *Protect and Survive*, a misconceived attempt to revive long defunct plans for civil defence against nuclear attack. Edward Thompson's response to this, a pamphlet entitled *Protest and Survive*, served to unlock the imagination of at least one inert activist (myself), and his public meetings up and down the country launched many a local group. The groups that mushroomed during 1980 were often initially resistant to accepting the CND identity, preferring to define themselves as single-issue, and often purely local, campaigns 'against the missiles'. Many of the new activists saw CND as a fossilized survivor from a remote era. In fact, CND had been growing since the mid-1970s, and had run an effective campaign against the deployment of the neutron bomb in 1978.[4] Under the skilful leadership of its General Secretary, Bruce Kent, the small CND apparatus made room for the new activists, thus preserving the continuity between the 1980s movement and its 1950s forerunner. In October 1980, when 70,000 people crowded into Trafalgar Square for CND's first London demonstration of the new wave, it was Thompson's phrase – 'feel your strength' – which best echoed the mood of the moment. The new Cold War had unleashed not only fear but also hope. Quite suddenly, it seemed, a moment of opportunity had arisen for popular protest to restrain and reverse the nuclear arms race.

Thompson also played a leading role in drafting the 1980 *Appeal for European Nuclear Disarmament*, a document which did much to define the political perspective of the new movement both in Britain and on the Continent. Returning to perspectives first developed in the late 1950s, Thompson aimed to 'replace Europe . . . at the centre of the story.'[5] During CND's first wave, the structures of the Cold War in

Europe had appeared immovable, forcing the New Left, in its search for a viable alternative foreign policy for Britain, to look overseas to the emerging non-aligned movement in the Third World. Subsequently, large sections of the left came to see in the anti-imperialist struggles of Third World peoples, and their post-imperial 'socialist' experiments, the decisive events of contemporary history. This was a salutary experience for Europeans whose inherited traditions, like those of pre-Copernican astronomy, had placed them at the centre of the universe. But it was also profoundly disabling. Imperialism might be crumbling at the periphery: but in the centre – and that included Britain – it remained unassailable. Practical internationalism became a matter of sympathy, solidarity and support. The real struggle was always somewhere else. History, it seemed, had finished with the Europeans, needing them neither as its victims nor as its agents.

The Pentagon's plans for 'limited' nuclear war restored Europe to History – as the killing ground of the Cold War. The fate awaiting Europeans, it suddenly appeared, was at least as awful as the worst degradations of imperialism in the Third World. Wars might start anywhere in the world. But they would finish in the detonation of the European powder-keg. Thompson's contribution was to outline a strategy by which Europeans, newly identified as victims, could re-appropriate historical agency. 'Within the threatening shadow of exterminist crisis, European consciousness is alerted, and a moment of opportunity appears.'[6] As the new disarmament movement leapt over national frontiers, spreading from one country to another, Thompson detected 'a spirit abroad in Europe which carries a transcontinental aspiration . . . for the first time since the wartime Resistance.'[7]

The decision to deploy land-based missiles in Western Europe provided a compellingly visible focus for this emergent 'European consciousness' to contest the hegemony of the superpowers. For European Nuclear Disarmament (END), the British organization established in 1980 to promote the Appeal, the campaign against the missiles was the growth point of a popular assertion of European self-determination. 'No Cruise – No SS20' carried a clear political message. Cutting short this latest twist in the spiral of the arms race could open the road to the ending of the blocs. 'We must commence to act', said the *END Appeal*, 'as if a united, neutral and pacific Europe already exists. We must learn to be loyal, not to 'East' or 'West', but to each other, and we must disregard the prohibitions and limitations imposed by any national state.'[8] The gathering crisis of Soviet rule in Eastern Europe opened the way for an unprecedented discourse between Western radicals and Eastern European dissidents, and END devoted much of its energy to advancing what was often a tense and difficult dialogue between Western European peace movements and unofficial groups in the Soviet bloc.

Despite the role played by Thompson in mobilizing the upsurge of the early 1980s, his vision did not become dominant within it. In part this reflected the reluctance of many peace activists to break altogether from the view that American imperialism – not the Cold War itself – was the main threat to world peace. Whatever might be said about the historical origins of the Cold War, Thompson argued, the bloc system had long since acquired a logic of its own in which both sides participated equally. The two superpowers were locked in an 'exterminist' confrontation driven forward by the power of their respective military–industrial complexes, and their rulers' need to legitimate their power by projecting the threat of 'the enemy'. No break with exterminism could be expected from either superpower. Only those caught between them now had the power to avert apocalypse. It was not only pro-Soviet opinion in the Communist Party and the Labour Left that rejected this analysis. The great majority of CND activists agreed that Russia bore some share of responsibility for keeping the Cold War going, and that it was vital for the new movement to be unaligned with either superpower. But resisting American cruise missiles was both more tangible and less problematic than seeking alliances with dissident forces in the East. And, however interesting Thompson's arguments about superpower equivalence, it usually seemed more important to make propaganda against popular misconceptions of the Soviet threat. CND was quite prepared to voice public criticisms of specific Soviet policies, notably the deployment of missiles in Eastern Europe after the collapse of the arms talks in 1983. But few activists shared Thompson's sense of an ongoing engagement against Soviet, as well as American, power in Europe.

It was not only the attitude to the Soviet Union that limited END's appeal. There was also opposition to Thompson's attempt to 'replace Europe at the centre of the story'. Though END was always sensitive to the accusation of Euro-centrism, this gave little reassurance to those wedded to the view that *any* conceivable 'common European consciousness' was likely to do more to aggravate the North/South divide than it was to appease the Cold War. Arguments of this sort were the tip of a familiar iceberg. Floating just below the surface of consciousness, the old imperial pacifist suspicion of continental Europe was a continuing obstacle to the spread of END's ideas in the British peace movement.[9]

In *Protest and Survive* Thompson insisted that END was a unilateralist movement: '. . . each national peace movement will proceed directly to contest the nuclear weapons deployed by its own state, or by NATO or Warsaw Pact Treaty obligations. . . . Its demands upon its own state for disarmament will be unilateral.'[10] But the *Appeal* itself made no such commitment to unilateralism, insisting rather on the autonomy of each national movement in deciding 'its own means and strategy' for contributing towards the denuclearization of Europe. For many END supporters the escape that it offered from CND's traditional fixation on Britain leading the world was precisely what attracted them. Raymond Williams, for example, looked for a campaign of resistance to specific escalations flanked by a broader European movement, rather than a return to CND's 'old-style unilateralism'. Given the decline of British power since the late 1950s, the old claims that Britain's unilateral renunciation of nuclear weapons held the key to world disarmament could not be revived. And given the urgency of the situation:

> campaigns against Cruise and Trident need not . . . involve, and often be politically limited by, the full unilateralist case. For to refuse the siting of Cruise missiles on our territories, as part of a process of demanding multilateral European negotiations for the removal of all such missiles and the related bombers and submarine bases from the territories of 'Europe from

Poland to Portugal', is not, in any ordinary sense, 'unilateralism'. It is the exercise of independence and sovereignty at a stage in a negotiating process for which there is still (just) time. Similarly in the case of the Trident purchase; it can be also a conscious entry into the negotiating process of strategic arms limitation, by refusing the . . . escalation of British-based missile-nuclear systems. *Positive campaigns for these specific initiatives can then in practice be very different from the relatively unfocused demand for 'unilateral renunciation', and should be kept rationally distinct.*[11]

Many of the activists agreed with this.

During the early 1980s CND concentrated its campaigning against cruise and Trident. Scottish CND successfully spawned an Anti-Trident Campaign, with a specific programme distinct from its own broader agenda. But the historic focus on British unilateralism may well have inhibited CND in its attempts to develop the other leg of the strategy outlined by Raymond Williams – an active Europeanism. It was not until the end of 1984 that CND got round to appointing an international worker. Until then, the CND leadership had usually allowed END to represent the British movement abroad – a division of labour which caused considerable confusion among Continental peace activists, not least because CND as a whole did not accept the END position on the Soviet Union. After 1983, when the anti-cruise movement appeared to have failed, strong pressure built up within CND to revert to a fundamentalist emphasis on British unilateralism. Despite Bruce Kent's involvement in launching the END Appeal and the leading role played by ex-END activists – Dan Smith, Meg Beresford and others – in CND's leadership, the 'END perspective' did not become the governing outlook of CND. Whether, in the new international situation of the Gorbachev era, END ideas will prove more acceptable to the wider peace movement is a question to which I shall return in the final chapter.

CND's relationship with the Labour Party was crucial to its strategy. Despite Gaitskell's victory of 1961, the first wave of CND, by its impact on the coming generation of trade union and Labour leaders, had created 'a dormant volcano' within the labour movement.[12] Although nobody took much notice at the time, the Labour Party had adopted unilateralist resolutions at successive Conferences since 1972. In 1976 the National Executive responded by commissioning a detailed elaboration of defence policy from a group of well-informed, pro-CND academics. Their 1976 Report, *Sense About Defence,* revealed a level of dissenting expertise which was to give the second wave of CND greater credibility among opinion formers than its more amateurish precursor.[13] Two of the authors of this report – Mary Kaldor and Dan Smith – were to play leading roles in the revived movement.

Following Mrs Thatcher's victory in the 1979 Election the Labour Left latched on to unilateralism as a major plank in their drive to radicalize the Party. It was, in fact, Labour's National Executive which, in a move calculated to put pressure on the Right, called the first mass demonstration of the new wave in June 1980. Thereafter the steadily hardening commitment of the Labour Party to unilateralism interacted with the burgeoning non-party movement to anchor nuclear disarmament, far more firmly than ever before, in British political life. In the early years of Thatcherism, nuclear disarmament was one of the few issues over which it seemed possible to put the new regime on the defensive. While trade unions went down like nine-pins, the peace movement even managed to inflict a small defeat on the Government, forcing it to cancel plans for a major civil defence exercise in the autumn of 1982. This success owed much to the emergence of the 'Nuclear-Free Zone' movement, which helped to combine the energy of local CND groups with the power of Labour-controlled local authorities and of unions organizing in local government.

For those whose energies were not absorbed in the Labour Party's crisis, the nuclear issue seemed to offer a way to mobilize opposition to Thatcherism on the broadest possible basis. Most CND activists were in no mood to trust the Labour Party. Tory revelations that £1000 million had been spent on the secret 'modernization' of Polaris warheads under successive Governments since the 1960s served merely to confirm the cynical belief that, whatever they might say about nuclear weapons in opposition, Labour politicians were easy game for the military-industrial complex once in office. Several of CND's leaders – notably Joan Ruddock – had close links with the Labour leadership and were gradually able to reassure the movement that Labour's unilateralist commitment was seriously intended, while steering CND away from linking its fortunes too closely to those of the so-called 'hard left', whose chance of capturing power in the Party receded dramatically after Tony Benn's failure to gain the Deputy Leadership in 1981.

But, while cynicism about the likely performance of a Labour Government may have diminished, skepticism about the possibility of Labour ever winning enough votes to be able to form a government was increasing. With anti-Tory politics in a state of upheaval following the breakaway of the SDP in 1981, peace activists needed little convincing of the importance of maintaining CND as a broad, non-party movement. Since no-one could be sure of Labour's ability to reconstruct its dominant position as *the* anti-Tory party, the consolidation of CND's long-standing support within the Liberal Party was generally understood to be a least as important as pinning Labour down on the finer points of unilateralist doctrine. The Liberal Assembly, which had opposed British nuclear weapons since the 1950s, came out against cruise missiles in November 1979. The threat to these positions represented by the Liberal alliance with the pro-nuclear SDP in the mid-1980s helped to shift the argument about nuclear weapons into the centre-ground of British politics.[14] Equally important, in this respect, was the work of CND supporters in the Christian Churches, especially the Anglican Church whose report on *The Church and the Bomb* in 1982 did something to prevent nuclear disarmament from being identified in the public mind as simply a party political issue.[15]

However important it was to win the parties, for most CND members – especially the two thirds of them who belonged to no political party[16] – the primary object was to convince the ordinary voting public. There was no point in persuading parties to adopt unilateralist platforms if this merely prevented them from getting elected. During the early 1980s, opinion polls suggested that, despite majority opposition to both cruise and Trident, most people remained firmly committed to the retention of existing nuclear weapons as the basis of British defence policy.[17] In the run-up to the 1983 Election, a CND campaign of door-to-door canvassing helped to convince activists that what the opinion polls said was correct.[18] During the Election itself CND mounted a major leafletting and poster campaign, but proved quite unable to prevent Mrs Thatcher from presenting the electorate with an apparent choice between defencelessness or the status quo, rather than the choice actually on offer: nuclear escalation or a shift towards non-nuclear defence. CND's own intervention was greatly weakened by an electoral law which prevented it from printing materials containing any message that could be remotely seen as supporting the Labour Party – not that any amount of outside help could have saved Labour from the consequences of entering the Election with a leadership in total disarray over what its defence policy actually was. After June 1983, with Mrs Thatcher safely back in Downing Street, the deployment of cruise missiles was just a matter of time. It was to be some months, however, before the peace movement accepted that it had been defeated.

Since 1981 CND had been supporting 'well-considered non-violent direct action' at the bases, and had even organized a blockade of its own as part of the Easter 1983 activities. Peace camps and actions at the bases were widely supported in the CND groups, and the leadership, despite some private reservations about the efficacy of such activity, was generally positive. Many activists felt a deep loyalty to the Greenham women. Moved by their endurance in appalling physical conditions, campaigners frequently visited the camp bringing money, food, clothing and even caravans to sustain them. Others joined the vigil for a night, a week or more. All this coming and going rapidly created a network of women who identified with the camp, linking it into the existing peace and women's movement networks.

Despite this the relationship between Greenham and CND was never a comfortable one. While Greenham owed much to the women's movement of the 1970s, part of its strength was that it also drew on an older, maternalist, tradition. This alienated some feminists, but it appealed to many more women who responded to Greenham's invitation to 'take pride in your womanly values'.[19] Greenham addressed itself not simply to cruise missiles and the nuclear threat, but equally to the patriarchal structures which, they asserted, underpinned the arms race. There was also a strong ecological emphasis, often expressed in an identification of women with the creative Life Spirit of nature, counterposed to the destructive, masculine Anti-Life forces represented by the base itself. Above all Greenham claimed the right to exclude men from its activities. A vociferous few felt that the sex as a whole was at the root of the problem: most expressed the need for 'space to find our own ways of working . . . to find our strengths, how to assert ourselves'.[20]

Many CND members, and some of its leaders, had little sympathy with the separatist philosophy underpinning the women's peace camp. The effect on public opinion of media stereotyping of Greenham women led some in CND to believe that the women were doing more harm than good. The major problem, however, arose from the women's opposition to mixed actions at the base. As the date for cruise deployment drew closer after the 1983 Election, it became increasingly difficult for CND to balance the women's claim for 'space' at Greenham against the widespread demand for the movement as whole to demonstrate its determination to refuse cruise missiles at Europe's first deployment site. The resulting conflict became a major distraction at the time of deployment, seriously weakening CND's capacity to respond. There was a moment, during the hectic autumn of 1983, when CND came close to splitting over this issue. The price of avoiding a split was a failure by CND to organize any large scale protest to mark the actual arrival of cruise; and this in turn caused frustrations which, during the early months of 1984, gave mounting prominence to attempts to revive a Committee of 100 style of direct action.

In the event it was the tracking of cruise missile convoys, not mass sit-downs in central London, that proved the most effective way of taking direct action against the new weapons. In a phrase that NATO officials must have come deeply to regret, the missiles were said to be invulnerable to Soviet attack because, in a crisis, they would simply 'melt into the countryside'. Quite apart from the unfortunate connotations of the word 'melt', the commitment to secretly exercise large and cumbersome convoys in narrow country lanes was quickly perceived to be the Achilles heel of the new weapons. Much energy, imagination and initiative went into the construction of Cruisewatch – a highly effective network of people organized to track and harass deployment exercises from the Greenham base. Even Cruisewatch, however, could not hide the fact that the movement had failed in its primary objective: preventing the deployment of cruise missiles.

In the debate which followed, some CND leaders urged the campaign to concentrate for the time being on the more modest goal of a nuclear freeze, while others attempted to persuade the movement to address itself directly to the voters' anxiety about 'defencelessness' by taking up the issue of non-nuclear defence. The running, however, was made by some of the more active local groups who mobilized to persuade national CND to 'get back to basics'. Believing that CND's early-1980s concentration on protest against particular weapons systems had let the arguments for complete British unilateralism go by default, these groups pressed for – and experimented with – a new style of 'Basic Case' campaigning, intended to win majority support for unilateralism as such. The Basic Case campaign raised difficult questions about the degree to which CND's involvement in actively *resisting* nuclear weapons contradicted its attempts to *persuade* ordinary members of the public. There was much talk of 'changing our image'. Some proponents of the Basic Case were hostile to direct action, but most were looking for ways of integrating all aspects of CND's work. After a faltering start, the new emphasis was effectively embodied in a campaign around the British Bomb in the autumn of 1986. Decentralized local actions designed to draw public attention to the routes of nuclear convoys were combined with billboards and mass leafletting, and followed up by a cinema advertisement. Technically, the British Bomb campaign marked a new level of sophistication in CND's approach to reaching the public. Politically, however, it shared the fundamental weakness of all Basic Case thinking. By concentrating on the case against

British nuclear weapons it failed to connect effectively with those changes in the international context which increasingly appeared to be making an anachronism of CND's panacea: British unilateralism. The active internationalism which had informed anti-cruise campaigning before 1983 was sadly lacking from CND's activity just before the 1987 election.

Despite its disorientation after 1983, CND did not disintegrate. As a national lobbying organization – which is what many of the more passive members wanted it to be – CND functioned with growing effectiveness. The national membership held up remarkably well, and groups soldiered on doggedly, learning to function effectively with lowered expectations. Life in the groups might not be as exciting as in the early 1980s, but there was still plenty to do: mounting the regular street stall; letter-writing to the local press; lobbying the MP; sorties to watch out for nuclear convoys; visits to Greenham or a nearby peace camp; local campaigns against nuclear bunkers, the transport of nuclear weapons or waste, the building of new nuclear power stations; occasional public meetings; corresponding with linked local peace groups in the US or Europe; filling the coaches for national CND demonstrations; persuading the membership to join in nationally initiated high-street activities and door-to-door leafletting; organizing instant responses to crisis – notably the 1986 bombing of Libya from USAF bases in Britain which was followed, almost immediately by the Chernobyl accident.

Attendance at group meetings – and national demonstrations – was well down from the highpoint of the early 1980s, and the activists were tired. But this did not appear to be a movement on its last legs. In May 1988 local CND groups distributed two million copies of a leaflet contrasting super-power disarmament talks with Britain's Trident programme. This was CND's biggest leaflet drop since the 1983 election. More importantly, there were signs, during 1987–88, that CND was beginning to move beyond the defensive and fundamentalist mentality represented by the Basic Case. Rather late in the day, perhaps, the campaign began to discuss seriously new ways of linking its activity with the dramatic changes taking place in Europe, as what appeared to be a new era of *détente* broke out between the superpowers.

16

Prospects

Ultimately the prospects for the British peace movement depend on international events. In the early 1960s the immobility of the bloc system effectively marginalized attempts to win even peace movement support for the goal of discovering a new British identity in the struggle for a neutral and pacific Europe. Today, the prospects of movement towards the eventual dissolution of the blocs are much more substantial. In 1982 Edward Thompson listed the signals of change: the decline of American economic and diplomatic power; intensifying economic rivalries in the capitalist world; growing isolationism in the United States and, on the other side, the loss of Soviet hegemony over a growing variety of Communisms (China, Italy, etc), the growing crisis of Soviet power in Eastern Europe (Poland), increasing signs of the integration between Eastern bloc economies and Western Europe – Eastern European indebtedness to Western banks; the construction, against fierce American opposition, of a pipeline to carry Soviet natural gas to the West; 'vodka–cola' deals between Soviet planners and capitalist firms. In this situation, he argued, cruise missiles were just the tip of an iceberg. What was at issue was the survival of West European Atlanticism:

> An inherited ideological formation, the Atlanticist dogma, has come under challenge; the challengers are not pro-Soviet although they are the inheritors of the grumblers and the third wayers who lost out at the Cold War's origins; they are looking for a new alternative, but they cannot yet spell its name.[1]

Subsequent events have done much to validate Thompson's perspective. Economic relations between Europe and the United States continued to deteriorate, while Reaganite economics built up huge trade and budgetary deficits.

Important sections of US opinion have increasingly question-
ed the commitment to Europe during the 1980s. This involves
not only the far Right, but also much of the leadership of the
Democratic Party for whom a serious question mark has now
arisen over the continued wisdom of devoting up to thirty per
cent of the US military budget to the defence of Europe. In
part, this represents a concern to devote what must now be
recognized as limited budgetary resources to a more fruitful
pursuit of American power and profit elsewhere in the world.
The shift to the South and West in the internal balance of the
US economy has helped to undermine the power of the old
Eastern ruling class, whose informal, non-governmental ties
with the élites of Europe long provided a necessary shock-
absorber for the internal contradictions of Atlanticism.[2] The
growing 'Pacificism' of the new American establishment has
no connection, beyond the increasingly misleading name of an
ocean, with the goals of pacifism. Underpinning the formidable projection of American military power in the Pacific is
not only its confrontation with the Soviet Union, but also the
belief that the 21st century will belong to the economies not of
Europe but of Asia:

> When we measure the near optimised markets of Europe
> and its 250 million persons against the near unoptimised
> 1.5 billion to 2 billion people of the Pacific basin, Europe
> seems a puny affair.[3]

Whatever the rise of American 'Pacificism' may mean for the
future of the world as a whole, it seems likely to open up new
opportunities for the peace movements of Europe.

Developments in the Soviet bloc have diverged significantly from Thompson's expectations: but with no less
favourable consequences for the project of European non-
alignment. In his analysis of 'exterminism', Thompson saw
the Soviet pursuit of nuclear 'parity' with the West as a key to
the incorporation of the dynamic thrust of the American
military-industrial complex into the heart of the Soviet
system. One of the most significant aspects of Soviet 'new
thinking' has been its questioning of the need to maintain
nuclear parity with the West. It was Soviet readiness to accept

disproportionate reductions in nuclear warheads which opened the way to the INF agreement. It is too soon to assess the significance of this Treaty for the nuclear arms race itself. It may turn out that the new veneer of civilized discourse merely disguises the unrelenting logic of technological escalation – in the East as in the West. Nevertheless, to the extent that the USSR pursues the implications of 'reasonable sufficiency', it may be able to break out of the economic trap laid by Western advocates of the arms race – bankruptcy induced by the imposition of unrestrained armaments expenditure. This trap is, in any case, beginning to close in on its perpetrators, as the competitive disadvantage caused by military over-commitment becomes increasingly apparent to analysts of the US (and of course the British) economy. Be that as it may, Gorbachev has already disproved Thompson's 1980 prediction that there was nothing to be hoped for from the superpowers themselves, and that the fate of the world hinged on the capacity of the European peoples to rebel. The sight of East German teenagers chanting the name of the General Secretary of the CPSU as an act of defiance against policemen of a Communist regime attempting to prevent them from listening to Western pop music across the Berlin Wall, indicates the existence of a new alignment of forces in Europe, and one unanticipated in the 'exterminist' analysis.[4] The major upheavals now occurring in the Soviet Union are beginning to stimulate significant changes in Eastern Europe. Democracy, perhaps, can come from the East as well as the West. The most decisive test of the viability of Gorbachev's 'revolution from above' over the coming years is likely to be managing the relaxation of the Soviet grip on Eastern Europe, without unleashing nationalist and revolutionary upheavals that would in turn trigger a new Soviet intervention and, perhaps, an end to the reform movement in the Soviet Union itself. For the moment, however, the Gorbachev phenomenon seems set to continue, alongside the growing crisis of Atlanticism, to open up opportunities for new dialogues about non-alignment across the Cold War divide in Europe.

In Western Europe the Right has been thoroughly alarmed by the willingness of the United States to conclude disarmament deals with the Soviet Union over their heads and with scant regard for their perceived interests. The prime object of cruise, after all, was not to 'balance' Soviet SS–20s, but to demonstrate conclusively that US nuclear forces were 'coupled' with the defence of Europe. Fears of an American betrayal of long-standing friends in Europe can hardly have been appeased by the spectacle of President Reagan aligning himself with the West German peace movement in the summer of 1987, to force Chancellor Kohl to abandon resistance to the INF deal. This was not a scenario that could have been anticipated in 1980 either. And the subsequent reversal of roles between West Germany and the US over the question of the post-INF 'modernization' of nuclear weapons in Europe, indicates the continuing impact of the peace movement's response to the 1979 decision to install INF weapons in the first place. Chancellor Kohl is forced, for electoral reasons, to resist attempts to install new nuclear weapons on the potential German battlefield.

Faced with this many-sided crisis in the Atlantic relationship there are two options open to the European Right. The first is to attempt to patch up Atlanticism: the second to embark on a thorough-going Europeanism. Simple inertia, and the conservatism of established institutions, suggest that the first option will not be lightly abandoned. Moreover the right-wing advocates of closer European unity face some difficult dilemmas. It seems probable that, in the long term, only a European state capable of co-ordinated intervention in the market economy can prevent the economic Balkanization of Europe by Japanese and American capital. Unfortunately for the Right, the degree of state intervention necessary to achieve this goal, is hardly compatible with the pursuit of free market economics. They face a parallel problem over defence.

In 1982 leading European Governments revived a defunct body – the Western European Union – as a forum within which to strengthen the European pillar of the NATO alliance. So far, progress has been modest and hedged around with protestations of loyalty to NATO. It is indeed difficult to see how European states could increase their defence spending sufficiently to fill the gap left by a withdrawal of American troops. And the only alternative – a drastic downward assessment of the 'Soviet threat' – is unappealing to the Right.

Pro-nuclear advocates of West European federalism have, since the 1950s, advocated the development of some kind of joint European nuclear force based on French and British expertise in this area, and discussion of a possible 'eurobomb' has revived in recent years. By such means Western Europe could enter a post-Atlantic world wielding its own strategic nuclear deterrent. However, in the absence of any equivalent popular sentiment to the nationalisms which sustain the French and British bombs, a move to 'Europeanize' the bomb is more likely to undermine, than to enhance, the popular acceptability of nuclear weapons in those two countries.

For the Right, the danger of openly raising the prospect of a post-Atlantic Europe taking care of its own defence is that it points irresistibly towards the need to reassess the relationship with the Soviet Union. It takes two to manufacture a satisfactory Cold War psychosis – a state of public paranoia about the 'enemy' sufficient to outweigh the political appeal of social as against military spending. Stalinism was an essential ingredient of the Cold War; and it was precisely the attempt to get up a New Cold War in the late 1970s which triggered the rise of the mass peace movements. In the face of dramatically shifting perceptions of the Soviet Union under Gorbachev, it seems improbable that Western Europe's élites will be able to whip up a new cold war psychology among their publics.

Britain's rulers have been most reluctant to confront the fundamental strategic choice between Europe and America. Their delay in joining the EEC in the first place has been matched by a consistently minimalist approach to economic and political integration since Britain joined in 1973. In particular, Britain's status as a nuclear power has been used to sustain the illusion of a viable middle way between mere Atlanticism and full integration into Europe. As the economy, the social services and the education system slide precipitously down the league tables of the industrialized world, British Governments have clung to the bomb as a hedge against complete subordination to more powerful allies – on either side of the Atlantic. The humiliation of Chancellor Kohl in 1987 must have given Mrs Thatcher food for thought, despite her third successive election victory. Britain's Trident programme may yet prove to be as vulnerable to a superpower deal on stategic weapons as Kohl's Pershings were to the INF negotiations. If the US administration was prepared to betray allies who had invested so much political capital in the need to deploy land-based missiles in Europe, how can it be trusted to uphold Mrs Thatcher's political investment in Trident? The absurdity of seeking to sustain Britain's prestige – and her own – by *renting* missiles from the United States is dangerously close to being exposed.

During the first wave of CND, Britain still had a larger industrial output than West Germany, France and Italy combined.[5] In the last 25 years Britain's relative economic decline has been so precipitate that it would now be difficult for either the right or the left to construct a popular base for 'going it alone' in the 1990s. It is true that the Falklands War of 1982 revealed the continuing power of British nationalism, and it undoubtedly did much to boost Mrs Thatcher's popularity.[6] But its long-term impact on popular attitudes to Britain's role in the world was probably negligible. Certainly it had no more than a temporary effect on the growth of support for CND. The fate of socialist attempts in the early 1980s to construct an alternative economic strategy around the reassertion of national sovereignty against the Treaty of Rome suggests that there is little to be gained by disputing the common sense view that, for a small and declining industrial economy, national economic sovereignty is no longer a viable option.[7]

During the early 1980s, CND was adept at exploiting mass anti-American sentiment in its campaign against cruise missiles. But it was far less ready to follow the lead given by END towards the elaboration of a positive alternative to Atlanticism. Despite the inspiration they drew from the cross-European mass demonstrations of 1981 and 1983, most British peace activists remained stubbornly insular. Even when the annual END Convention occurred in Britain, in 1987, they showed little interest. When Mrs Thatcher out-flanks the peace movement's appeal to anti-Americanism by pinning national independence to the British Bomb, CND has tended to fall back on technical arguments about absence of a genuinely *independent* nuclear capacity, and simple moral opposition to nuclear weapons. What it has generally failed to do is to elaborate or propagate its own political alternative to continuing dependence on the United States.

Can the peace movement succeed, where the pro-European Right has so signally failed: in creating popular enthusiasm for 'Europe'? This is a misleading question. However important it is to retain the peace movement's independence from political parties and its power to mobilize millions of people around the overriding issue of survival, the movement cannot rely simply on its own efforts to create the conditions necessary for its success. A new Europe will not be built by the peace movement alone. Equally important is the development of an alternative Europeanism focused on social and economic questions. The relative enlightenment of the European Commission and the European Court on issues of women's rights points to the possibility of a dialogue between popular movements and an emergent 'European state power capable of outflanking bastions of reaction anchored in the larger nation states. Questions of the upward equalization of social welfare benefits throughout the EEC are beginning to edge onto the agenda of the British Left, alongside the use of Common Market regional policy to tackle some of the grosser inequalities in the UK. Increasingly the debate on alternative economic strategy is looking to joint European action to tackle unemployment and recession, driven forward by the failure of French, Greek and Spanish attempts to discover an independent national road away from monetarism. With the coming of the single internal market in 1992, pressures for a common social and economic policy across the community are bound to increase. There are ways for the peace movement to engage with these topics, notably by raising demands for a co-ordinated policy of demilitarizing the European economy.

It is often argued that the EEC is too narrow a basis on which to seek to construct an alternative Europeanism. Indeed it is. But we must start from where we are, and there is nothing to be gained by exaggerating either the reactionary character of the Community, or its incapacity for change and renewal. As Raymond Williams pointed out, contesting the renewed emphasis of the Labour Left on the need for national economic sovereignty in the late 1970s:

> If we are seriously proposing a collaborative campaign for European Nuclear Disarmament, is it sensible at the same time to propose simple withdrawal from the EEC? What is necessary and possible, in both cases, is a radical negotiation, and this can only really be undertaken on a European rather than simply a British scale.[8]

The success with which the Federal Republic has pursued a policy of economic *Ostpolitik* within the EEC confounds notions of the Community as simply an economic arm of Cold War politics – as do recent moves by the Soviet Union towards full recognition of, and direct dealing with, the Community. There are exciting new opportunities for the peace movement to campaign jointly with the ecological movements which have sprung up in Eastern Europe and the USSR in the wake of Chernobyl, demanding greater East – West co-operation in controlling environments, pollution and developing a safe energy policy. In all this there is a danger that the opening up of economic relations with the East will tend to subordinate the interests of Eastern European citizens to those of Western capital – that *Ostpolitik* could become 'roll-back', the restoration of an unfettered market economy in Eastern Europe.[9] It would be a mistake, however, for the left to respond by advocating a return to the historically discredited project of building 'socialism in one country', or even one bloc. The reintegration of the Soviet bloc into a global economic order dominated by capitalism has worrying features, but the way to combat these is not by looking back to the alliance between socialism and nationalism, but by seeking to construct new transnational agencies to counter the power of international capital, and to build alliances amongst the popular forces mobilized by trade unions, peace movements, women's organizations, green movements and the political parties of the Left. Socialists need a strategy linking all these levels, one that firmly rejects the idea that there can be any viable socialism, democracy or peace that rests on attempts to fence off the socialist experiment within a self-sufficient 'post-capitalist' world.

Similar considerations apply to the relationship between Europe and the Third World. The fact that the EEC operates to restrict Third World access to European markets does not mean that a reformed European Community could not play an important role in helping to sustain a realistic path of development. As Lucio Magri wrote in 1982:

> Western Europe today possesses – as it did not thirty years ago – the economic, technological and cultural resources to assert its own political autonomy and to help sustain another path of development for the Third World. . . . But for this to occur, of course, two fundamental conditions would be necessary. Firstly, European unification would itself have to advance, as a collective project of the Left. . . . [Secondly], it is not possible to confront the problem of underdevelopment seriously without putting into question our own ways of producing and consuming, our whole system of values. Any new relationshp with the Third World presupposes a qualitative change in our own type of development.[10]

It is by conceiving of itself as part of this process of transformation both within Europe and in Europe's relationship to the South, that the British peace movement can most effectively combat the legacies of imperialism in Britain's political culture.[11]

While the EEC may turn out to be part of the solution, NATO – the other powerful international organization to which Britian belongs – is intrinsically part of the problem. Despite the incontestable moral case that Britain could not be genuinely non-nuclear while continuing to retain membership of a nuclear alliance, CND has given a low priority to campaigning for British withdrawal from NATO. So long as the dissolution of the blocs remained a merely utopian goal for the distant future, this was sensible – since there was nothing for Britain to withdraw *into*. Now that changes in the superpower relationship are moving beyond-the-blocs politics on to the practical political agenda, the peace movement can no longer evade the issue of NATO. It would be foolish to adopt doctrinaire positions about the best way for

particular existing NATO states to contribute to the dissolution of Cold War policies and structures. Certainly the
withdrawal of a major NATO country from the alliance
would, in present circumstances, precipitate far-reaching
change in Europe. But the election of a Government
committed to withdrawal remains a long way from the
practical political agenda. Making propaganda in the wilder-
ness has its uses, but it may, in this case, be even more useful to
pursue a policy of de-escalation and progressive denuclearization within NATO, particularly when developments in the
East – including persistent rumours of a Soviet intention to
withdraw significant numbers of troops from Eastern Europe
– seem set to undermine radically the credibility of the
exaggerated threat assessments on which present NATO
force levels and strategic doctrine are based. Demanding
changes in NATO policy, within a perspective of bloc
dissolution, has more to be said for it than a campaign for a
British withdrawal which would probably prove impossible
in practice. It is difficult to believe that Britain, acting alone,
and against the united opposition of both America and the
major Western European states, would be capable of withdrawing from the alliance. A reassertion of national
sovereignty on *that* scale would seem to require a degree of
economic independence not available to post-imperial Britain.
This does not, of course, mean that NATO is invulnerable:
merely that unilateral action by Britain, unsupported by other
major European states, is not a promising line of attack.

In 1962 when the Right abandoned the defence of national
sovereignty in favour of Europe, both the Left and the peace
movement moved unhesitatingly into the empty trenches of
nationalism. Today there is some reason to hope that the
deep-rooted affinity between socialism and nationalism,
which peaked in Britain during the Second World War, may at
last be disintegrating. As the Right dithers between attempting to shore up a decaying Atlanticism and the pursuit of a
greater European independence, which seems hardly compatible with its own militarist and free market assumptions, a
historic opportunity is opening up for the Left and the peace
movements to project an alternative vision of Europe.

So long as the Right remains in power in the major Western

European countries, the tasks of the peace movement will remain those of resistance to new weapons, and the patient work of lobbying and public education. But if, in the early 1990s, left and left-of-centre Governments come to power, then the possibilities of a transformative break from Cold War politics would be greater than ever before. In 1913 H. N. Brailsford advised pacifists – 'When we think of peace, we must learn to think as Europeans.'[12] After Europe collapsed into anarchy in 1914, most pacifists (Brailsford included), looked to one or other of the emerging superpowers to bring peace to Europe. Confronted by the problem of Nazism in the 1930s, peace campaigners again turned to the superpowers for salvation. Only in the 1940s, and then only marginally, did advocacy of an independent and pacific Europe revive, to be quickly crushed by the Cold War. The attempt to link the new nuclear disarmament movement of the late 1950s to the vision of a non-aligned Europe appears, in retrospect, to have had little chance of success. But since 1979 the democratic European vision has re-emerged. This time it is unlikely to slip away. Britain may no longer have the power to save the world, as successive peace movements believed. But the peace movement may have a major role to play in saving Britain from the debilitating consequences of Mrs Thatcher: global pretension and domestic decay. By throwing itself into the struggle for a democratic, non-aligned and pacific Europe, the British peace movement will be confronting directly those insular and imperialist traditions which, in the last analysis, remain the most serious obstacles to its success.

Contemplating the history of peace movements is an effective antidote to facile optimism, perhaps to optimism of any sort. All the movements failed, swept aside by forces far beyond their control. The progressive internationalism of pre-1914 bourgeois – and socialist – Europe never entirely disappeared. The European vision of the liberal socialists survived through the hurricanes of two World Wars and the Cold War, though only as a dissident voice, often with little influence on events. Even that foothold on sanity was frequently obscured by the seductions of a falsely global pacifism left over from the Pax Britannica. And many, while clinging to the wreckage of old Europe, placed their hopes in alien gods – the New World across the Atlantic, or the New Class erupting from the East. Neither Pax Americana nor Proletarian Revolution brought salvation.

Today a disintegrating bi-polar world system discloses no open road to the Utopia of world government. The super-powers and their simplistic ideologies are failing, leaving Europeans to confront the legacies of their own political cultures. In Britain something positive may yet be built from the old imperialist connections with the Third World. But the primary resource for the peace movement lies in Europe. The point is not to replace British nationalism with a spurious Euro-nationalism. Each of us belongs simultaneously to many different communities and we create our identities in complex ways.[13] As the peace movement sets out to build an active non-alignment in Europe, it should do so, not in the belief that a united Europe can 'lead the world', but with a deep sense of its responsibility to put its own house in order. We should act where we are. We should remember, always, the old socialist truth – the enemy is at home. And we should not abandon hope.

Notes to Preface

1 I take the phrase from Raymond Williams, *Towards 2000*, Part V, 1983.
2 S. White, *Britain and the Bolshevik Revoluton*, 1979, p. 217.
3 The peace organizations which survived longest in the twentieth century either rested on a particular narrow constituency (like the Quakers) or acted mainly to circulate information among other campaigning organizations, rather than to initiate campaigns of their own (like the National Peace Council).
4 George Orwell, *The Road to Wigan Pier*, 1962, p. 143.
5 E. Halevy, *Imperialism and the Rise of Labour*, p. 66; M. Ceadel, *Pacifism in Britain*, pp. 3–5, 144–46.
6 As someone who has spent a good deal of time helping to run CND's national apparatus over the last few years, I hesitated before describing myself as an 'activist' in the first sentence of this Preface. Real 'activists' might consider me something of a 'bureaucrat'. But what I do feels like 'activism' to me!
7 A. J. P. Taylor, *The Trouble Makers*, 1985, pp. 51n.

Notes

1: Victorian Visions: Imperialist Pacifism

1 The phrase is used in Karl Polanyi, *The Great Transformation*, 1944.
2 The Crimean War came close but, as Olive Anderson remarked, despite 'great expectations' it remained 'a great war which failed to materialize'. *A Liberal State at War. English Politics and Economics during the Crimean War*, 1967, p. 26.
3 J. A. Hobson, *Richard Cobden, The International Man*, 1918, p. 37.
4 R. Cobden, *Speeches on Questions of Public Policy*, 1908, p. 187.
5 Quoted in D. Read, *Cobden and Bright. A Victorian Political Partnership*, 1967, p. 110.
6 *Ibid.*, p. 114.
7 R. Cobden, *ibid.*, p. 187.
8 Quoted in R. Hyam, *Britain's Imperial Century, 1815–1914*, 1976, p. 52.

9 *Ibid.*, p. 54.
10 Sir Eyre Crowe, January 1907, quoted in J. Joll, ed., *Britain and Europe, 1793–1940*, 1961, p. 205.
11 G. Orwell, *The Lion and the Unicorn*, 1982, p. 43.
12 M. Gilbert, *Plough My Own Furrow*, 1965, p. 105.
13 Quoted in M. Howard, *War and the Liberal Conscience*, 1978, pp. 48–9.
14 E. H. Carr, *Nationalism and After*, 1945, p. 16.
15 Quoted in D. Read, *ibid.*, p. 111.
16 B. Porter, *Britain, Europe and the World, 1850–1982. Delusions of Grandeur*, 1983, Ch. 1.
17 A. J. P. Taylor, *The Troublemakers. Dissent over Foreign Policy, 1792–1939*, 1985, p. 52.
18 D. Read, *ibid.*, pp. 111–12.
19 *Ibid.*, p. 110.
20 A. J. P. Taylor, *ibid.*, pp. 53–4.
21 D. Read, *ibid.*, p. 32.
22 'God's ends can rarely be attained in politics without passion: and there is now, the first time for a good many years, a virtuous passion.' Gladstone to Granville, 29 September 1876, quoted in R. T. Shannon, *Gladstone and the Bulgarian Agitation, 1876*, 1963, pp. 106–07.
23 Quoted in A. J. P. Taylor, *ibid.*, p. 59.
24 M. Howard, *War and the Liberal Conscience*, 1978, p. 44. In 1851, speaking on the same platform as Kossuth, he had argued that only an England not tainted by meddling in other nations' internal affairs would have the moral authority to demand that the Russians 'stop' – not a very convincing attempt to have it both ways. N. C. Edsall, *Richard Cobden, Independent Radical*, 1986, p. 253.
25 R. Harrison, *Before the Socialists*, 1965, Ch. 2.
26 W. T. Stead, quoted in S. Koss, *The Anatomy of an Anti-War Movement: The Pro-Boers*, 1973, p. 77.
27 Speech in House of Commons, 6 February 1900, quoted in *ibid.*, p. 94.
28 Quoted in J. H. Grainger, *Patriotisms: Britain 1900–1939*, 1986, p. 166.
29 J. Vincent, *The Formation of the British Liberal Party, 1857–68*, 1966, pp. 211-38, 246–50.
30 J. L . Hammond, *Gladstone and the Irish Question*, 1938, Ch. V.
31 Quoted in A. J. P. Taylor, *ibid.*, p. 86.
32 H. N. Brailsford, *The War of Steel and Gold. A Study of the Armed Peace*, 1914, p. 104.
33 J. L. Hammond, *ibid.*, pp. 53–4.

2: Victorian Protests: Organizing the Virtuous Passion

1 P. Brock, *Pacifism in Europe to 1914*, 1972, Chs. 9, 10; M. Ceadel, *Pacifism in Britain, 1914–1945*, 1980, pp. 31–2.

2 J. Bright, *Selected Speeches*, 1907, p. 216.

3 D. Read, *Cobden and Bright*, 1967, p. 45.

4 R. Anstey, *The Atlantic Slave Trade and British Abolition, 1760–1810*, 1975, pp. 406–07.

5 John Morley justified his own quietist position during the Boer War by quoting this statement. S. Koss, *The Anatomy of an Anti-War Movement: The Pro-Boers*, 1973, p. 99; N. C. Edsall, *Richard Cobden, Independent Radical*, 1986, p. 273.

6 Quoted in S. Koss, *ibid.*, p. 85.

7 *The Right to Free Speech*, 1900, quoted in S. Koss, *ibid.*, p. 120.

8 A. J. P. Taylor, *The Troublemakers*, 1957, p. 40.

9 H. Jephson, *The Platform. Its Rise and Progress*, Vol. II, 1892, p. 483.

10 Quoted in R. T. Shannon, *Gladstone and the Bulgarian Agitation, 1876*, 1963, p. 23.

11 *Ibid.*, pp. 136–37.

12 S. Koss, *ibid.*, p. 152.

13 *Ibid.*, p. 73. Such rhetoric did not, however, go down at all well with working-class audiences, whose loyalty to 'our lads' outweighed any masochistic desire to participate in organized shame about the misdeeds committed in their name. R. Price, *An Imperial War and the British Working Class*, 1972, pp. 82ff.; D. J. Newton, *British Labour, European Socialism and the Struggle for Peace, 1889–1914*, 1985, pp. 113–123.

14 S. Koss, *ibid.*, p. 71.

15 *The Speaker*, 22 June 1901, quoted in *ibid.*, p. 206.

16 R. Shannon, *ibid.*, p. 100.

17 R. Price, *ibid.*, pp. 24, 160–1; D. J. Newton, *ibid.*, pp. 123ff.

18 D. Howell, *British Workers and the Independent Labour Party, 1888–1906*, 1983, pp. 250, 369; K. O. Morgan, *Keir Hardie*, 1975, pp. 106–08.

19 'I do not trust Radicals, nor Liberals as such. If they are with us let them come to us. . . . To me it seems that Hardie always does the wrong thing. Now he is ready to break the socialist line to form an anti-war party. The war is a detail. Someday it will be over. We are for socialism. I do not trust Hardie. He does not steer straight.' Robert Blatchford, quoted in D. J. Newton, *ibid.*, p. 131.

20 *Ibid.*, pp. 101–118.

21 D. Howell, *ibid.*, pp. 345–46.

3: Hobson and Angell

1 R. Robinson and J. Gallagher, *Africa and the Victorians*, 1961, Ch. 1.
2 R. Koebner and H. D. Schmidt, *Imperialism: the Story and Significance of a Political Word*, 1964, Ch. 8. Kipling's poem was written in 1899 and addressed to the United States, which had just embarked on its own imperial career in the Philippines.
3 P. Warwick, 'Did Britain Change? An Inquiry into the Cause of National Decline', *Journal of Contemporary History*, 20, 1985; B. Porter, *Britain, Europe and the World, 1850–1982*, Ch. 2.
4 J. R. S. Granvile, *Lord Salisbury and Foreign Policy*, 1964; G. W. Monger, *The End of Isolation*, 1963; C. J. Lowe and M. C. Dockrill, *The Mirage of Power*, Vol. 1, 1972.
5 A. Sykes, *Tariff Reform in British Politics*, 1903–1913, Oxford, 1979; B. Semmell, *Imperialism and Social Reform*, 1960.
6 J. A. Hobson, *Confessions of an Economic Heretic*, 1938; T. Kemp, *Theories of Imperialism*, 1967, Ch. 3; B. Porter, *Critics of Empire*, 1968, Ch. 6.
7 J. A. Hobson, *Richard Cobden, The International Man*, 1918, p. 400.
8 J. A. Hobson, *Imperialism: A Study*, 1902, pp. 71–2.
9 *Ibid.*, p. 70.
10 *Ibid.*, p. 52.
11 *Ibid.*, p. 60.
12 *Ibid.*, p. 332. Hobson was one of the few Edwardian pacifists to place 'civilized' in inverted commas. Despite the anti-semitism of his attack on finance capital, his attitude towards the black victims of imperialism was a great deal less racist than most of his contemporaries.
13 H. N. Brailsford, *The War of Steel and Gold*, 1914, p. 308.
14 J. A. Hobson, *ibid.*, pp. 335–6, 385–89.
15 B. Porter, *ibid.*, pp. 58, 63.
16 D. Canadine, 'The British Monarchy', in E. J. Hobsbawm and T. Ranger (eds), *The Invention of Tradition*, 1983, pp. 127–28.
17 Graham Wallas, *Human Nature in Politics*, 1908, p. 80. H. Cunningham, 'The Conservative Party and Patriotism', in R. Colls and P. Dodd, *Englishness: Politics and Culture, 1880–1920*, 1986. At the end of the Second World War, perhaps the apex of popular British nationalism, E. H. Carr remarked: 'there is no name for the citizen of the entity officially known as "the United Kingdom of Great Britain and Northern Ireland"', *Nationalism and After*, 1945, p. 36.
18 B. Semmell, *ibid.*, p. 147.

19 N. Angell, *The Great Illusion. A Study of the Relation of Military Power in Nations to Their Economic and Social Advantage*, 1911, p. 68.

20 A. J. P. Taylor, *A Personal History*, 1983, p. 27.

21 N. Angell, *ibid.*, p. 269.

22 P. Brock, *Pacifism in Europe to 1914*, 1972, pp. 385–86.

23 G. Dangerfield, *The Strange Death of Liberal England*, 1966, p. 21.

24 N. Angell, *ibid.*, p. 191.

25 A. J. Morris, *Radicalism Against War, 1906–1914. The Advocacy of Peace and Retrenchment*, 1972, pp. 90–1.

26 H. N. Brailsford, *ibid.*, p. 250.

27 Quoted in A. J. P. Taylor, *The Troublemakers*, 1957, p. 125.

28 N. Angell, *ibid.*, pp. 306–07.

29 M. Swartz, *The Union of Democratic Control in British Politics During the First World War*, Oxford, 1971, pp. 21–2.

30 N. Angell, *ibid.*, pp. 304, 314–7; K. Robbins, *The Abolition of War. The 'Peace Movement' in Britain, 1914–1919*, Cardiff, 1976, pp. 16–17.

31 Morel to Cadbury, 4 July 1905, quoted in C. A. Cline, *E. D. Morel, 1873–1924. The Strategies of Protest*, 1980, p. 43. My discussion of this campaign is entirely based on this excellent book.

32 E. D. Morel, *The Morrow of the War*, n.d.

33 This was Lord Cromer's characterization of the Congo Reform Association, quoted in C. A. Cline, *ibid.*, p. 62.

4: Socialism, Liberalism and Peace before 1914

1 C. Attlee, *The Labour Party in Perspective*, 1937, pp. 200ff.

2 B. Semmell, *Imperialism and Social Reform. English Socialist and Imperialist Thought, 1895–1914*, 1960; C. R. Searle, *The Quest for National Efficiency*, 1971.

3 R. J. Scally, *The Origins of the Lloyd George Coalition. The Politics of Social Imperialism, 1900–1918*, 1975. The illiberal implications of the Liberal Imperialist reconciliation with state power was already fully evident before the war when, in 1910, they used the spy mania generated by the arms race to push through the Official Secrets Act. The Act equated the 'interests of the State' exclusively with those of the state apparatus and was, from the start, intended to defend Whitehall against the impudent curiosity of British citizens, as much as that of German spies. R. Colls and P. Dodd (eds), *Englishness: Politics and Culture, 1880–1920*, 1986, p. 52.

4 D. J. Newton, *British Labour, European Socialism and the Struggle for Peace, 1889–1914*, Oxford, 1985, pp. 140–1, 147–55, 212–15, 226–27.

5 *Ibid.*, pp. 208–11.

6 R. Colls and P. Dodd (eds), *ibid.*, pp. 52–3.

7 P. F. Clarke, *Lancashire and the New Liberalism*, 1971; N. Blewitt, *The Peers, the Parties, and the People*, 1972.

8 S. Yeo, 'Socialism, the State and some Oppositional Englishness', in R. Colls and P. Dodd (eds), *ibid.*, p. 349.

9 J. A. Hobson, *Confessions of an Economic Heretic*, 1938, p. 53.

10 F. M. Levanthall, *The Last Dissenter: H. N. Brailsford and his World*, Oxford, 1985.

11 H. N. Brailsford, *The War of Steel and Gold,*. 1914, pp. 203–04.

12 *Ibid.*, p. 311.

13 O. J. Hale, *Publicity and Diplomacy: England and Germany 1890–1914*, 1940, pp. 30–1.

14 H. N. Brailsford, *ibid.*, p. 296.

15 *Ibid.*, p. 297.

16 Irene Cooper Willis, *England's Holy War*, New York, 1919–21, p. 5, quoted in J. Vellacott, *Bertrand Russell and the Pacifists in the First World War*, Brighton, 1980, p. 5. Though Cooper was discussing Liberals, her comments apply equally well to Socialists – (*cf.*) J. R. Macdonald's remark in November 1914: 'Our feebleness consisted in the fact that Great Britain was asleep in foreign matters. . . . Our people are indifferent to Foreign Office transactions. . . . The result has been that we have never been able to get up popular interest in foreign policy . . ., quoted in D. Marquand, *Ramsay MacDonald*, 1977, p. 182.

17 A. J. Morris, *Radicalism Against War, 1906–1914*, 1972, p. 266.

18 H. N. Brailsford, *ibid.*, pp. 225–230; A. J. Morris, *ibid.*, pp. 59–70, 176–189; F. M. Levanthall, 'H. N. Brailsford and the Search for a New International Order', in A. J. Morris (ed.), *Edwardian Radicalism, 1900–1914*, 1974, pp. 208–9; D. J. Newton, *ibid.*, pp. 169–174. In taking up the issue of loans to the Tsar, the pacifists were following a precedent set by Cobden in 1850: 'What shall we say of England if we have to record that, in the year 1850, there were found men in London ready to endorse the desperate wickedness of Russia by lending her money to continue the career of violence she has hitherto maintained?' R. Edsall, *Richard Cobden, Independent Radical*, 1896, p. 237. More than 40 years later Koni Zilliacus, the left-wing Labour MP, was still arguing that the failure of Britain 'to let the Russian Revolution of 1905–6 succeed, instead of lending money to the Tsar to strangle it', was a major contributory factor to the outbreak of the First World

War:'The liberalisation of Russia would have made it impossible to retain semi-autocracy in Imperial Germany, and we should probably have avoided the first world war.' *I Choose Peace*, 1949, p. 278. Whatever the merits of this argument it seems unlikely that Brailsford's rather conspiratorial depiction of the role of British bankers can be sustained. J. Harris and P. Thane, 'British and French bankers 1880–1914, an "aristocratic bourgeoisie"?', in P. Thane, *et al*, (eds), *The Power of the Past*, p. 223.

19 '. . . it is true to say that for many (Trades) councils, their excursions into the area of foreign policy began and ended with criticisms of the Russian autocracy and the British connections with it.' D. J. Newton, *ibid.*, p. 83.

20 G. H. Perris, quoted in M. Ceadel, *Thinking About War and Peace*, Oxford, 1987, p. 105. On Perris see Ch. 5, n. 1, below.

21 K. Robbins, *The Abolition of War*, Cardiff, 1976, p. 26.

22 H. N. Brailsford, *ibid.*, p. 17.

23 *Ibid.*, pp. 70–2, 268.

24 D. J. Newton, *ibid.*, pp. 183–4, 206, 236–45, 314–5, 345.

25 A. J. Marder, *The Anatomy of British Sea Power*, 1964, p. 30.

26 G. Haupt, *Socialism and the Great War. The Collapse of the Second International*, 1972, pp. 150–1.

27 D. J. Newton, *ibid.*, p. 263.

5: Sustaining Pacifism, 1914–15

1 G. H. Perris, *Our Foreign Policy and Sir Edward Grey's Failure*, 1912, quoted in M. Ceadel, *Thinking About Peace and War*, 1987, pp. 110–11. Perris was a Cobdenite internationalist who joined the ILP in 1908 and became a leading socialist writer on pacifist issues. In 1914 he published a widely read pamphlet exposing the machinations of the *The War Traders*.

2 The Peace Society itself refused to condemn the war, 'relapsed into a coma', and has hardly been heard of since. M. Ceadel, *Pacifism in Britain*, 1980, p. 32. It did, however, show fleeting signs of regaining consciousness in the agitation for a negotiated peace during 1916. K. Robbins, *The Abolition of War. The 'Peace Movement' in Britain, 1914–19*, Cardiff, 1976, pp. 99–100.

3 G. D. H. Cole, *History of Socialist Thought*, Vol. IV, Part 1, 1958, pp. 27ff.

4 Quoted in J. Liddington, *Generations to Greenham. Feminism and Anti-Militarism in Britain*, Virago, forthcoming.

5 M. Kamester and J. Vellacott, eds, *Militarism versus Feminism. Writings on Women and War*, 1987, p. 40.

6 A. Wiltsher, *Most Dangerous Women. Feminist Peace Campaigners of the Great War*, 1985; J. Vellacott, 'Feminist Consciousness and the First World War', *History Workshop*, 23, 1987.

7 My account of the UDC is largely based on: K. Robbins, *ibid.*; M. Swartz, *The Union of Democratic Control in British Politics During the First World War*, Oxford, 1971; C. A. Cline, *E. D. Morel, 1873 – 1924. The Strategies of Protest*, 1980.

8 R. W. Clarke, *The Life of Bertrand Russell*, 1975, p. 252.

9 E. D. Morel, *The Morrow of the War*, n.d., in P. Stansky, ed., *The Left and the War. The British Labour Party and World War One*, 1969, p. 89.

10 Quoted in Lord Elton, *The Life of Ramsay MacDonald*, 1939, p. 252.

11 K. E. Miller, *Socialism and Foreign Policy*, The Hague, 1967, p. 83; T. Wilson, *The Downfall of the Liberal Party, 1914–1935*, 1966, pp. 25–8; S. Koss, *Nonconformity in British Politics*, 1975, Ch. 6.

12 Source mislaid. The UDC had no such hesitations about the Quakers, who were active, respected and, some of them, rich.

13 This orientation, however, enabled the Fellowship to survive all disasters, which is probably why the historian of British pacifism describes it as 'Britain's most thoughtful pacifist society'. In 1918 it had 8000 members. It still exists today. M. Ceadel, *ibid.*, pp. 35–6.

14 But there appears to have been some tension between Swanwick and some of her fellow feminists over the degree to which women should organize autonomously in their peace campaigning. J. Liddington, *ibid.*

15 In 1918 Wake became Labour's National Agent. R. McKibbin, *The Evolution of the Labour Party, 1910–24*, 1974, pp. 23, 94, 125.

16 Quoted in M. Swartz, *ibid.*, p. 102.

17 P. Stansky, *ibid.*, p. 92.

18 *Ibid.*, p. 103.

19 H. N. Brailsford, *The War of Steel and Gold*, 1914, p. 172.

20 Quoted in M. Swartz, *ibid.*, p. 59.

21 *Ibid.*, p. 152.

6: Resisting War and Militarism, 1916–17

1 T. Wilson, *The Downfall of the Liberal Party, 1914–1935*, 1968, pp. 33–5, 42, 84–5.

2 S. and B. Webb, *The History of Trade Unionism*, 1920, pp. 636–40.

3 M. Swartz, *The Union of Democratic Control in British Politics During the First World War*, Oxford, 1971, pp. 235–37.

4 G. D. H. Cole, *History of the Labour Party*, 1948, pp. 26–8; M. Cole, ed., *Beatrice Webb's Diaries, 1912–1924*, 1952, pp. 53 – 5.

5 Quoted in J. Hinton, *The First Shop Stewards Movement*, 1973, p. 210.

6 The following account of the NCF is based on J. Vellacott, *Bertrand Russell and the Pacifists in the First World War*, 1980; J. Rae, *Conscience and Politics*, 1970; D. Boulton, *Objection Overruled*, 1967; J. W. Graham, *Conscription and Conscience*, 1922.

7 M. Gilbert, *Plough My Own Furrow. The story of Lord Allen of Hurtwood as told through his writings and correspondence*, 1965, p. 37.

8 *Ibid.*, p. 46.

9 J. W. Graham, *ibid.*, p. 181.

10 J. Rae, *ibid.*

11 M. Gilbert, *ibid.*, p. 55.

12 *Ibid.*, p. 71.

13 T. C. Kennedy, 'The Quaker Renaissance and the Origins of the Modern British Peace Movement, 1895–1920', *Albion*, 16, 1984.

14 M. Gilbert, *ibid.*, p. 14.

15 Quoted in F. M. Levanthall, *The Last Dissenter*, 1985, p. 136.

16 Quoted in M. Ceadel, *Pacifism in Britain*, 1980, p. 78.

17 M. Gilbert, *ibid.*, p. 129; J. W. Graham, *ibid.*, p. 23; T. C. Kennedy, 'Public opinion and the Conscientious Objectors, 1915–1919', *Journal of British Studies*, 12, 2, 1973, p. 111.

18 J. W. Graham, *ibid.*, pp. 15, 23.

19 J. Vellacott, *ibid.*, pp. 87, 109–10; K. Robbins, *The Abolition of War. The 'Peace Movement' in Britain, 1914–19*, Cardiff, 1976, Ch. 5; *The Call*, June-July 1916.

20 M. Swartz, *ibid.*, p. 214.

21 D. Marquand, *ibid.*, 1977, p. 200.

22 A. Link, *Wilson – Campaigning for Progressivism and Peace, 1916–1917*, 1965, pp. 265–66.

23 D. Birn, *The League of Nations Union, 1918–1945*, 1981, p. 7.

24 K. Robbins, *ibid.*, pp. 52, 136.

25 A. J. P. Taylor, *The Troublemakers*, 1985, p. 86.

26 H. N. Brailsford, *A League of Nations*, 1917, pp. 34, 36, 41.

27 *Ibid.*, p. 45.

28 B. Russell, *Which Way to Peace*, 1936, pp. 151–2; A. Ryan, *Bertrand Russell. A Political Life*, 1988, pp. 67–8, 144–5.

29 J. Vellacott, *ibid.*, p. 12.

30 B. Russell, *Autobiography*, Vol. 2, 1968, p. 30.

31 D. Birn, *ibid.*, p. 8.

32 H. N. Brailsford, *ibid.*, p. 312.
33 M. Swartz, *ibid.*, pp. 25, 42.
34 J. R. MacDonald, *National Defence*, 1917, p. 60; A. J. P. Taylor, *ibid.*, p. 144.

7: Pacifism, Revolution and the Labour Party, 1917–18

1 J. Vellacott, *Bertrand Russell and the Pacifists in the First World War*, 1980, p. 155.
2 D. Marquand, *Ramsay MacDonald*, 1977, p. 208.
3 On the Leeds Convention see J. Hinton, *The First Shop Stewards Movement*, 1973, pp. 239–41; S. White, 'Soviets in Britain', *International Review of Social History*, 19, 1974.
4 P. Snowden, *An Autobiography*, Vol. 1, 1934, pp. 450–1.
5 *What Happened at Leeds*, 1917, reprinted as *British Labour and The Russian Revolution*, Nottingham, n.d., p. 22.
6 D. Marquand, *ibid.*, p. 216.
7 P. Snowden, *ibid.*, p. 456.
8 *What Happened at Leeds*, *ibid.*, p. 32.
9 M. Swartz, *The Union of Democratic Control in British Politics During the First World War*, Oxford, 1971, pp. 153, 159, 166–8.
10 R. Harrison, 'The War Emergency Workers National Committee', in A. Briggs and J. Saville, eds, *Essays in Labour History, 1886–1923*, 1971; R. McKibbin, *The Evolution of the Labour Party, 1910–24*, 1974, Ch. 5.
11 My discussion of Henderson's visit to Russia, and its consequences, is largely based on J. Winter, *Socialism and the Challenge of War*, 1974, pp. 240–259.
12 Special Conference of the Labour Party, 10 August 1917, *Report*, p. 13.
13 J. Liddington, *Generations to Greenham. Feminism and Anti-Militarism in Britain*, Virago, forthcoming.
14 L. Woodward, *Great Britain and the War of 1914–1918*, 1967, pp. 148, 150, 288–90, 294.
15 P. Fussell, *The Great War and Modern Memory*, 1975, pp. 181–3.
16 B. Waites, *A Class Society at War. England 1914–18*, 1987, pp. 230–31.
17 J. Cronin, *Labour and Society in Britain, 1918–1979*, 1984, p. 31. Contrast R. McKibbin and H. Mathew, 'The Franchise Factor in the Rise of the Labour Party', *English Historical Review*, 1976, where it is suggested, somewhat implausibly, that nothing that happened during the war had any significant effect on working-class attitudes. See also R. McKibbin, *ibid.*, pp. xiii–xiv, Ch. 5.

18 W. Gallacher, *Revolt on the Clyde*, 1936, p. 177.

19 J. Hinton, *ibid.*, pp. 243ff.

20 *Ibid.*, pp. 236–38; B. Waites, *ibid.*, pp. 229–30.

21 K. Robbins, *The Abolition of War*, 1976, Ch. 5. In late February, Lansdowne, aided by Francis Hirst, the editor of the *Economist* with many friends in the City, was trying to get up a conspiracy with Labour leaders to oust Lloyd George and establish a peace-making Government.

22 D. Toye, 'The War Aims of the Labour Party', Warwick MA Thesis, 1971.

23 M. Swartz, *ibid.*, p. 199.

24 For the differences, see *The Herald*, 19 January 1918.

25 J. Hinton, *ibid.*, p. 256.

26 F. L. Carsten, *War Against War: British and German Radical Movements in the First World War*, 1987, p. 174.

27 M. Cole, ed., *Beatrice Webb's Diaries, 1912–24.*, 1952, p. 107; A. Henderson, letter to *The Times*, 1 February 1918.

28 D. Toye, *ibid.*

29 Labour Party Conference, January 1918, *Report*, p. 133.

30 *What Happened at Leeds*, 1917, reprinted as *British Labour and The Russian Revolution*, Nottingham, n.d., p. 22.

31 D. Marquand, *ibid.*, p. 223.

32 J. Bromley speaking at Labour Party Conference, January 1918, *Report*, p. 117.

33 *Ibid.*, p. 129.

34 Quoted in D. Howell, *A Lost Left. Three Studies in Socialism and Nationalism*, 1986, p. 188. Maclean was speaking at the BSP conference in March 1918, after the German offensive had ended the unrest. There is no record of his speeches during January and February, but it is probable that he was saying the same things. N. Milton, *John Maclean*, 1973, p. 158.

35 J. Hinton, *ibid.*, pp. 261ff.

36 D. Toye, *ibid.*

37 H. Swanwick, quoted in A. Wiltsher, *Most Dangerous Women*, 1985, p. 194; G. Lansbury in *The Herald*, 30 March 1918; W. F. Watson, *Workers Dreadnought*, 6 April 1918.

38 R. Harrison, *ibid.*, pp. 254–5.

39 *Ibid.*, pp. 255–6.

40 B. Waites, *ibid.*, p. 68.

41 D. Howell, *ibid.*, p. 182.

42 A. Henderson, *The Aims of Labour*, 1917, p. 24.

43 Morel, Russell and John Maclean, among others, were all jailed for offences under the Defence of the Realm Act.

44 J. R. MacDonald, *Socialism After the War*, 1917.

45 A. W. Wright, *G. D. H. Cole and Socialist Democracy*, 1979; G. D. H. Cole, *Self-Government in Industry*, 1917, G. D. H. Cole, *Social Theory*, 1920.

46 J. Winter, *ibid.*, pp. 124, 129–31; J. Vellacott, *ibid.*, pp. 159–60, 167, 169.

47 A. Henderson, *ibid.*, p. 91.

8: 'Figs Cannot be Gathered from Thistles': the 1920s

1 K. Robbins, *The Abolition of War*, 1976, p. 172; D. Birn, *The League of Nations Union, 1918–1945*, 1981, pp. 8–11. The latter book is the main source for the following account of the LNU.

2 D. Birn, *ibid.*, p. 51.

3 M. Cowling, *The Impact of Labour*, 1971.

4 Lord Grey of Falloden, *Twenty Five Years*, quoted in K. Zilliacus, *I Choose Peace*, 1949, p. 23.

5 D. Birn, *ibid.*, p. 24.

6 E. H. Carr, *The Twenty Years Crisis, 1919–1939*, 1984, p. 35.

7 D. Birn, *ibid.*, p. 198.

8 C. A. Cline, *Recruits to Labour*, 1963, Ch. 4.

9 D. Marquand, *Ramsay MacDonald*, 1977, p. 251.

10 K. Robbins, *ibid.*, p. 188.

11 A. J. P. Taylor, *The Troublemakers*, 1985, p. 160.

12 C. A. Cline, *E. D. Morel, 1873–1924. The Strategies of Protest*, 1980, pp. 126–27.

13 B. C. Woodward, 'Elite Migration from the Liberal to the Labour Party', Oxford B. Phil, 1984, pp. 80–2.

14 D. Birn, *ibid.*, pp. 44–6.

15 R. W. Lyman, *The First Labour Government, 1924*, 1957.

16 The Foreign Office greatly embarrassed the Government by releasing the text of what purported to be a letter from the Communist International, inciting revolution in Britain on the eve of the Election. In fact, it seems, Conservative Central Office already had copies of the (forged) 'Zinoviev letter' before the Foreign Office released it. J. Ramsden, *The Age of Balfour and Baldwin*, 1978, p. 205.

17 R. Skidelsky, *Politicians and the Slump*, 1967, p. 39.

18 F. M. Leventhall, 'Towards Revision and Reconciliation', in A. Briggs and J. Saville, eds, *Essays in Labour History*, Vol. 3, 1977, p. 170.

19 *New Leader*, 2 February 1923, quoted in R. E. Dowse, 'The ILP and Foreign Politics, 1918–23', *International Review of Social History*, 1962.

20 E. Halevy, *The Era of Tyrannies*, 1967, pp. 158–59.
21 C. P. Kindleberger, *The World in Depression, 1929–1939*, 1973; R. W. D. Boyce, *British Capitalism at the Crossroads, 1919–1932. A Study in Politics, Economics and International Relations*, 1987.
22 R. Skidelsky, *ibid.*, D. Marquand, *ibid.*, pp. 554–56, 560–63.
23 M. Ceadel, *Pacifism in Britain*, 1980, pp. 70–79.
24 M. Kamester and J. Vellacott, eds, *Militarism versus Feminism. Writings on Women and War*, 1987, pp. 47, 50–1.
25 A. Wiltsher, *Most Dangerous Women*, 1985, p. 185.
26 ILP Conference *Report*, 1920, p. 55.
27 M. Gilbert, *Plough My Own Furrow*, 1965, p. 90.
28 M. Ceadel, *ibid.*, p. 71. Ceadel criticizes pacifists for seeking to make compromises with the revolutionary currents unleashed by 1917, and expresses astonishment that warnings about the dangers of revolutionary violence were so muted: *ibid.*, p. 54. This remark reveals more about Ceadel (who on his own account is a 'defencist', not a pacifist: M. Ceadel, *Thinking About Peace and War*, 1987, p. 6) than it does about pacifists. It seems to me not in the least surprising that pacifists, most of whom were radicals searching for ways to transform the world, should be drawn to revolutionary ideas. Ceadel's book, indispensable though it is, is marred by the author's presupposition that pacifists ought to abstain from politics and seek spiritual purity in quietist sects. This attitude appears to flow from the fact that, as a historian, Ceadel wishes to treat pacifists with respect, while, as a citizen, he believes that their prescriptions are dangerous delusions., Hence they are most admirable when most ineffective.
29 K. Middlemass, ed., *Thomas Jones, Whitehall Diaries, 1916–1925*, 1969.
30 The following account is largely based on S. White, *Britain and the Bolshevik Revolution. A Study in the Politics of Diplomacy, 1920–24*, 1979.
31 Quoted in R. Miliband, *Parliamentary Socialism*, 1972, p. 79.
32 H. Pollitt, ed., *Lenin on Britain*, 1934, pp. 204–5.
33 E.g. H. Pollitt speaking at the Trafalgar Square rally to protest about British intervention in Greece in December 1944, *Daily Worker*, 18 December 1944. I have heard it said from CND platforms in the 1980s.
34 L. J. Macfarlane, 'Hands off Russia in 1920'. Past and Present, 38, 1967.
35 A. J. P. Taylor, *ibid.*, p. 164; A. Bullock, *The Life and Times of Ernest Bevin*, Vol. 1, 1960, pp. 137–38.
36 S. White, *ibid.*, pp. 92–3.
37 *Ibid.*, p. 93.

38 *Ibid.*, p. 228.
39 *Idem.*
40 *Ibid.*, p. 45.
41 R. E. Dowse, *Left in the Centre*, 1966, pp. 130ff.
42 D. Howell, *A Lost Left. Three Studies in Socialism and Nationalism*, 1986, p. 255.
43. *Ibid.*, p. 261. On another occasion Wheatley remarked: 'I would use the navy were I in power, to sink the ship that brought from abroad the product of sweated labour to reduce the standard of life here.' *Ibid.* p. 275.
44 *Ibid.*, pp. 261–2.
45 *Ibid.*, p. 269.
46 R. Skidelsky, *Oswald Moseley*, 1975, Chs. 7–12; H. Thomas, *John Strachey*, 1973.
47 Source mislaid.
48 M. Newman, *Socialism and European Unity*, 1983, p. 185.

9: 'The Necessary Murder'? – Facing Fascism

1 J. A. Thompson, 'Lord Cecil and the Pacifists in the League of Nations Union', *Historical Journal*, 20 (4), 1977, p. 319.
2 The National Peace Council, a loose umbrella organization first established in 1904, exists to this day.
3 Quoted in M. Ceadel, 'The Peace Movement Between the Wars: Problems of Definition', in R. Taylor and N. Young (eds), *Campaigns for Peace*, 1987, p. 89.
4 Quoted in D. Birn, *The League of Nations Union, 1918–1945*, Oxford 1981, p. 183. It was not until the actual coming of war, however, that large numbers of ex-'Peace-Week' organizers were prepared to turn their energies into mounting local 'Defence Weeks' and 'Red Army Days'.
5 Quoted in M. Ceadel, *Thinking about Peace and War*, Oxford, 1987, p. 20.
6 Vera Brittain, *Testament of Experience*, 1980, pp. 164–5.
7 He used this phrase in an article in *The Guardian* in, I think, 1984.
8 G. M. Young, *Stanley Baldwin*, 1952, p. 174.
9 Bertrand Russell, *Which Way to Peace*, 1936, p. 48.
10 Studs Terkel, *The Good War. An Oral History of World War Two*, 1985.
11 E.g. Gollancz's agonizing, related in R. D. Edwards, *Victor Gollancz, A. Biography*, 1987, pp. 268, 301–2; M. Ceadel, *Pacifism in Britain*, 1980, p. 197.
12 B. Russell, *ibid.*, p. 51.

13 Much of this work is reviewed in W. J. Mommsen & L. Kettenacker, eds, *The Fascist Challenge and the Policy of Appeasement*, 1983. See also G. Schmidt, *The Politics and Economics of Appeasement. British Foreign Policy in the 1930s*, 1986; G. C. Peden, *British Rearmament and the Treasury*, 1979; R. Shay, *British Rearmament. Politics and Profits*, 1977.

14 For a particularly scurrilous example see *30 questions and (honest) answers about CND*, a broadsheet published by The Coalition for Peace Through Security in the early 1980s.

15 M. Ceadel, 'The King and Country Debate, 1933: student politics, pacifism and the dictators', *Historical Journal*, 22, 1979.

16 M. Ceadel, *Pacifism in Britain*, 1980, pp. 139–40.

17 Labour Party Conference, *Report*, 1933, p. 186.

18 C. T. Stannage, 'The East Fulham By-Election, 25 October 1933', *Historical Journal*, 14, 1971.

19 'War and Peace', statement by the National Council of Labour, 1934.

20 D. S. Birn, *ibid.*, *passim*; M. Pugh, 'Pacifism and Politics in Britain, 1931–35,' *Historical Journal*, 23, 1980.

21 Dame A. Livingstone and M. S. Johnston, *The Peace Ballot: the Official History*, 1936, p. 5. The following account of the Peace Ballot is largely based on D. Birn, *ibid.* and M. Ceadel, 'The First British Referendum: the Peace Ballot, 1934–5,' *English Historical Review*, 1980.

22 To this end, a proposal to ban national air forces and place military aircraft exclusively in the hands of an International Police Force controlled by the League had been widely canvassed. The LNU leaders were inclined to agree, but their efforts to move the Union towards supporting a more coercive policy met with fierce resistance from a united front of Tories and pacifists, both of whom supported the League only to the extent that it did not threaten to involve Britain in new military commitments. J. A. Thompson, *ibid*; M. Ceadel, *Pacifism in Britain*, 1980, pp. 157, 162.

23 A further sop to them was an extra option added after canvassing was underway – 'I accept the Christian Pacifist attitude'. Very few people took advantage of this clause.

24 M. Ceadel, 'The First British Referendum,' *ibid.*, p. 834.

25 B. Russell, *ibid.*, p. 196.

26 E. H. Carr, *The Twenty Year Crisis*, 1981, pp. 114ff., 131–2.

27 Quoted in M. Ceadel, *ibid.*, pp. 835n (my italics).

28 P. M. H. Bell, *The Origins of the Second World War in Europe*, pp. 204–08.

29 D. Birn, *ibid.*, p. 151.

30 C. T. Stannage, *Baldwin Thwarts the Opposition. The British General Election of 1935*, 1980, p. 155 and *passim*.
31 A. J. P. Taylor, *The Troublemakers*, 1957, p. 189.

10: Against Fascism *and* War

1 M. Ceadel, *Pacifism in Britain*, 1980, pp. 123, 144–6.
2 C. R. Bisceglia, 'Norman Angell and the "Pacifist" Muddle', *Bulletin of the Institute of Historical Research*, 45, 1972, pp. 104–121.
3 M. Gilbert, *Plough My Own Furrow*, 1965, p. 334.
4 S. Cripps to Lord Ponsonby, September 1935, quoted in J. F. Naylor, *Labour's International Policy in the 1930s*, Boston, 1969, p. 93.
5 F. Brockway, *Inside the Left*, 1942, p. 326.
6 H. Pollitt in *International Press Correspondence*, 28 September 1935.
7 F. Brockway, *ibid.*, p. 329.
8 M. Ceadel, *ibid.*, *passim*; D. C. Lakowitz, 'British Pacifists and Appeasement: The Peace Pledge Union', *Journal of Contemporary History*, 9 (1), 1974.
9 A. Huxley, *What Are You Going To Do About It? The Case For Constructive Peace*, 1936, p. 31.
10 M. Ceadel, *ibid.*, p. 246.
11 A Huxley, *ibid.*, p. 27. George Lansbury was the foremost proponent of this idea, under the title 'truce of God': R. Postgate, *Life of George Lansbury*, 1951, pp. 311–2. For Clifford Allen's version of the same see M. Gilbert, *ibid.*, p. 387.
12 *Peace News*, 1 October 1938.
13 *Labour Monthly*, August, 1938, p. 470. There was nothing new about the Communist attack on pacifism. In 1932 Tom Wintringham wrote: 'The struggle against war is first and foremost a struggle against pacifism.' *Labour Monthly*, May 1932, p. 290, quoted in M. Ceadel, 'The Peace Movement Between the Wars: Problems of Definition', in R. Taylor and N. Young, *Campaigns for Peace*, Manchester, 1987, p. 98.
14 M. Ceadel, *ibid.*, p. 93; and see the article by Patrick Richards in *Peace News*, 29 October 1938.
15 Kenneth Nicholson, letter to *Peace News*, 1 October 1938.
16 'Vigilantes', *Why The League Failed*, 1938, pp. 93–5.
17 F. M. Levanthall, *The Last Dissenter*, 1986, p. 243.
18 R. Palme Dutt at 14th Congress of Communist Party of Great Britain, May 1937, *Report*, p. 126ff.

19 Examples include the Left Book Club leaflet of November 1938, *There Is Grave Danger*, 10 million of which were printed. The leaflet is reproduced in J. Lewis, *The Left Book Club*, 1970, p. 99. See also the Communist Party's superb 1939 propaganda film, *Peace and Plenty*, discussed in D. Macpherson, *Traditions of Independence: British Cinema in the Thirties*, 1980, pp. 86ff.

20 H. Francis, *Miners Against Fascism. Wales and the Spanish Civil War*, 1984; B. Alexander, *British Volunteers for Liberty: Spain 1936–39*, 1982.

21 E.g. Fenner Brockway, *Inside the Left*, 1942, pp. 339–40.

22 B. Russell, *ibid.*, p. 192.

23 N. Branson, *Britain in the Nineteen Thirties*, 1971, pp. 312–3.

24 C. Cook and J. Stevenson, *The Slump*, 1979, Ch. 13.

25 B. Pimlott, *Labour and the Left in the 1930s*, 1977; J. Jupp, *The Radical Left in Britain, 1931–41*, 1982.

26 T. Kennedy, 'The Next Five Years Group and the Failure of the Politics of Agreement in Britain', *Canadian Journal of History*, 11, 1974; S. Koss, 'Lloyd George and Non-Conformity: the Last Rally', *English Historical Review*, 1974.

27 D. Birn, *The League of Nations Union*, 1981, Ch. 10; N. Thompson, *The Anti-Appeasers. The Conservative Opposition to Appeasement in the 1930s*, 1971, Ch. 7.

28 J. Jupp, *ibid.*

29 J. Lewis, *ibid.*, *passim*.

30 G. D. H. Cole, *The People's Front*, 1936, *passim*.

31 J. F. Naylor, *ibid.*, 1969, pp. 247ff.; B. Pimlott, *Hugh Dalton*, 1985, pp. 256–7.

32 In a letter to Party members, Palme Dutt condemned them for indulging in 'speculating' about whether the Party should support Chamberlain if he did go to war. This was characteristic of Dutt's contemptuous attitude to the normal processes of democratic politics, and his powerful disciplinarian role in the Party helps to explain the incapacity of otherwise highly intelligent activists to trust their own judgements in a crisis, including the crisis of September–October 1939. See *The New Situation and the Next Stage of the Fight*, 5 October 1938. Dutt papers in the British Library, Dutt MSS K3.

33 *Peace News*, 29 October 1938.

34 *Idem.*

35 M. Gilbert, *ibid.*, p. 418; T. Kennedy, *ibid.*

36 M. Ceadel, *ibid.*, p. 279.

37 J. Lewis, *ibid.*, pp. 93–4; D. Edwards, *ibid.*, pp. 276, 280, 295. By contrast, according to Mass Observation, the Labour Party 'consistently misjudged public opinion throughout the crisis,

were always about two days late.' T. Harrison and C. Madge, *Britain by Mass Observation*, 1986, p. 98.

38 *Ibid.*, p. 106.

39 L. MacNeice, *Autumn Journal*, 1939, pp. 55–6.

40 I. McLean, 'Oxford and Bridgewater', in C. Cook and J. Ramsden, eds, *By-elections in British Politics*; R. Eatwell, 'Munich, Public Opinion and the Popular Front', *Journal of Contemporary History*, 6, 1971.

41 B. Pimlott, *Hugh Dalton*, 1986, pp. 257–61.

42 F. M. Levanthall, *ibid.*, p. 259.

43 H. Thomas, *John Strachey*, 1973.

44 N. Thompson, *ibid.*, Ch. 11.

45 B. Pimlott, *Labour and the Labour Left in the 1930s*, 1977.

46 H. Dalton, *The Fateful Years*, 1957, pp. 215–16.

47 J. F. Naylor, *ibid.*, pp. 228–31.

48 *Ibid.*, p. 160.

49 K. Morgan, 'Against War and Fascism. Ruptures and Continuities in British Communist Politics,' Manchester PhD, 1987, Chs. 1, 4.

50 Labour Party, *Conference Report*, 1937, p. 209.

51 *Left News*, 20 October 1938.

52 'The Labour Movement has a powerful weapon in its hands. The National Government's policy of depending on rearmament to protect them from the consequences of their own political errors, presupposes the co-operation of the Trade Unions. This means that the Labour movement now holds the reality of power in its own hands and is in a position to compel the Government to abandon its plans of co-operation with the Aggressors.' F. Elwyn Jones, *The Battle of Peace*, 1938, p. 317.

53 R. A. G. Parker, 'British Rearmament 1939–39; Treasury, Trade Unions and Skilled Labour', *English Historical Review*, 1981, pp. 322–33.

54 F. M. Levanthall, 'Towards Revision and Reconciliation: H. N. Brailsford and Germany, 1914–1949', in A. Briggs and J. Saville, eds, *Essays in Labour History*, Vol. 3, 1977, p. 184.

55 K. Morgan, *ibid.*, pp. 127–30.

56 E. Bullock, *The Life and Times of Ernest Bevin*, Vol. 1, 1969, pp. 637–8; J. F. Naylor, *ibid.*, Ch. 8.

57 K. Morgan, *ibid.*, p. 111; D. Birn, *ibid.*, p. 198.

58 P. Bell, *The Origins of the Second World War in Europe*, 1986, pp. 258–262.

11: Socialist Patriotism and People's War

1 'The International Post-War Settlement', in Labour Party, *Report of Annual Conference*, 1944, pp. 4, 5.
2 F. M. Levanthall, *The Last Dissenter*, 1985, pp. 268, 279.
3 F. Borkenau, *Socialism – National or International*, 1942, pp. 39, 104.
4 *Ibid.*, p. 157.
5 E. H. Carr, *Nationalism and After*, 1945, pp. 19, 20, 23; *cf.* Barbara Wooton, *Socialism and Federalism*, 1941: '. . . "socialism in our time" has been degraded into the bastard parody known as national Socialism – the socialism of the battlefield and the War cabinet.'
6 J. Ramsden, *The Age of Balfour and Baldwin*, 1978, p. 331.
7 K. Middlemass, *Politics in Industrial Society*, 1979; S. Tolliday & J. Zietlin, eds, *Shop Floor Bargaining and the State*, 1985.
8 Labour Party, *Let Us Face the Future*, 1945.
9 T. Wintringham, *Left Review*, September 1935, quoted in D. Fernbach, 'Tom Wintringham and Socialist Defense Strategy', *History Workshop*, 14, 1982.
10 J. Klugman, in J. Clark *et al*, eds, *Culture and Crisis in Britain in the 1930s*, 1979, p. 25.
11 T. Nairn, *The Enchanted Glass: Britain and Its Monarchy*, 1988.
12 Quoted in R. Terrill, *R. H. Tawney*, 1973, p. 173.
13 J. B. Priestley, *Postscripts*, 1940, pp. 4, 20.
14 E.g. R. Calder, *Carry on London*, 1941.
15 G. Orwell, *The Lion and the Unicorn*, 1982, pp. 84–5, 101.
16 *Ibid.* p. 40.
17 G. Claeys, '*The Lion and the Unicorn*, Patriotism and Orwell's Politics', *Review of Politics*, 47, 1985.
18 G. Orwell, *ibid.*, p. 49.
19 *Ibid.* p. 102.
20 P. Addison, *The Road to 1945*, 1982, pp. 156–7.
21 P. Grafton, *You, You and You. The People Out of Step with World War II*, 1981. Certainly, as Mass Observation reported at the time, there were moments when the bombing seemed to come close to destroying popular 'morale'. But, as Tom Harrison pointed out, these moments of panic were misleading. It is fleeing armies, not aerial bombardment, that destroys civilian 'morale'. T. Harrison, *Living Through the Blitz*, 1978, p. 332.
22 This thought is prompted by, among other things, some interesting speculations in D. Vaughan, *Portrait of an Invisible Man. The working life of Stewart McAllister, film editor*, 1983, pp. 104–05, 132.

23 P. Addison, *ibid.*, Ch. 5; J. Hinton, 'Coventry Communism: A Study of Factory Politics in the Second World War', *History Workshop*, 10, 1980, p. 94.

24 The following discussion of Common Wealth is based on A. Calder, 'The Common Wealth Party, 1942-45', Sussex PhD, 1968; G. McCulloch, 'The Politics of the Popular Front in Britain, 1935-45', Cambridge PhD, 1980; P. Addison, 'By-Elections of the Second World War', in C. Cook and J. Ramsden, eds, *By-elections in British Politics*, 1975.

25 Priestley to Kingsley Martin, 9 April 1968, quoted in G. McCulloch, *ibid.* Martin felt much the same way as Priestley about the inconvenient distractions created by mass activity. M. Jones, *Chances: An Autobiography*, 1987, p. 161.

26 G. McCulloch, *ibid.*

27 *Left News*, July 1942.

28 A. Calder, *ibid.*, Vol. 2, p. 202.

29 J. Attfield & S. Williams, *1939. The Communist Party and the War*, 1984; N. Branson, *History of the Communist Party of Great Britain*, 1985, Chs. 19-21; K. Morgan, 'Against Fascism and War. Ruptures and Continuities in British Communist Politics, 1935-1941', Manchester PhD, 1987, Chs. 5-7.

30 J. Hinton, *ibid.*; S. Tolliday, 'Government, Employers and Shop Floor Organisation in the British Motor Industry, 1939-69', in S. Tolliday and J. Zeitlin, *ibid.*, pp. 108-117; R. Croucher, *Engineers at War, 1939-45*, 1982.

31 Communist Party, *The Case for the Second Front: And The Arguments Against It*, May 1942. H. Cantril, *Public Opinion, 1939-1946*, 1951, pp. 1062-65; Mass Observation, *File Report 1297*, 1 June 1942; A. J. P. Taylor, *Lord Beaverbrook*, 1972, Chs 19-21; M. Foot, *Aneurin Bevan*, Vol. 1, 1966, pp. 292-6, 314-9, 330-4.

32 Olive Anderson, *A Liberal State at War*, 1967.

33 A. J. P. Taylor, *The Troublemakers*, 1957, pp. 60-1.

34 T. D. Burridge, *British Labour and Hitler's War*, 1976, pp. 30-1, 41.

35 V. Brittain, *Testament of Experience*, 1980, p. 221. Brittain's pacifist anti-Sovietism looked ultimately to the US for salvation, *ibid.*, pp. 222-3. For further elaboration of this theme see the discussion of George Catlin's role in K. van der Pilj, *The Making of an Atlantic Ruling Class*, 1984, pp. 111ff. Catlin was Brittain's husband. Perhaps there is a continuity with the Atlanticism of the SDP here?

36 J. Eglin, 'Women and Peace: from the Suffragists to the Greenham Women', in R. Taylor and N. Young, eds, *Campaigns*

for Peace, 1987, pp. 234–5; and see Jill's book on Selina Cooper – respectable Radical – which might say a little more about this.

37 P. Brock, *Pacifism in the Twentieth Century*, 1970, p. 184.

38 Vera Brittain, *ibid.*, pp. 296–304, 324–329, 352. After the war this was continued in Gollancz's Save Europe Now movement, whose organizer, Peggy Duff, was, of course, to become Organizing Secretary of CND. P. Duff, *Left, Left, Left*, 1971, has an account of Save Europe Now.

39 D. Hayes, *Challenge of Conscience. The Story of the Conscientious Objectors of 1939–45*, 1949, Foreword by Brockway.

40 M. Ceadel, *Peace and War*, 1987, p. 163; M. Gilbert, *Plough My Own Furrow*, 1965, p. 46.

41 Quoted in M. Ceadel, *ibid.*, p. 165.

42 B. Pimlott, *Hugh Dalton*, 1986, p. 296.

43 T. D. Burridge, *ibid.*, p. 167.

44 *Ibid.*, pp. 71–2, 95–6.

12: A 'Third Force': Vision versus Cold War

1 T. D. Burridge, *British Labour and Hitler's War*, 1976, Ch. 9; F. M. Levanthall, 'Towards Revision and Reconciliation: H. N. Brailsford and Germany, 1914–1949', in A. Briggs and J. Saville, eds, *Essays in Labour History*, Vol. 3, 1977.

2 D. Fernbach, 'Tom Wintringham and Socialist Defence Strategy', *History Workshop*, 14, 1982, pp. 84–5; T. Wintringham, 'Common Wealth', *Left News*, September 1942, p. 2228.

3 Labour Party, *Conference Report*, May 1945, p. 114.

4 See also G. D. H. Cole: 'The sovereign state which cannot defend itself, even for a time, against foreign attack is an obvious impostor, laying claim to an authority which it does not in fact possess.' *Europe, Russia and the Future*, 1941, p. 102. W. Friedmann, *The Crisis of the National State*, 1943, p. 149 makes a similar argument.

5 E. H. Carr, *Conditions of Peace*, 1942, p. 272.

6 D. Thompson, *The Proposal for Anglo-French Union in 1940*, Oxford, 1966. Churchill was not, however, offering to substitute the *Marseillaise* for *God save the King*!

7 R. A. Wilford, 'The Federal Union Campaign', *European Studies Review*, 10, 1980.

8 M. Newman 'British Socialists and the Question of European Unity, 1939–45,' *European Studies Review*, 10, 1980, p. 97; A. Spinelli, 'European Unity and the Left,' *New Europe*, 5, 3, 1977; W. Friedmann, *ibid.*, pp. 166–69. E. P. Thompson's elder

brother, Frank, who was later killed serving as a liaison officer with Bulgarian partisans, wrote in 1943: 'I am not yet educated to a broader nationalism, but for a United States of Europe I could feel a patriotism far transcending my love for England.' E. P. Thompson, *Beyond the Cold War*, 1982, p. 4.

9 E. H. Carr, *Nationalism and After*, 1945, p. 49.

10 E. H. Carr, *Conditions of Peace*, 1942, p. 209; J. A. Hobson, *Imperialism*, 1902, pp. 384–5.

11 E. H. Carr, *Nationalism and After*, 1945, p. 63.

12 G. D. H. Cole, *Europe, Russia and the Future*, 1941, pp. 169–71, 180–1.

13 *Ibid.*, pp. 105, 174; G. D. H. Cole, *Social Theory*, 1920.

14 W. Churchill, *The Second World War*, Vol. 6, 1954, p. 258. The account which follows is based on the following sources: Sir L. Woodward, *British Foreign Policy in the Second World War*, Vol. 3, 1971; D. Eudes, *The Kapetanios. Partisans and Civil War in Greece, 1943–1949*, 1972; C. M. Woodhouse, *The Struggle for Greece, 1941–49*, 1976.

15 *The Times*, 18 December 1944; *Daily Worker*, December 1944, *passim*; *Socialist Appeal*, January 1945; J. Hinton, 'Coventry Communism', *History Workshop*, 10, 1980, p. 51. After the event Harry Pollitt remarked: 'We must not brand as Trotskyist every worker who demanded strike action on such questions as Greece, we should welcome such evidence of strong feelings, but should find other and more effective channels for their expression.' Report of CP National Industrial Conference, 13 January 1945.

16 Mass Observation, 'Greece: December 1944', File Report 2190.

17 A. J. P. Taylor, *Beaverbrook*, 1972, pp. 561–62.

18 Labour Party, *Conference Report*, December 1944, pp. 143–50. For details of the manœuvring see the minutes of Labour's National Executive Committee, and Dalton's *Diaries*.

19 *Ibid.*, p. 147.

20 *What We Saw in Greece. Report of the Trade Union Delegation to Athens*, February 1945. Some of the atrocities no doubt occurred. Others appear to have been faked for the eyes of the TUC delegation. H. Richter, *British Intervention in Greece. From Vakizea to Civil War*, 1985, pp. 28–9.

21 *Tribune*, 29 December 1944.

22 G. D. H. Cole, *Great Britain in the Post-War World*, 1942, pp. 66–71, 164; G. D. H. Cole, *Europe, Russia and the Future*, 1941, pp. 10, 131.

23 G. Kolko, *The Politics of War. Allied Diplomacy and the World Crisis of 1943–45*, 1969, Chs. 11, 12; T. Anderson, *The United States, Great Britain and the Cold War, 1944–47*, 1981.

24 D. C. Watt, *Succeeding John Bull. America in Britain's Place, 1900–1975*, 1984, p. 161. The point can be put more harshly. Condemning the Labour Government's sacrifice of socialist planning to the special relationship with America, Tom Balogh remarked: '"Internationalism" thus turns out to be the negation of the socially positive state . . . it . . . deteriorates into a feeble agreement with the highest common platitude of the most reactionary Great Power.' T. Balogh, *The Dollar Crisis. Causes and Cure*, 1949, p. 55.

25 K. Worlpole, *Dockers and Detectives*, 1983, Ch. 2; P. Stead, 'The People and the Pictures', in N. Pronay and D. Spring, eds, *Propaganda, Politics and Film, 1918–45*, 1982.

26 *World News and Views*, 22 January 1944, 1 March 1944.

27 *Victory, Peace, Security*, Report of the 17th Congress of the CPGB, p. 17.

28 E. Burns in *World News and Views*, 13 January 1945.

29 *World News and Views*, 7 April 1945, 8 September 1945.

30 F. Claudin, *The Communist Movement: From Comintern to Cominform*, 1975.

31 *Tribune*, 29 December 1944.

32 B. Crick, *George Orwell, A Life*, 1982, pp. 521, 546, 550, 582.

33 G. Orwell, *Nineteen Eighty-Four,* p. 173.

34 *Tribune*, 7 April 1944.

35 C. Barnett, *The Audit of War*, 1986, pp. 38–40.

36 H. Dalton, *High Tide and After*, 1962, p. 73.

37 T. Balogh, *ibid.*, pp. 34, 50, 93–5.

38 For a survey of recent literature on this topic see D. Reynolds, 'Britain and the New Europe: The Search for Identity since the 1940s', *Historical Journal*, 31, 1988.

39 M. Newman, *Socialism and European Unity*, 1983, p. 123.

40 *Ibid.*, pp. 133–4.

41 Quoted in D. F. Fleming, *The Cold War and its Origins 1917–1960*, Vol. 1, 1961, p. 446.

42 K. Morgan, *Labour in Power, 1945–51*, 1984, Ch. 6.

43 K. Morgan, *ibid.*, Ch. 5; P. S. Gupta, 'Imperialism and the Labour Government', in J. Winter, ed., *The Working Class in Modern British History*, 1983.

44 P. N. Weiler, 'British Labour and the Cold War', *Journal of British Studies*, 26, 1, 1987, pp. 78–9.

45 D. Reynolds, *ibid.*, p. 233.

46 B. Pimlott, *Hugh Dalton*, 1986, p. 436.

47 T. Brett, *et al*, 'Planned Trade, Labour Party Policy and US Intervention', *History Workshop*, 13, 1982, p. 139.

48 S. Orwell and I. Angus, eds, *The Collected Essays, Journalism and Letters of George Orwell*, Vol. 4, 1970, p. 426.

49 B. Porter, *Britain, Europe and the World 1850 – 1982: Delusions of Grandeur*, 1983, pp. 124, 126.

50 House of Commons, *Debates*, 1946 – 47, Vol. 430, cols.536-7.

51 R. J. Jackson, *Rebels and Whips*, 1968, pp. 55–6.

52 M. Newman, *ibid.*, p. 139. Zilliacus was contemptuous of the 'Phantom third alternative', describing it as 'the illusion of a Western Union run by Social Democrats and independent of both the USA and the USSR – what I call the policy of a little grey home in the West for pinks scared white by the reds.' Newman, *ibid.*, p. 145.

53 T. Balogh, *ibid.*, pp. 34, 50, 67–8, 93–5.

54 J. Schneer, 'Hopes Deferred or Shattered: The British Labour Left and the Third Force Movement, 1945–49', *Journal of Modern History*, 56, 1984, p. 202; M. Newman, *ibid.*, p. 146.

55 P. N. Weiler, *ibid.*, p. 78.

56 Note, however, that even the wartime thinkers had been unduly optimistic about the possibility of combining a European and a global role – e.g. E. H. Carr, *Nationalism and After*, 1945, pp. 71–3.

57 P. Duff, *Left, Left, Left*, 1971, pp. 29ff.

58 J. Wood, 'The Labour Left in the CLPs, 1945–51', Warwick MA thesis, 1977.

59 J. Schneer, *ibid.*, p. 210; A. J. P. Taylor, *A Personal History*, 1984, p. 234.

60 Mass Observation, 'It Isn't There', File Report 2415, 3 August 1946.

61 R. J. Jackson, *ibid.*, pp. 59–60. In 1948 the compromise was scrapped, after threats of resignation over the issue from the chiefs of staff. R. Miliband, *Parliamentary Socialism*, 1972, p. 297.

62 Though the Liberal Party consistently opposed it. P. Chivall, *Liberals, Defence and Disarmament*, 1984, p. 14.

63 J. Cox, *Overkill*, 1982, pp. 192–94.

64 Mass Observation, *ibid.*.

13: 'Damned Fools in Utopia': CND's First Wave

1 N. Walter in *New Left Review*, 14, 1962, pp. 119, 128.

2 Or perhaps one should say 'After the Russians acquired nuclear weapons in 1949. . . .' So long as the United States had a monopoly of these weapons, Bertrand Russell urged the Americans to use nuclear blackmail – or even actual pre-emptive

war – against the Soviet Union to establish world government on the basis of a Pax Americana. Such thinking stemmed partly from the belief that Stalin was another Hitler, bent on limitless expansion. But its primary source was the conviction that unless the US used its fleeting moment of omnipotence to create an effective Empire of the Earth, then the inevitable proliferation of nuclear weapons in conditions of international anarchy would inexorably lead to the self-destruction of humanity. While the ruthless logic of his prescription is perhaps open only to philosophers with an aristocratic disdain for the common herd, Russell's underlying diagnosis remains alarmingly plausible. R. W. Clark, *The Life of Bertrand Russell*, 1975, pp. 519–527; A. Ryan, *Bertrand Russell. A Political Life*, 1988, pp. 173, 177–80.

3 H. Macmillan, *Memoires*, Vol. 3, 1971, p. 164.

4 M. Foot and M. Jones, *Guilty Men*, 1957, p. 222. The title of this book, of course, echoed the famous pamphlet Foot had co-authored in the aftermath of Dunkirk. Unlike Eden, Foot knew the difference between appeasing Hitler and withdrawing from empire: until, that is, he forgot it during the Falklands War in 1982.

5 Quoted in P. Worsley, 'Imperial Retreat' in E. P. Thompson, ed., *Out of Apathy*, 1960.

6 'There is no doubt that the moods of Suez and the emotional force behind the founding of CND are related.' H. Steck, 'The Re-emergence of Ideological Politics in Great Britain: the Campaign for Nuclear Disarmament', in R. Kimber and J. J. Richardson, eds, *Pressure Groups in Britain: a Reader*, 1974, pp. 130–31.

7 This debate is surveyed by A. J. R. Groom, *British Thinking About Nuclear Weapons*, 1974.

8 Rev. D. C. Wilkins to V. Gollancz, 6 July 1954, in Gollancz Papers, Modern Record Centre, University of Warwick, MSS 157/3/ND/1; L. J. Collins, *Faith Under Fire*, 1966, pp. 294–5.

9 R. Taylor, 'The British Nuclear Disarmament Movement of 1958–65 and its legacy to the Left', Leeds PhD, 1983, Ch. 7. In this chapter I have relied heavily on Taylor's thesis. At the time of writing I have not yet seen his book.

10 J. Liddington, '1955. The Roots of CND', *Sanity*, June 1986; J. Eglin, 'Women and Peace: from the Suffragists to the Greenham Women', in R. Taylor and N. Young, *Campaigns for Peace*, 1987, p. 236.

11 Jacquetta Hawkes, quoted in E. Wilson, *Halfway to Paradise*, 1980, pp. 178; J. Eglin, *ibid.*, pp. 238–9. Women, however, were probably much more prominent in organizing local CND

groups than they were in other mixed organizations. M. Jones, *Chances. An Autobiography*, 1987, p. 150.

12 R. Taylor, *ibid.*, Ch. 1. For the role of the churches in CND see the brief survey in D. Ormrod, 'The Churches and the Nuclear Arms Race, 1945–85,' in R. Taylor and N. Young, *ibid.*, pp. 208–10.

13 R. Taylor, *ibid.*, Ch. 4.

14 *Daily Worker*, 7 October 1957. For a sympathetic account of the Communist position see R. Taylor, 'The Marxist Left since 1945', in R. Taylor & N. Young, *ibid.*, pp. 163–173.

15 These sentiments of imperialist pacifism were to be widespread throughout the first wave of CND. Among the forest of banners which lent colour to Aldermaston marches, York CND's was a favourite: 'Britain's unilateral action ended the slave trade: let Britain lead again.' (L. Lloyd and N. A. Sims, *British Writing on Disarmament, 1914–1978*, 1979, p. 12.) No doubt the endorsement of the coercive power of the Royal Navy implied in this statement was hidden from its authors. 'Let Britain Lead', was the theme of a national CND campaign in 1959.

16 *New Statesman*, 2 November 1957. The reference to 1940 was not a personal idiosyncrasy. Alex Comfort – biologist, anarchist and future Committee of 100 supporter – spoke in almost identical terms at the founding meeting of CND in 1958. (D. Widgery, *The Left in Britain*, 1976, p. 116.) And so did Zilliacus, one of the few older socialist intellectuals to align himself with the New Left. (*New Reasoner*, 4, Spring 1958, p. 37.)

17 C. Driver, *The Disarmers. A Study in Protest*, 1964, p. 62.

18 P. Duff, *Left, Left, Left*, 1971.

19 Quoted in R. Taylor, *ibid.*, p. 137.

20 R. Taylor, *ibid.*, Ch. 3; H. J. Steck, *ibid.*, P. Duff, *ibid.*

21 *Peace News*, 25 August 1961.

22 C. Driver, *ibid.*, p. 47.

23 R. Taylor, *ibid.*, pp. 107–08, 194. Russell, indeed, favoured British unilateralism just because it would leave America and Russia with a nuclear monopoly opening the way to a joint condominium as the basis for world government. R. W. Clark, *ibid.*, p. 562.

24 '. . . introducing the moral element into the centre of politics and a political realism into the heart of moral conviction'. J. Collins, *ibid.*, p. 349.

25 *New Statesman*, 2 July 1960.

26 J. Collins in *The Listener*, 23 March 1967, quoted in G. Wooton, *Pressure Groups in Britain, 1720–1970*, 1975.

27 C. Driver, *ibid.*, pp. 98–99.

28 R. Taylor, 'The Marxist Left Since 1945', in R. Taylor & N. Young, *ibid.*, pp. 166–67.

29 This account of CND's struggle within the Labour Party is mainly based on R. Taylor's PhD thesis; L. Minkin, *The Labour Party Conference*, 1978; P. Williams, *Hugh Gaitskell. A Political Biography*, 1979; F. Parkin, *Middle-class Radicalism: the Social Bases of CND*, 1968.

30 P. Williams, *ibid.*, p. 582.

31 'Some Notes on the Present Position of CND', n.d., Summer 1963. I am grateful to Sheila Jones for drawing my attention to this document.

32 R. Taylor and C. Pritchard, *The British Nuclear Disarmament Movement of 1958–1965: Twenty Years On*, Oxford, 1980, p. 115.

33 L. Freedman, *Britain and Nuclear Weapons*, 1980, pp. 24–5, 31–2. Just after the Scarborough conference in 1960, Wilson had publicly alleged that Gaitskell was secretly planning to resuscitate the independent deterrent once in office. Gaitskell's biographer, who relates this fact with some delight, could find no evidence to support it in Gaitskell's papers. P. Williams, *ibid.*, p. 616. The record proves that Wilson was a turncoat. But what would Gaitskell have done, had he lived?

34 N. Young, 'What is Wrong with the Nuclear Disarmament Movement', July 1963. CND Archive. I am grateful to Sheila Jones for drawing my attention to this document.

35 J. Collins, *ibid.*, p. 321. The following account of the Committee of 100 is largely based on Taylor's thesis.

36 April Carter to Mike Randall, 28 September 1960, quoted in R. Taylor, *Thesis*, p. 670.

37 George Clark, quoted in *ibid.*, p. 671.

38 Quoted in *ibid.*, p. 708.

39 *Peace News*, 25 August 1961.

40 E.g. M. Randall in *Peace News*, 10 March 1961. For an effective defence of the DAC approach and a rather different account of Schoenman's attitudes, see M. Randall, 'Non-Violent Direct Action', in R. Taylor and N. Young, *ibid.*

41 Russell to Schoenman, 16 August 1960. Bertrand Russell Archive, McMaster University, Ontario.

42 J. Collins, *ibid.*, pp. 335–36.

43 *Peace News*, 11 August 1961.

44 *Ibid.*, 22 September 1961.

14: The New Left and the Politics of Unilateralism

1 E. P. Thompson, 'Outside the Whale', in E. P. Thompson, ed., *Out of Apathy*, 1960. Thompson's critique of Orwell's political pessimism in this essay involves what, in retrospect, appears to be an astonishing blindness to the things he shared with Orwell: the sense of a valued Englishness of the common people; insistence on the importance of the rule of law to the maintenance of liberty; the search for a progressive Europeanism to counterpose to the Blocs. In 1960 it clearly seemed more important to demolish Orwell than to claim him back from the Natopolitans. And perhaps Thompson's loyalty to his own Communist past was interfering with his eyesight?

2 P. Sedwick, 'The Two New Lefts', in D. Widgery, *The Left in Britain, 1956–68*, 1976, pp. 131ff. N. Young, *An Infantile Disorder? The Crisis and Decline of the New Left*, 1977.

3 E. P. Thompson, 'An Essay in Ephology', *The New Reasoner*, Spring 1959, p. 5.

4 D. Widgery, *ibid.*, pp. 131–2, 140–2.

5 E. P. Thompson, 'The New Left', *The New Reasoner*, Summer 1959, p. 17.

6 Nearly 10% of a sample of ex-CND activists interviewed in the 1970s claimed to have been active in Left Clubs, a not inconsiderable proportion. R. Taylor and C. Pritchard, *The Protestmakers. The British Nuclear Disarmament Movement of 1958–65*, 1980, p. 26.

7 *Peace News*, 6 October 1961.

8 In 1955 Richard Acland (the organizer of the 1938 Bridgewater by-election, and the leader of Common Wealth during the war) who was then a Labour MP, resigned his seat in order to fight a by-election on the single issue of nuclear weapons. His gesture was swallowed up in the General Election. C. Driver, *ibid.*, pp. 28–9. But it does establish a clear link in the tradition Thompson was trying to evoke. In 1958 Acland had been co-opted onto the CND Executive.

9 M. Jones, 'Shifting the Mule', *New Left Review*, 15, 1962.

10 D. Widgery, *ibid.*, p. 136.

11 R. Taylor, *Thesis*, pp. 180–82.

12 *Peace News*, 10 March 1961.

13 *Anarchy*, 13 March 1962, quoted in C. Driver, *The Disarmers*, 1964, p. 71.

14 *Peace News*, 6 October 1961.

15 M. Jones, *ibid.*

16 'Can We Have a Neutral Britain?' *New Reasoner*, Spring 1958, p. 10.

17 R. Taylor, *ibid.*, pp. 107ff. J. Collins, *ibid.*, pp. 310ff. P. Duff, *ibid.*, pp. 226ff.

18 C. Driver, *ibid.*, pp. 139–40. Zhukov was to earn an international reputation for ideological brutality over the next 25 years, until Mr Gorbachev finally put an end to his career in the Soviet peace apparatus.

19 E. P. Thompson, 'Outside the Whale', *ibid.*, pp. 171, 186; E. P. Thompson, 'An Essay in Ephology', *ibid.*, pp. 7–8; C. Bourdet, 'The Way to European Independence', *New Reasoner*, 5, Summer 1958, pp. 12–24. This impressive essay reads today like a first draft for the END Appeal of 1980.

20 R. Taylor, *ibid.*, p. 108.

21 E. P. Thompson, *New Reasoner*, Summer 1959, p. 7.

22 Editorial in *New Reasoner*, Spring 1958.

23 C. Bourdet, *ibid.*, pp. 15–18.

24 P. Worsley, 'Imperial Retreat', in E. P. Thompson, ed., *Out of Apathy*, 1960, p. 138; M. Newman, *Socialism and European Unity*, 1983, pp. 181–83.

25 P. Worsley, *ibid.*, p. 135.

26 P. Duff, *ibid.*, pp. 233–237; D. Widgery, *ibid.*, pp. 142–44; A. MacIntyre, 'Is a neutralist foreign policy possible?' *Peace News*, 16 June 1961.

27 M. Jones, *Chances. An Autobiography*, 1987, pp. 179–80. Compare Louis MacNeice's characterization of the post-Munich protesters – 'the nicest people in England . . . those who by their habit hate politics', L. MacNeice, *Autumn Journal*, 1939, pp. 55–6.

28 D. Shelley, 'If you read this, then presumably we are both alive', *Sanity*, October 1987; R. Taylor, *ibid.*, pp. 188ff.

29 P. Duff, *ibid.*, pp. 204–5.

30 N. Young, *ibid.*, p. 148.

31 P. Anderson, 'The Left in the 1950s', *New Left Review*, 29, 1965.

32 P. Williams, *Hugh Gaitskell. A Political Biography*, 1979, pp. 734–35.

33 *Ibid.*, p. 736.

34 Both the Communist Party and the Labour Left's 'Forward Britain Movement' took a strongly anti-German line. The Communists asserted that MacMillan's application for EEC membership was 'worse than Munich'! M. Newman, *ibid.*, pp. 179, 194.

35 *Encounter*, February 1963, p. 65.

36 S. Hall and P. Anderson, *New Left Review*, 10, 1961, p. 1.

37 A. J. P. Taylor, *A Personal History*, 1984, p. 291.

38 'The Left Against Europe', *New Left Review*, 75, 1972, p. 62.

15: Protest and Survive: CND's Second Wave

1 F. Halliday, *The Making of the Second Cold War*, 1983.

2 It may be helpful to mention some personal history at this point. I have been actively involved throughout the new wave of the peace movement – as a local group activist and a member of British END in the early 1980s, and as the chair of the National CND committee responsible for its mass campaigning activity for most of the years since 1983. This makes it difficult for me to attain a proper distance from the events related in this chapter, and I would urge readers to bear in mind that the same story can be – and no doubt will be – told from many different angles of vision. However, since it is probably too early for anyone to attempt a balanced historical account of CND's second wave, I have felt justified in extending this book into the 1980s despite the fact that my account will eventually be seen to contain distortions and silences of which, at the time of writing, I am unaware. What follows is a provisional settling of accounts with a very recent past. Much of the detail in this chapter is based on papers in my possession. These papers will, eventually, be deposited in an appropriate archive.

3 For a survey of the Continental movements see D. Johnstone, *The Politics of Euromissiles*, 1984.

4 J. Cox, *Overkill*, 1982, pp. 230–1.

5 *New Left Review*, 121, 1980, p. 3.

6 *Ibid.*, p. 29.

7 *Beyond the Cold War*, 1982, p. 25.

8 The *Appeal* is printed in E. P. Thompson and D. Smith, eds, *Protest and Survive*, 1980.

9 For some sharp comments on the tendency of some activists to substitute anti-imperialist rhetoric for political analysis, see E. P. Thompson in *END Journal*, 31, 1987, pp. 22–4.

10 *Ibid.*, p. 30.

11 *New Left Review* 124, pp. 35–36 (my italics).

12 B. Pimlott, 'Trade Unions and the Second Coming of CND', in B. Pimlott, and C. Cook, eds, *Trade Unions in British Politics*, 1982, p. 232.

13 This expertise has been built on in the 1980s by a number of academic institutions and by the Alternative Defence Commission, whose two *Reports* represent the most detailed peace movement elaborations of the wider implications of British nuclear disarmament. Other professional groupings have also been important to CND's credibility, notably The Medical Campaign Against Nuclear Weapons and Scientists Against

Nuclear Arms (SANA), which have been especially effective in contesting Home Office claims about the efficiency of Civil Defence.

14 S. Hughes, *et. al*, *Across the Divide. Liberal Values for Defence and Disarmament*, 1986; P. Chival, ed., *Liberals, Defence and Disarmament*.

15 For a brief account of the debate in the Churches see D. Ormrod, 'The Churches and the Nuclear Arms Race, 1945–85', in R. Taylor and N. Young, eds, *Campaigns for Peace*, 1987, pp. 211–15.

16 I am grateful to Paul Byrne for giving me a copy of the results of his survey of national CND members.

17 R. Taylor, 'CND and the 1983 election', in I. Crewe and M. Harap, eds, *Political Communications: The General Election Campaign, 1983*, 1986, p. 211.

18 The Peace Canvass, an idea initiated by the present writer, was originally conceived as a re-run of the 1934–5 Peace Ballot. But persuading activists to knock on doors turned out to be very much harder in the 1980s than it had been in the 1930s. In the end only 55,000 responses to the canvass were returned to national CND – a mere 0.5 per cent of the numbers reached by the Peace Ballot. So much for the inspiration provided by misleading historical precedents!

19 For a critique of Greenham feminism see Jane Lewis in *END Journal*, Aug.–Sept. 1983.

20 L. Jones, *Keeping the Peace*, 1983, p. 88.

16: Prospects

1 E. P. Thompson, *Beyond the Cold War*, 1982, p. 16.

2 D. C. Watt, *Succeeding John Bull. America in Britain's Place, 1900–1975*, 1984, pp. 116, 159–62.

3 Quoted in J. Palmer, *Europe Without America? The Crisis in Atlantic Relations*, 1987, p. 157. My thinking about current prospects for the peace movement has been greatly helped by this book.

4 Though not, it may be said, in the original perspectives of the New Left – and of Thompson himself, who took a rather more favourable view of the Soviet Union in 1959 than he did in 1980. *New Reasoner*, Summer 1959, p. 6.

5 J. Palmer, *ibid.*, p. 82.

6 But not as much as is often assumed. See D. Saunders, *et al*, 'Government Popularity and the Falklands War: a Reassessment' *British Journal of Political Science*, 17, 1987.

7   A. Gamble, *Britain in Decline*, 2nd Ed., 1985, pp. 173–4, 220; M. Newman, *Socialism and European Unity*, 1983, pp. 245–7, 255–6.

8   *New Left Review*, 124, 1980, p. 37.

9   S. Bromley and J. Rosenberg, 'After Exterminism', *New Left Review*, 168, 1988, p. 76.

10   *New Left Review*, 131, 1982.

11   The acute reader may notice an apparent contradiction between this argument and my earlier approval of the *New Reasoner's* argument that the politics of survival took precedence over the politics of socialist revolution. If there is a contradiction it is of the dialectical kind – we cannot mobilize a mass peace movement except on a survivalist basis; but final victory for this movement will be inseparable from the revolutionary transformation of our society. My disagreement with revolutionary critics of the peace movement is that there are very substantial steps down the road to final victory – including a nuclear-free and non-aligned Europe – which do not have to await some irreversible moment of revolutionary transformation.

12   H. N. Brailsford, *The War of Steel and Gold*, 1914, p. 296.

13   This is a Guild Socialist thought, and I owe it to G. D. H. Cole's First World War writings. For a compelling modern statement of a similar view, see R. Williams, 'The Culture of Nations' in *Towards 2000*, 1983.

Index